CURRENT
REFORM RESPONSA

CURRENT
REFORM RESPONSA

by

SOLOMON B. FREEHOF, D.D.
Rabbi Emeritus, Rodef Shalom Temple, Pittsburgh

THE HEBREW UNION COLLEGE PRESS

1969

Library of Congress Catalog Card Number: 68-57979
Manufactured In The United States of America

CONTENTS

iii

ACKNOWLEDGMENTS

In rabbinic works such as Responsa the acknowledgments are usually headed by a phrase derived from Deuteronomy (27:11): "These stand to pronounce the blessing." The passage refers to the six tribes who are to gather on Mt. Gerizim to bless the people of Israel. What a vast multitude there must have been crowding the mountain to proclaim their benediction!

Whenever an author reflects on the various influences which contributed to his life and work he will soon realize that there has been a multitude of people who have blessed and helped him. There are far too many who have earned his gratitude for him even to record his full indebtedness. He can only mention the few whose help has been direct and recent.

I thank my many colleagues who have directed their halachic inquiries to me. The answers to their questions constitute almost the entire contents of the book. My special thanks go to the Alumni Asociation HUC-JIR which had accepted the responsibility of publishing not only this book (*Current Reform Responsa*) but also the two previous ones of the series (*Reform Responsa* and *Recent Reform Responsa*). I am deeply grateful to the Board of Rodef Shalom Congregation of Pittsburgh which, with its usual generosity, has aided in the publication of this volume.

Dr. Fritz Bamberger has earned my gratitude for contributing his specialized skill to the Alumni Association in planning and arranging the publication of this book. Each responsum separately and then the book as it developed were under the care of my friend and secretary, Esther Tyrnauer. I cannot thank her sufficiently for her efficient help and her loyal devotion.

My own devotion to the task of finding the halachic path for our movement in Judaism was constantly strengthened by the unflagging enthusiasm and the loving encouragement of my dear wife Lillian, to whom I now gratefully dedicate this book.

Solomon B. Freehof

FOREWORD

This is the third volume by Dr. Freehof on Responsa published by the Alumni Association of the Hebrew Union College-Jewish Institute of Religion. For many years alumni of the College-Institute have consulted Dr. Freehof concerning the propriety of procedures and practices within the framework of Jewish law. The answers to the questions asked of Dr. Freehof now collected and published in these three volumes constitute an important body of definitive and authoritative literature.

The Alumni Association, upon the recommendation of its Publication Committee and the approval of the Executive Committee has published volumes by Drs. Kaufmann Kohler, Jacob Z. Lauterbach, Samuel Sandmel, Sheldon Blank, Julian Morgenstern and Henry Slonimsky.

The Alumni Association through its Quinquennial Fund, supported by the members of the organization, makes possible the publication of these books.

The publication of this volume was hastened by a significant contribution by the Rodef Shalom Temple in Pittsburgh.

The author is an alumnus of the College, ordained in 1915. During the First World War he was a chaplain in the American Expeditionary Force. After his ordination he continued as a member of the faculty of his alma mater; in 1924 he became rabbi of Kehillath Anshe

Maariv Temple in Chicago; and in 1934 he became rabbi of Rodef Shalom Temple in Pittsburgh, of which he is now Rabbi Emeritus. He is a former president of the Central Conference of American Rabbis, and Honorary Life President of the World Union for Progressive Judaism. He is the author of *Stormers of Heaven*; *The Book of Psalms, A Commentary*; *Modern Jewish Preaching*; *The Small Sanctuary*; *Reform Jewish Practice* (2 vols.); *Preface to Scripture*; *The Responsa Literature*; *Book of Job, A Commentary*; *Reform Responsa*; and *Recent Reform Responsa*.

INTRODUCTION

The first *Yearbook of the Central Conference of American Rabbis* was issued in 1890. Since then for these seventy-seven years the *Yearbook* has appeared without interruption. This sequence of volumes now constitutes a longer succession than that of any Jewish magazine in existence and the most uninterrupted record of any existing organization. Add to this significant continuity the fact that it contains the record of a conference of rabbis who, by training and dedication, are alert to the changing moods and needs of the American and world Jewish communities. By its very extensiveness and its seriousness the Conference *Yearbook* has become a valuable repository of contemporary Jewish history.

More specifically, of course, it is a record of the inner history of the Reform movement in America. The sequence of *Yearbooks* should be evaluated as a totality. The themes of the successive Conference lectures, sermons, and essays and certainly the changing moods of the discussions from the floor, chart the varying emphases in our lives as American Jews. The listing and analysis of those matters which had once agitated us and then have faded into insignificance and those other matters which grew up to an overshadowing importance would provide source material for a number of doctoral theses. It has, I believe, already served such a purpose to some extent.

There are many themes whose development could profitably be traced through the *Yearbooks*. The changing relationship of Zionism to world Jewry could be illustrated in the successive resolutions and debates of the Conference. The dedication of the Conference to social progress beginning with its general assertions of the ideals of the prophets and continuing through all the specific causes which the Conference aided and advocated is certainly significant as a part of American social history. The interrelationship of American Jewry with world Jewry and specifically with European Jewry is likewise traceable. The first three *Yearbooks* recorded all the decisions of the German synods for our guidance. The later *Yearbooks* give evidence of our increasing independence as an American Jewry and then reveal our responsibility for the survival and reestablishment of the Jewries in the Old World.

The theme which underlies this volume, *Current Reform Responsa,* and its predecessors, *Recent Reform Responsa* and *Reform Responsa,* likewise appears in the *Yearbooks* in an evolutionary sequence. In the early days there were the usual expressions of deprecation for the *Shulchan Aruch* and the other legal codes; the usual contrast between the Priestly, i.e., the ceremonial form of Judaism and the Prophetic, ethical, which Reform was proud to represent. Then slowly there began to appear papers on Jewish Talmudic themes and sporadic discussions of the legal literature. Soon there were expressions of regret that the strong discipline of Orthodoxy is no longer ours, that Reform Judaism, strong though it be in ethics, lacks the sense of *Halacha,* of the Divine mandate which once covered every detail of Jewish daily life. Papers and discussions began to appear demanding some specific code of practice which might bring the older concepts of the older discipline into our Reform life.

All these new voices express a strong feeling which grows from many roots. There was first a realization that Judaism had always been a religion of law and that Reform somehow had lost a great deal of inner strength when it veered away from the old sense of a religiously organized life and put its sole emphasis on the less specific ethical ideals. Then also these newer feelings rise from a sense of a greater appreciation of the rabbinic past. Since modern biblical criticism has shown the Bible to be a human book, it deprived it of a special uniqueness. It was now not necessarily different in status from the confessedly human, argumentative Talmudic literature. Since God speaks in "the language of human beings," He may be speaking through both literatures. If hitherto God had revealed Himself through the writers of the Bible by the flame of the human conscience then He revealed Himself through the debating scholars of the Talmud, by the light of human intellect; and it may well be that the intelligence is as worthy a vehicle of revelation as the conscience. Also perhaps the facts of our own progress as a Reform movement have affected our relationship to the older legal literature. In the early days of Reform we were fighting against an overmastering Jewish legal authority. We could not attain our independence without denying and defying that authority. But now we are strong and we can afford to be much more tolerant of the authoritative past. We no longer need to fight our historical parent for our independence. We are adult enough now and independent enough to begin to appreciate him. All these influences are perhaps the source of the mood that has been working in the Conference in recent years to turn it in the new direction which may be described as pro-Halachic.

Yet so far this mood is chiefly a vague stirring and not yet a march upon a clearly marked out road. It is at most a feeling of direction with the goal, however, not yet clear. The reason for the slow pace of our evolution towards a clear Halachic point of view is that we hold to certain counter ideas which to us are likewise important. In the first place, we are still strongly aware of our independence from many burdensome old restrictions. Our independence and our modernity are precious to us and we would not risk it by surrendering them to others. We find it easier to honor the learning and wisdom of the rabbis of the past than to imagine our bowing to the pronouncements of the Orthodox rabbis of the present. Our pioneers had freed us from Orthodox control and we will do nothing now that might restore any authority to it. Having been freed from older customs, we have had an opportunity to become creative, to transform old ceremonies, to invent new ones. In the totality of Jewish religious life this inventive creativity of Jewish ceremonial observance may well be our true and specific function. At all events we cherish it and would not give it up by binding ourselves too closely to ceremonial codes.

Moreover, we and most Jews of the modern world, having moved away so long from obedience to a large bulk of the ceremonial and ritual law, now find it almost impossible to believe again that certain parts of it can possibly represent the Divine Will. There would be no sense and no meaning in having a code, even a new code, which would describe to any degree of detail the handling and the preparation of food or the details of garments or hundreds of other such *mitzvos* which seem absurd to us. Our people simply could not muster the slightest faith that these matters are God-commanded. After all, a code in Judaism is not a code of manners; it is a code of mandates. It is almost impossible for us to include any part of vast sections of the *Shulchan Aruch* in a code and say that these "doth the Lord require of thee."

Above all, our objections to much of the law are protests of conscience. The laws which will never be acceptable to us are those which concern chiefly the status of the Jewish woman. Aside from all the special tragedies in the life of Jewish women with regard to marriage and divorce, the very concept of her inferior legal status tends to turn us against the legal tradition.

We have, then, two opposite tendencies in our movement, one which leads us toward the law and one which repels us from it. It is certain that a long period, and we might say many *Yearbooks* of the Conference, will stretch before us before we will be able to arrive at a philosophy of Jewish law suitable for us. It would seem to the present writer that with regard to matters of conscience we will never yield or even compromise. Perhaps the grandest achievement of Reform Judaism is its liberation of the Jewish woman. As for the practical commandments, many of which are simply unbelievable to us as Divine mandates, as the years go by there will be a certain process of selectivity. Actually it is a social-psychological evolution which must take place. We will have to search our hearts and minds and find out which of the many practices in Jewish life we can believe or come to believe to be Divine commands. We have long held that the ethical doctrines and ideas are a God-given mandate and that we are bound to obey them.

May we not come to believe that the worship of God in the sanctuary is likewise a demand on our conscience? That to worship regularly must not depend upon the attractiveness of the sermon or the choir but must rest upon a command-ment which we have accepted and which we will obey? It may also be that due to our increasing efforts Jewish adult education will grow to be a widespread habit, and then perhaps it will come to be considered to be not only an intellectual gain but also a spiritual blessing. Thus the habit of regular home study might attain the stature of a duty, and we will have rediscovered one of the noblest and most unique *mitzvos* of the Torah.

Thus it may develop with us. Worthy actions may grow into religious duties, and so our Reform code will develop *mitzvah* by *mitzvah,* as each action achieves its sanctity. Some of these may be new *mitzvos,* but most of them will be rediscoveries of actions which our tradition has cher-ished. We will have to find out which elements in the Jewish traditional life-style we can truly accept as a mandate and which will remain merely custom and therefore changeable. All this social psychology must be explored and experi-enced before we can ever attain a clear-cut philosophy or well-defined ceremonial discipline.

Because we have not yet arrived at the stage of sure selection and clarification, our increasing discussions at the Conference are still chiefly yearnings, hopes and anticipa-tions. Nevertheless as is bound to be the case with men of our profession, trained to earnest thought, there will be in-creasing clarification and evolution toward a viable point of view.

Towards this attainment the studies in this volume and in its predecessors may perform some service. Almost every one of the themes discussed in this volume and in its two predecessors was based upon a question asked by a member of the Conference and only rarely by someone not a member of the Conference. So in a sense this sequence of questions might be looked upon as a parallel series to the *Yearbooks* themselves, and the nature of the questions asked reveal the varying and changing concerns of these leaders of Reform Judaism.

As for the doctrine underlying the answers, that too, like that underlying the questions themselves, has not yet, it must be confessed, evolved itself into clarity. What principle there may be underlying the answers, may be described as follows: The great legal literature in its vast extent embodies the best thinking of the best minds in Judaism on the problems and the duties of Jewish life. Even though we do not agree that all the matters which these thousands of scholars discuss are truly mandated, nevertheless God's Will somehow speaks through their earnest devotion and dedicated thinking. The Halachic literature is the grandest repository of Jewish thinking and feeling and what we may find in it as answer to the various questions which we ask may not, indeed, govern our lives but will at least serve us as a guide. Beyond this guidance in the various problems which arose in our congregational life, may the material here derived from the records of loyal and devoted Jewish intellectual experience help our movement in its progress towards increasing self-discipline and self-dedication.

1

THE ETERNAL LIGHT

Is it actually required by Jewish legal tradition that there
be an eternal light in front of the ark? Would it be a
serious violation if the light is extinguished when, let us
say, it is necessary to change gas pipes or electrical con-
nections? (From Vigdor Kavaler, Rodef Shalom Temple,
Pittsburgh, Pennsylvania.)

THE Eternal Light (*ner tamid*) is one of the most beloved
symbols of the synagogue. When a synagogue is dedicated
in modern times, one of the most impressive ceremonials is
the first lighting of the Eternal Light. Since the use of an
Eternal Light in the synagogue is based upon the Eternal
Light commanded by God of Moses for the Tabernacle
(Exodus 27:20 and Leviticus 24:2), one would imagine

that this beloved symbol, with such ancient roots, would continually come up for discussion in the long sequence of Jewish legal literature. Yet the astonishing fact is that it is not mentioned at all as part of the synagogue appurtenances in any of the historic codes, the Mishnah, the Talmud, the *Shulchan Aruch,* or the others. One might say there is not a single classic mention of it (as far as I can find).

All the references that are usually cited as referring to an Eternal Light actually refer to an occasional light in the synagogue or else, more generally, to lights lit all over the synagogue during services, but not specifically in front of the Ark. This is the case with the various references in the Midrash. Numbers *Rabba* 4:20 speaks of the merit of Peultai (mentioned in I Chronicles 26:5) who lit a light before the Ark in the Temple in the morning and then again in the evening. Thus this reference speaks of a light kindled twice a day, but not burning permanently. The same reference is in *Shir Rabba* 2:5. Nevertheless, Heyman, in his *Otzar Divre Chachamim,* quotes this reference as saying (*"Hamadlik,"* etc.): "He who kindles an eternal light before the Ark is blessed." Heyman may have seen a manuscript or some edition from which this is an exact quotation, but since the midrash in *Shir Rabba* quotes the same story as Numbers *Rabba* about Peultai, it would seem that Heyman's quotation is only a paraphrase. At all events, I have been unable to find that exact quotation which does speak of an Eternal Light. So also, Isaac Ashkenazi in his *Va-ya'an Yitzchok* (published Ancona, 1932) says that the Eternal Light is an old custom and gives various references among which are the *Kol Bo* 15 and the Responsa of Asher ben Jehiel, *K'lal* 5. Yet both these references speak merely of lighting a light in the synagogue for worship, but not necessarily before the Ark or a single light. So very likely it is with the other reference he gives to the *Shelah.* However a clear reference is found in the eighteenth century. Jedidiah Samuel Tarika in his responsa *Ben Jedid,* Chapter 7, in discussing a church lamp says of it, "It is just like ours which we hang before the Ark and which we call 'eternal' (*t'midim*)."

Actually the earliest definite reference that I have come across is in the Talmudic encyclopedia, *Pachad Yitzchok,* by Isaac Lamperonti, Rabbi of Ferrara, seventeenth-eighteenth century. Ismar Elbogen, in his *Gottesdienst,* p. 476, says that the first literary mention of the synagogue *ner tamid* is in the seventeenth century. He may be referring to this citation in *Pachad Yitzchok,* which actually uses the expression *"ner tamid"* for the Eternal Light in the synagogue. None of Elbogen's reference notes indicate that he saw an earlier mention than this one. Also Krauss (*Synagogale Altertuemer,* p. 391, Note 3) who discusses every detail of the appurtenances in the older synagogues, has made only this single reference (i.e., to *Pachad Yitzchok*).

This absence of any earlier reference to the synagogue Eternal Light is all the more remarkable because the general subject of lights in the synagogue is frequently discussed, from the time of the Tosefta through the Talmud, the Gaonim, and the later legalists. These discussions deal with the donation of lights and lamps to the synagogue (*Tosefta Megilla* III:3 and b. *Arachin* 6b) and whether these gifts may be changed for other purposes more needful to the synagogue at the time. Other discussions are on the question of whether a person may study by the light of the synagogue candles or lamps on the Sabbath, since it is generally prohibited to use the Sabbath lights for study, lest the person tilt them to improve the oil flow (b. *Shabbas* 12a). In recent years the discussion has been whether petroleum may be used instead of olive oil, the question being inspired by the fact that the petroleum, although it burns longer, does not have a pleasant odor (see Moses Schick, *Orah Hayyim* 83). Or there are discussions as to whether the synagogue lights may be used for secular purposes (to light one's way home, for example; *Shulchan Aruch, Yore Deah* 151:19; 154:13, 14). Further references to the question of whether the purpose intended by the donor of lamps and lights may be changed are: Meir of Rothenburg, ed. Berlin, 299; David ben Zimri (*Radbaz* II: 644); *Shulchan Aruch, Yore Deah* 151:19. Additional references to the question of studying by the synagogue lights are the *Responsa of the Gaonim*, ed. Lyck, 59, *Chemda Genuza,* 7. These references are discussed in such broad variety and so fully in the literature that we can hardly dismiss, as mere chance, the omission of any mention of the "Eternal" Light.

Of course, it is conceivable that although an Eternal Light may have been used in the synagogue right from the beginning, it just happens that no question ever arose about it. This is hardly believable because the various problems constantly discussed in reference to synagogue lights could very well have arisen with regard to the Eternal Light, had it actually been in general use. Clearly, it must have become an honored symbol only in recent centuries.

Because of this complete absence of earlier and classical reference to the synagogue Eternal Light in the legal literature, J. Wiesner (in *Ben Chananiah,* III, p. 581) surmises that it was borrowed from the use of an eternal light in Christian churches. But Wiesner is rather extreme in these matters. Leopold Loew, the editor of the magazine *Ben Chananiah* adds a note saying, "Why not say that the Jews derived it from the *ner tamid* in the Tabernacle and the Ancient Temple?" It well may be, therefore, that when the Eternal Light became customary a few centuries ago, it was seen to be analogous to the Eternal Light mentioned in the Bible for Tabernacle and Temple.

Be that as it may, the synagogue Eternal Light certainly has been in use for three centuries, and that is long enough for it to have become a beloved symbol. Evidently, its association with the biblically ordained Eternal Light for Tabernacle and Temple gave this symbol of the synagogue (whenever it did arise) an immediate and now a continuous sanctity. Therefore, to answer the question as to how uninterruptedly it must burn, we must consider it by analogy with the Eternal Light of the Tabernacle and Temple, with which it has now been for centuries associated.

How eternal was the original Tabernacle-Temple Eternal Light meant to be? Was it to burn without any interruption at all? We know that the *fire* on the altar is described as "not to be extinguished" (Leviticus 6:5). But the two biblical references to the Eternal Light, *ner tamid,* do not say that it is not to be extinguished. It is quite possible that the word *tamid* here does not mean "eternal," but "regular." In other words, the lights were to be kindled every day, but not necessarily to burn all of the day, so that one day's light should continue into the next, uninterrupted. In fact, Rashi to the passage in Exodus simply says that *"tamid"* here means "every night." Rashi's statement is an epitome of his argument in b. *Hagiga* 26b. The Tosfos there partially disagrees with Rashi and says that one of the two Tabernacle and Temple lights did miraculously stay alight permanently.

The Talmud also (in *Tamid* 30b) describes how the lamps were cleaned every day at dusk. The priest cleaned every one except one which remained alight until the others were cleaned and rekindled. This one light was called "the western light," and it is presumed that our single, eternal light is derived from (or is analogous to) this.

At all events, Isaac Lamperonti, in the first reference which I have found to *ner tamid,* used in the synagogue (s.v., *ner tamid*) says that since Rashi has explained that *"tamid"* in relation to the Tabernacle and Temple Light did not mean "continuous," but "regular," therefore we must conclude from Rashi that the *ner tamid* which we now have in the synagogue, which is to us "the small sanctuary," need not burn at all except at the hour of prayer. (The phrase, "the small sanctuary," for the synagogue, comes from b. Megilla 29a, based upon Ezekiel 11:16.) Here we have then, a clear statement that the light may even be extinguished.

But, of course, we must bear in mind that two centuries ago they had only oil lamps or tallow candles, and to keep a light continuous would be a difficult task. This may be an additional reason for assuming that they never had an Eternal Light in the synagogue in the past, namely, the technical difficulty involved. At all events, nowadays, with gas or electricity, it is easily possible to have the Eternal Light actually continuous, except for some accident. In that case, it should certainly be maintained as such. But should it be necessary, for purposes of rewiring or pipe refitting, to extinguish it, then there is no actual violation of the law involved at all. It is for us to maintain the general ideal of an eternally burning light, but we must remember that the authorities doubt whether even the original light in the Tabernacle and Temple itself was actually meant "never to be extinguished."

2

MEMORIAL CANDLES ON YOM KIPPUR

I have been asked concerning an older custom of burning candles in the synagague on Yom Kippur in memory of departed parents. Is this custom widespread and is it well established? (From Rabbi Walter Jacob, Rodef Shalom Temple, Pittsburgh, Pennsylvania.)

IN THE *Shulchan Aruch, Orah Hayyim* 610:4, Joseph Caro says that it is the custom on the Day of Atonement to light many candles in the synagogues and to spread beautiful cloths. To this Isserles adds that it is a custom that each individual, adult or minor, should kindle a light for himself in the synagogue and also a light for the soul of his father and mother who died. Then he adds: "And so it is proper to do, for thus some of the great scholars have written."

Thus Caro does not mention the custom of memorial candles at all, but it is Isserles who mentions it. This would indicate that it was a custom which did not develop among the Sephardim, but only among the Ashkenazim. Furthermore, the fact that even Isserles merely recommends it as something worth doing because "some of the scholars recommend it," would indicate that even among the Ashkenazim it was not a well-established or widespread custom.

It would, therefore, be worthwhile to trace the evolution of this custom and perhaps explain how and why it developed.

It is clear that the custom developed as an elaboration of earlier and related practices with regard to the Day of Atonement. The Talmud (b. *Shabbas* 119a) speaks of how to honor the Day. The verse from Isaiah 58:13 reads: "Do honor to the Holy Day of God," and the Talmud says this verse refers to honoring the Day of Atonement. The Talmud continues to the effect that since it is impossible to honor the Day of Atonement in the way in which the Sabbath is honored, namely, by extra meals, therefore it should be honored by fine garments. (That is why Caro says that it is the custom to spread handsome cloths in the synagogue on the Day of Atonement.) Asher ben Jehiel (thirteenth century) in his commentary to the Talmud (*Yoma,* the last chapter) adds another way of honoring the Day of Atonement besides with handsome cloths. He cites the verse in Isaiah 24:15: "In regions of light (*b'urim*) honor the Lord," and he calls attention to the fact that Targum (Jonathan) translates the word "*urim*" as candles or lanterns. Therefore he says there is a custom also to increase the number of candles kindled in the synagogue.

Another reason for increasing the lights of the synagogue besides "honoring the Day," is given by the *Kol Bo* (an early Halachic source of debated date, possibly thirteenth or fourteenth century; see *Jewish Encyclopedia,* Vol. VII, p. 538). The *Kol Bo* says that since people stay all day and all night in the synagogue and have to read all the time, they need many more lights.

Jacob ben Asher in the *Tur* quotes his father's opinion (*Orah Hayyim,* 610) but neither father nor son speaks of individuals each lighting a candle for himself, but merely of increasing the lights of the synagogue. Then how did the idea arise of having individual lights for each person on Yom Kippur? The *Kol Bo* quotes Asher ben Jehiel that individuals used to light lights for each person. Jacob Weil (fourteenth century) in his Responsa 191 and 192, speaks of the fact that Moses brought down the second tablets of stone on Yom Kippur. Therefore the day represents the "complete" availability of the Torah. Therefore, since men and not women are in duty bound to study the Torah, only the men have individual lights on Yom Kippur. He also says that on this day the judgment is completed for the souls of men, and since the verse (Proverbs 26:27) says: "The soul of man is the light of God," the lights also began to signify the redemption of the soul of the individual worshiper. Thus the *Kol Bo* says, "God says, 'Light a light before Me that I might protect your soul which is also called light.' " The parallelism of God's light (the Torah) and our light (our lives) is based upon the Midrash (Deuteronomy Rabba 4:4).

From the concept that the individual Yom Kippur light was for the redemption of the souls of the living, it was easy to move over to the additional idea that it should also signify a memorial or a redemption for the departed, because it was long held that the dead need redemption, as do the living. This is based upon the verse in Deuteronomy, 21:8: "Atone for Thy people Israel which Thou hast redeemed." The closing words, "which Thou hast redeemed," refer to those who came out of Egypt. They were already dead and yet the verse asks that they, too, be given atonement. Therefore the *Sifre* at the end of *Shoftim* says, "This teaches us that the dead, too, need atonement." So the *Kol Bo* (68) among the various reasons for lighting the extra lights, mentions also that it is a custom that each one lights a light or a lantern at his place in the synagogue to atone for his father or mother. Gaguine, in his *Keser Shem Tov,* Vol. I, p. 115, Note 153, quotes the *Sefer Chassidim* as speaking of this custom of the memorial candle on Yom Kippur, but I have been unable to verify the reference in any edition of the *Sefer Chassidim.* If it is indeed found in the *Sefer Chassidim,* this would perhaps be the oldest reference. The *Kol Bo* seems to have the earliest mention of this memorial custom. Few of the other codes mention it, but by the sixteenth century it is found, as we have said, in Isserles and also it is found in Mordecai Jaffe's *Levush* (*Levush Ha-chor* 610). Gaguine in his *Keser Shem Tov,* Vol. VI, p. 235, in the heading, speaks of this as a world-wide Jewish custom. He would not say so unless he knew of it, since he carefully preserved all these Sephardic customs. But since Joseph Caro does not mention it, while Isserles does mention it, and since none of the Sephardic codes mention it, it may be that Sephardim have picked up the custom from Ashkenazim in recent times.

While all the elements of the observance are already found in the *Kol Bo,* yet most later codes omit the memorial candle until the sixteenth century (Isserles and Mordecai Jaffe). Evidently the custom spread rather slowly. At all events, the process of the development of the custom of memorial lights for parents in the synagogue seems, therefore, clear enough. Yom Kippur was to be honored by special clothes and garments. Then it was honored by extra lights. Then the custom arose to have *individual* lights, either because reading had to be done all day or, later, because the soul "which is a light" is redeemed on that day. From the latter idea it spread (chiefly among the Ashkenazim) that the soul of the departed should also have redemption on the Day of Atonement; hence the memorial candles which became known in Jewish parlance as *neshomah licht.*

3

THE TORAH DECORATIONS

A high-minded worshiper, during the Holy Days, was rather repelled by what he considered to be the over-decoration of the Torah. The pomp of the whole Torah ritual seemed idolatrous to him. He consulted a scholar who raised the further question, whether in the responsa literature there is a discussion of the legal or spiritual status of these Torah ornaments; whether, for example, there was anything equivalent to the iconoclastic movement in Christianity; in other words, whether any of the scholars felt that there was an idolatrous admiration of these objects. (From J. R. M.)

BEFORE discussing the spiritual or legal status of the Torah ornaments, it might be well to see how much actual mention there is of them in the legal literature. Those who write about these objects in modern times frequently indicate that the decorations are meant to symbolize the garments of the priest as described in Scripture, chiefly in Exodus 28. The crown is the priest's mitre, the breastplate, the priest's breastplate, the bells were symbolic of the bells on the garment of the priest. This analogy is, as far as I know, mentioned nowhere in the older literature, and might easily mislead us into the belief that the ornaments which we now use were an ancient transfer of the priestly garments into synagogue worship; just as, for example, the hours of the priestly sacrifices were transferred to the synagogue as the hours of the three-times-a-day worship. This is a mistake. In fact, nowhere in the earlier literature are these ornaments mentioned at all. One could assume a priori that these objects are not ancient, from the very fact that they differ so greatly between Sephardic and Ashkenazic Jews. We use a mantle of velvet with the various objects hung on it, whereas they use a solid silver case and only occasionally do they have crowns on the tops of the staves protruding from the solid case. So it would, therefore, be important to see what references there are to them in the literature.

The Talmud (b. *Megilla* 26b) discussing which of the synagogue appurtenances may be sold, mentions the receptacle or case (*tik*) of the *Sefer Torah*. Maimonides' *Yad* (*Hilchos Sefer Torah* X:4) speaks, however, of "the pomegranates of gold and silver" that are brought for decoration to the synagogue. So Asher ben Jehiel in Tur, Yore Deah 282; so, also, the *Shulchan Aruch* in *Yore Deah* 282:16 speaks of "apples of silver and gold." The *Shulchan Aruch* in *Orah Hayyim* 138:18 speaks of the holy vessels of silver (using our usual term for the ornaments, *k'ley kodesh*) which people are accustomed to bring to the synagogues on the festivals. Isserles to *Orah Hayyim* 154:6 speaks of reworking the wooden rod on which the Ark curtain hangs into pointers to guide in the reading, and cites Isserlein (in his *Pesakim* 225). Yair Chaim Bachrach, in his *Responsa Chavos Yair*, 162, speaks of the permissibility of melting up unusable silver Torah ornaments and converting them into a silver candelabrum for use in the synagogue. The fullest discussion and perhaps the most interesting is found in the Responsa of Eleazar Fleckeles in his *Responsa Teshuva M'Ahava,* Vol. II, 232, p. 11. The responsum is dated 1814. The Austrian Empire had issued an order that all sacred silverware in churches and synagogues be brought to the royal mint where they would be purchased. Fleckeles, who was in the Klauss Synagogue which had many such ornaments, decided that it was Halachically permissible to obey the government order and to replace the ornaments with new ornaments from the money received from the mint. In the process of the discussion, he lists all the objects that we use today, the pointer, the crown, the breastplate, etc. Thus, by chance, we have a full description of the Torah ornaments, and it is only by the chance that Fleckeles was a little more wordy than usual in this responsum.

Now to the essence of the question: What was the status of these silver objects, and did anybody object to them as idolatrous? In the first place, as to the general attitude of the *people* towards them, it cannot be compared to the mood of the Christian people in the ninth century in Constantinople, when iconoclasm became strong. There the people adored statues of the Virgin and of saints, an adoration which easily could be considered idolatry, and therefore would evoke protest on the part of the puritanical-minded. But here these were inanimate objects that resembled no living thing and could hardly be personified by the ignorant as the Christian statues were. Besides the mood of the people, the actual status of these objects in the law kept them from being superstitiously adored. Beginning with the discussion in the Talmud, *Megilla* 26b, the main legal debate concerning these objects was under what circumstances they could be sold; how much sanctity they had, when sold. Generally the decisions were that the authorities could sell them and use the money for any proper purpose. This was certainly true of the objects that were individually owned. Furthermore, the fact that they *could* be individually owned and brought to the synagogue for holidays (*Orah Hayyim* 153:18) made them more or less private possessions. In fact, in *Orah Hayyim* 154:10 it is seen that at the end of Succos, the Hassan Torah was often crowned with the Torah crown. The whole burden of the argument of Fleckeles in the responsum mentioned above was that these objects could be sold. There is an interesting comment in the heart of the responsum, in which he says as proof of his decision, that we have so few of these objects left from the times "before the Expulsion," and therefore it is clear that the earlier people of Prague, "before the Expulsion," sold the objects.

The only status of sanctity which these objects had was a reflection of the sanctity of the Torah on which they were hung. The Torah had *kedusha,* and these objects were *tashmishey kedusha,* "appurtenances of the sacred." What the Torah's sanctity amounted to was, as indicated in *Yore Deah* 282, that it should be respected, but even the Torah could be sold for certain specific purposes.

So the status of these objects in the law is clear: They receive a "reflected respect" from the respect due to the Torah, nothing more than that.

4

EMBROIDERED NAME OF GOD ON ARK CURTAIN

The Tetragrammaton is embroidered on an Ark curtain in a synagogue in Buenos Aires. A colleague objected that it is not permitted. (Question discussed by Dr. Nathan Blum, Buenos Aires, Brazil.)

THE book which the colleague quoted as source for the objection is *Leket Ha-Kemach Ha-Chodesh,* a work recently collected by Jacob Zvi Katz, who was Rabbi in Sabasia and now is Rabbi of the Ashkenazic congregation in Amsterdam. Being in Amsterdam, he saw the great library of the Etz Chaim Yeshiva, containing many books of Shaalos-u-Teshuvos that he had never seen before. Therefore he decided to enlarge and to modernize the collection *Leket Ha-Kemach* made by Moses Hagiz.

The *Berech Yitzchok* which he quotes is by Isaac of Fass,

published in Salonika in 1803. Responsum 2 in this book is by Chaim Abulafia who says, quoting the *Shach,* that embroidery is forbidden only on a *tallis,* because appurtenances of a *mitzvah (tashmishey mitzvah)* may be thrown aside and the Name of God on it thus defiled, but that it is not forbidden on Torah covers and *peroches,* which are appurtenances of holiness *(tashmishey kedusha).* Isaac of Fass, in the next *Teshuvah,* answers him to the effect that the *Shach* meant to permit it only on the Torah mantles and not on the curtain, which is only the appurtenance of appurtenances *(tashmishey tashmishey)* of holiness. However, this distinction is artificial, and we can certainly rely on Abulafia that it is permitted. Your arguments are sound, therefore. The curtain is never in danger of being brought to an unclean place, and that is all that is important here.

But, of course, there still remains the basic question, whether in the first place *(l'chatchilla)* it is permitted to embroider the Name of God on the curtain even if one could be sure that it would be carefully protected against being taken to an unclean place. The whole discussion should be based on the Talmud passage in *Arachin* 6a, where the question comes up of a Gentile who gave a beam of wood for the Temple with the Name of God on it. The Talmud says that the Name of God should be erased and that the beam can then be used.

Now, the Talmud discusses the reason that the Name of God may be erased, and it says that this Name is not sacred because it is not written in the normal place for the writing of God's Name. Rashi gives two explanations of this reason, namely, that the Name of God is holy only when the text is written with the Name in its proper place, but the Name alone is not holy and, therefore, can be erased. Rashi admits that this is a sound explanation, but he prefers a more artificial reason. Yet the explanation as we have given it is sound, as we can tell from the fact that the Rambam says that the Name can be erased from metal vessels, etc. (See *Hilchos Yesodeh Torah* 6:1 ff.). This is based on *Messeches Sofrim* V. Therefore, even if the Name of God on the curtain were destroyed, it would not be a sin because the Name is not "in its proper place," as the Talmud says, and therefore is not holy.

But there is no reason why we should debate this ourselves, as if this were a new question. In the last generation the greatest Galician authority decided that there is no objection to embroidering the Name of God on the mantles, etc., namely, Shalom Mordecai Schwadron of Berzun (Maharsham). This responsum of the Maharsham is not found, as far as I know, in his regular *Teshuvos*, but is in a book called *Jerushalaim D'Dahava* by Benzion Katz, who was Rabbi of Czernovitz. He discusses a similar question, and the Maharsham says as follows, in clear words: "But as for sewing (as opposed to writing) there is no holiness involved at all in the sewn or embroidered Name, and therefore the Rambam did not concern himself about that in his Teshuva quoted by the Bes Joseph in Yore Deah 283." Because I am certain that this book (*Jerushalaim D'Dahava*) is not found in Buenos Aires, since it is a rare book, I am sending you the title page and the page of the *Teshuva* of Shalom Mordecai Schwadron.

Let us, then, sum up: The only possible objection to embroidering the Name is that it would be brought (as with a *tallis*) to an unclean place. This caution does not apply to the curtain, which is not carried around. The distinction of Isaac of Fass that it is permissible to embroider only the mantle of the Torah but not the curtain is an artificial distinction, because the important question is not whether one is *tashmishey* and the other is *tashmishey tashmishey* (an appurtenance of an appurtenance) but whether they are safe from being carried into unclean places. The essential fact is, according to the Talmud in *Arachin* 6a, that the Name, not written in the normal way, is not holy at all, and this is the basis of the clear answer of Maharsham in *Jerushalaim D'Dahava.*

5

WHITE TORAH COVERS

The congregation has been using the customary red or scarlet velvet Torah coverings throughout the year, except that for holidays, confirmations, and bar mitzvahs they have been using the white Torah coverings. Is it permissible to have the Ark and the Torahs covered with white throughout the year? (From Rabbi Harold L. Gelfman, Macon, Georgia.)

I HAVE searched through most of the books of *minhagim* and I have not succeeded in discovering a single reference to a well-established custom that the Torahs should be covered with white during the High Holy Days. I know that this is the custom in many of our congregations, yet the very fact that the overwhelming majority of the books of *minhagim* have no reference to this custom would indicate clearly that it is certainly not in any sense a requirement of the

Halacha. This silence as to white coverings is rather remarkable when one considers that a number of other questions concerning the Torah coverings are discussed in the legal literature and are codified with considerable details in the *Shulchan Aruch, Orah Hayyim* 147. As for the curtain of the Ark, its status is not very firm in the Halacha except as a vague analogy to the curtain in the Temple in Jerusalem in front of the Holy of Holies. In fact, Maimonides, when he carefully discusses the appurtenances of the synagogue makes no mention at all of an Ark curtain. (See *Yad Hilchoth, Tefillah* XIV.) The same is true of the *Tur* and the *Shulchan Aruch.* (See *Orah Hayyim* 150.) Of course the Ark curtain has become customary, certainly since the sixteenth century, where it is mentioned in various responsa, but it has no legal status. For a full discussion, see *Reform Responsa,* p. 62 ff. Therefore, speaking from the point of view of the strict letter of the law, there is no ground for decision, prohibition, or permission with regard to the color of either the Ark curtain or the coverings (the mantles) of the Torah.

Since there is no strict legal basis for any decision, we must rely for our conclusion on whatever analogies are available. There is considerable discussion in the law making a connection between personal garments and the Ark curtain and Torah coverings. For example, there are many questions as to whether worn garments can be converted into an Ark curtain or Torah covering, or whether used-up Torah coverings should be made into shrouds for the dead and thus decently disposed of by burial. Hence, in order to come closer to our subject, it would be logical to consider the white *garments* worn on the holidays and to draw whatever analogy we can.

There is, of course, a widespread custom firmly based in the legal literature that the white *kittel* (the East European name) or the *sargenes* (the West European name) be worn by the worshiper on the Day of Atonement. It is also obvious that the white *kittel* was associated with the shrouds worn by the deceased. This fact is referred to specifically, for example, in the *Hago'os Maimoniot* to the *Yad Hilchoth* Sabbath, Chapter 30, where it is called "the garment of the dead." Also, Moses Isserles in *Orah Hayyim* 610, where the Day of Atonement customs are discussed, says (4): "So it is the custom to wear the *kittel* which is white and pure and also is the garment of the dead." If this interpretation of the meaning of the white garment is the correct and the basic meaning, namely that it is the garment of the dead and therefore is worn in humility on the Day of Atonement, then we would have to conclude by analogy that the white Ark curtain and the white Torah covers should be used *only* on the solemn days of the High Holy Days.

However, this somber interpretation of the white garments clearly is not the original or the basic one. Even as a garment to be worn on the solemn Day of Judgment, the earlier sources give it a different interpretation. The classic source for the older meaning is in the Palestinian Talmud, *Rosh Hashonah,* Chapter 1:3, where it is said: "Normally when a man has to face judgment, he wears black garments (to be humble in the face of a stern judge) but we wear white garments in joyous confidence that God will perform a miracle for us." In other words, the white garments were garments of joy. This is also clear from the Babylonian Talmud, *Shabbas* 114a, in which it is said that brides and grooms wear white. This Talmudic understanding of white garments as garments of joy is borne out by early Jewish custom; for is not the white *kittel* worn by the head of the household at the Passover Seder and by the cantor who prays the *Mussaf* on the last day of Succoth and the first days of Passover (i.e., for rain and for dew)? Furthermore, one of the earliest of the Rhineland authorities, Eliezer ben Joel Halevi (first half of the twelfth century) says in his code *Raviah* (Sabbath 197) that the *sargenes* was made especially for Sabbath wear, which certainly is a day of joy.

All this indicates that the basic and original meaning of white and the white garment was not somber dread but confident joy. Nevertheless, it is true that for historical and psychological reasons the white garment began to be associated with sorrow, and even the non-High Holy Day uses of it were given a somber meaning. The wearing of the white by the bride and groom was now described as due to the fact that their marriage day was a fast day (they were required to fast). The fact that it was worn at the Seder and otherwise at holidays was explained as a solemn warning to think of death in the times of joy. In other words, the white garment, originally a joyous garment even for the Day of Judgment (according to the *Jerushalmi*) eventually became, in its every use, associated with the shrouds of the dead. (See the description of this process of change from joyous to gloomy in Berliner, *Jewish Life in the Middle Ages,* especially p. 48.)

How, then, should we decide our question? According to the law and the original meaning of the white garments, the white can be used for any occasion one wishes, and certainly for joyous occasions. But in accordance with the development of Jewish custom and mood, it has become associated with solemn and serious thoughts. I believe that we should respect the moods of the past few centuries (even though there is no strong *legal* ground for it) and keep the white garments primarily for the High Holy Days and perhaps for an occasional other holiday. It would be contrary to the mood of our tradition, though not of course of its strict law, to make the white coverings a permanent and common usage.

6

DESTROYING THE DIVINE NAME

At certain Jewish social affairs of a partially religious nature, such as Bar Mitzvahs, etc., cakes are served with the Name of God written in icing on them. How can it be permitted to eat such cakes, since it is forbidden to destroy the Name of God? (Asked by Professor Jacob Marcus, Cincinnati, Ohio.)

WHILE it may seem to be merely curious interest as to whether the Name of God may be put on cakes, many more serious problems are related to it, such as painting verses on synagogue walls, since when the time comes for the synagogue to be redecorated, the Names of God originally painted on the walls will have to be blotted out. Also, the question would involve the treatment of utensils, spoons, etc., with the Name of God engraved upon them. The question is a difficult one, not only because the law involved is highy complicated, but also because in the development of the law, there are two basically opposite tendencies. It is therefore necessary to go into the subject rather fully.

The basic prohibition of erasing the Name of God is derived from the verse in Deuteronomy 12:3–4, where we are told: "Thou shalt destroy their names (of the idols) but thou shalt not do so to the Lord thy God." The *Sifre* to the passage (ed. Friedmann, p. 87b) says that it is therefore forbidden to erase the Name of God. The Talmud in b. *Maccos* 22a uses the same verse as the basis for this prohibition. The Rambam in *Hilchoth Yesode Torah,* VI, 1ff., develops most of the law implied in this prohibition. He speaks also of engraving on a vessel and says that the Name of God (on the spoon or cup) must be cut out and hidden, put away (*ganuz*) before the article can be melted. The Name of God tattooed on the skin must be covered up when bathing. The prohibition of erasure applies to all sacred writings (not only the Torah scroll). Thus in *Sefer Ha-chinuch* (Aaron of Barcelona), commandment 437 likewise states that wherever the Name is found, in whatever commentary, etc., it may not be destroyed. This explains the habit of preserving old prayerbooks, etc., and burying them with a righteous man in the cemetery, as was originally done with the *Sefer Torah.*

The prohibition elaborates into questions such as this: If a verse containing the Name of God were painted on the walls of a synagogue, how can the walls later be repainted thus erasing the Name of God? This question was asked of Jonah Landsofer (Bohemia, seventeenth-eighteenth century) and he, in turn, asked it of Meyer Eisenstadt (see *M'il Zedaka,* 23 and 24, and *Panim Meiros* I, 45). They both are disinclined to permit the repainting, although both are troubled by the statement in *Sota* 35b that the Jews wrote the Torah on stone in seventy languages and then plastered the stone, hiding the writing.

All of the above is sufficient to indicate that the tendency of the law has been towards increasing carefulness with the Name of God, spreading the former sanctity of the written Name in Scrolls to the printed Name (prayerbooks, etc.), to the painted Name (on synagogue walls, etc.), to the engraved Name (on spoons, etc.).

While this tendency towards increasing caution as to the erasure of the Name is a definite development, nevertheless, there are so many limitations (which we will now mention) to the prohibition of erasure that they constitute an entirely opposite tendency. First of all, what does the law mean by "writing"? The Mishnah (in *Sabbath* XII, 4) discussing what sort of writing is prohibited on the Sabbath, says that if one writes with fruit juice or with any material that does not endure, this is not to be legally considered "writing," and therefore it is not prohibited on the Sabbath. Hence, a writing of the Name of God on a cake with sugar or whatever the icing is composed of, is not permanent writing at all and, therefore, not prohibited. Obviously, since (technically) it is not writing, one may destroy it.

A second consideration involves who the writer is. Even a *Sefer Torah,* if written by an *epikoros,* a *min,* i.e., an unbelieving Jew, must actually be burned with all the Names of God in it (see reference in the *Yad* 6, 8; this is based upon the Talmud in b. *Gittin* 45b). If it is written, however, by a non-Jew, it must be hidden away (i.e., not burned). The Rambam says that if written by a non-believing Jew, it is even a *mitzvah* to burn it. Who knows who the pastry chef was who wrote the Name of God? Only if he were a pious Jew could the Name have any sanctity (aside from the question of the temporary nature of the "writing").

Furthermore, and this perhaps is the most important element in the whole matter, not all writing of the Name of God, even by a pious Jew, is sacred. All the laws on this matter are derived from the writings of the Sefer Torah and other scrolls. Every writing of the Name of God, in order to be deemed sacred, has to be written with the conscious intent on the part of the scribe and his clear awareness that he is writing it for a sacred purpose (*l'shem kedusha*). Joseph Caro, based upon early authorities, even believes that he must actually *utter* the formula of consecration for every Torah Divine Name he comes to. At all events, either in mind or by actual words, the Name is not holy unless consciously consecrated (see *Shulchan Aruch, Yore Deah,* 274 and the long discussion by the Taz in the passage).

Suppose, then, the Names are not consciously consecrated. What is their status? May they be erased? The classic source of the discussion of this question is in Simon ben Zemach Duran (*Tashbetz I,* 177). He bases his argument on the Talmud in *Gittin* 20a, where we are told that if the scribe should have written "YHWH" but thought that he should have written "Judah," but by chance left out the *daled* and thus wrote the Name "YHWH" anyhow, the law is (with the Rabbis) that the Name is not sacred (at least not proper). Duran, upon this foundation, says that the Name is not sacred at all, unless written with conscious intent to make it sacred. (See, also, *Hagahot Maimoniot* to the *Yad* l.c.).

Upon this foundation, Joseph Babad (of Tarnopol) in his famous commentary to *Sefer Ha-chinuch* (*Minchas Chinuch*) says (l.c.) explicitly: It is the opinion of many of the earlier and later authorities that *no sin* is committed by erasing a Name which we know for certain was not consciously consecrated (cf. top of column 2, p. 42).

It is evident that the *mood,* especially of the later Halacha, is to avoid any erasure of any Name of God. Yet the basic law is absolutely clear that an impermanent writing by someone of whose piety we do not know, and which, at all events, has never been consciously sanctified, such a Name has no sanctity at all. The only conclusion one can come to, based upon the general mood of the law, is that in the case mentioned, no sin has been committed, but what was done is contrary to the spirit of reverence for God's Name.

7

SECULAR MUSIC IN THE SYNAGOGUE

A congregation has been asked to lend its building for a general concert of high-grade music, an operatic star leading the concert. Is it proper to lend the synagogue premises for this purpose? (From Rabbi Joshua O. Haberman, Trenton, New Jersey.)

THERE are a number of full discussions of music in the synagogue. The outstanding one among those discussions would be the famous one of Leon of Modena (Number 6 of his Responsa) on Jews and music. This responsum is to be found in *Treasury of Responsa,* p. 160.

Modena goes thoroughly into all the questions of music and the Jews and the synagogue. He deals with all the ancient prohibitions which seem to forbid instrumental or secular music in the synagogue on the ground that we are in perpetual mourning for the destruction of the Temple. He disposes of these general objections. Then he justifies the use of music as an aid to the fulfillment of a *mitzvah,* such as marriage (for which purpose instrumental music was permitted even on the Sabbath) and also as an aid in the service. He also says, in reference to his friend Solomon dei Rossi, who was a choir leader for the Duke of Mantua, that if one is under the command of the King or the Prince, one may study and make music. He ends up with saying that in order to fulfill these various *mitzvos,* a person is permitted to study music in general. Therefore it is possible to argue that increasing the standard of musical appreciation among our congregations would aid us in enhancing the musical beauty of our services which is, of course, a *mitzvah.*

In *Shulchan Aruch, Orah Hayyim* 561, 3, giving the old law, Caro says that we must not have instrumental music at all and that it is forbidden even to listen to it, but Isserles says at the end of the paragraph that for the needs of *mitzvos* as, for example, weddings, all is permitted. Similar permissions of dancing, etc., are recorded, generally by Isserles, indicating that the people have simply moved away from this excessive puritanism, and that these various pleasures hitherto frowned upon have gradually become permissible.

So we have to consider, in addition to the strictness of the law, what has "become permissible" in the mood of our day. We are now all accustomed to listening to good music and do not find it an hilarity but a cultural satisfaction. Of course, much depends upon the type of music which is to be permitted in the synagogue. To give a sensual, riotous jazz concert in the synagogue would insult the sanctity of the building and would be contrary to Jewish law, as could easily be proved. There are decisions, for example, against holding even temporary Holy Day services in hotel ballrooms where hilarious modern dances are given during the year.

But a high-grade musical concert is culture to us. We do not feel any more that it is a violation of the older objections against *any* singing and *any* music. Those objections were already refuted by Leon de Modena and by the life of the people in the time of Isserles.

A negative answer prohibiting secular concerts in the synagogue was given by the Orthodox Professor of the Hildesheimer Seminary in Berlin, Jehiel Weinberg. He calls to mind the prohibition of listening to music altogether, though there is justification for listening to religious music. He bases his opinion on the material referred to above. Even a religious concert which may be deemed permissible in the synagogue should be preceded by the reciting of a chapter of the Psalms, which would make it surely an act of study. But secular music should be resisted in the Orthodox synagogue and the rabbi should never yield to the congregation on the matter.

This strict, unyielding Orthodox opinion is of special historical interest because as Jehiel Weinberg explains, it was written in Berlin during the Nazi times, when Jews were forbidden to meet in any sort of assembly except in the synagogues. Since the German Jews loved music, and concerts of secular music were given in the Liberal synagogues, the inquirer was concerned about the danger that Orthodox Jews would go to the Liberal synagogues to hear music and thus, perhaps, be weaned away from their Orthodoxy.

At all events, it is clear that the Orthodox synagogues had some doubt about the permissibility of a secular concert in the synagogue, or the question would never have been asked, and Liberal synagogues had no objection. The responsum is in the newly published *S'riday Esh*, Volume II, 12.

Our answer, however, would be that just as we have lectures on general culture in the synagogue and do not feel that they contradict the mood of the institution, so can we have music as an expression of general culture, specifically since raising the standard of musical appreciation may aid us in our efforts to enhance the beauty of the service, which is a direct *mitzvah*.

8

CHANGING THE TORAH ROLLERS

There are two Torah rollers, *Etz Chaims,* which are no longer in use. The congregation desires to keep them in a case for historical purposes; but the rollers, in order to fit the case, need to be taken apart (i.e., the perpendicular part has to be removed from the plate). Is it permissible to do this? (From Rabbi Martin B. Ryback, Evansville, Indiana.)

THE question is, first of all, to what degree of sacredness are the *etz chaims* to be assigned? The *Shulchan Aruch, Orah Hayyim* 153 ff., discusses the disposal of sacred objects and in 154 discusses the various degrees of sanctity of sacred synagogue objects. It is evident that the parts of a *Sefer Torah* have a rather high sanctity. They are "appurtenances of sacredness" (*tashmishey kedusha*) rather than the lower degree of *tashmishey mitzvah*. The question, then, is what rights are there of the disposal of *tash-mishey kedusha*, which the *etz chaims* clearly are. The *Mogen Avraham* (paragraph 14 to *Shulchan Aruch* 153) says that such objects may, of course, be sold by the consent of the leaders of the community ("the seven notables of the city"), in this case, of course, the Board of Trustees of the congregation. But although they may be sold and the money used, the objects sold nevertheless retain some sanctity.

Most of the later discussions are based upon this observation of the *Mogen Avraham*. The chief discussion is by Joel Ashkenazi, in his Responsa published in Muncazc, 1893, in which he deals with a case very much like the one with which you are dealing. In his Responsa (*Orah Hayyim* 15) the following question is asked: A man donated a *Sefer Torah* to the synagogue; the *etz chaims* were of copper, but the *Sefer Torah* with the *etz chaims* of copper proved too heavy for use. The question asked was, what may be done with those copper *etz chaims*? Ashkenazi bases his discussion and his decision primarily upon the *Mogen Avraham's* decision, cited above. He also cites Maimonides in *Hilchos Sefer Torah* X:4, to the effect that these appurtenances of the *Sefer Torah* are *tashmishey kedusha* and so, even when no longer in use, still have sanctity. However, though they still have sanctity, Ashkenazi continues, the officers of the congregation may remove them from their sacred use (if they are worn out). But since they still remain sacred, he suggests that some respected use be made out of these unused copper *etz chaims*. They could be cut up to make smaller *etz chaims* for smaller Torahs or be made into a copper menorah.

Shalom Mordecai Schwadron, the great Galician authority of the last century, in his Responsa (IV:135) cites this whole discussion with approval.

This applies to your problem in the following way: The Board of the congregation can decide that these *etz chaims* need no longer be used in worship, but they cannot strip them of their sacred status entirely. Is, then, the purpose for which you intend to use them a worthy one and in consonance with their residual sacredness? Certainly it is. To preserve them for historical purposes is certainly a worthy purpose. In fact, the law in Maimonides, which was cited above, says that they should be *hidden away* (*ganuz*) which is exactly what you are doing. Now, if in order to hide them away, it is necessary to take them apart, there is no objection to it. You will notice that Joel Ashkenazi, whose responsum is crucial in the whole discussion, would permit the cutting up of the copper *etz chaims* to make smaller *etz chaims,* or to remold them entirely to make a menorah.

Since the tradition requires that the change in the status of a sacred object be done by "the seven notables of the city," i.e., the Board of the congregation, it would be in accord with the mood of tradition if a resolution be introduced at the Board meeting, and the Board pass a decision formally to make this change.

9

HOW TO CARRY THE TORAH

"It occurs to me that the Torah is held on the left shoulder (heart side) if a person is right-handed and on the right side if a person is left-handed, following the custom of the Tefillin wrapping." (From Dr. Floyd Fierman, El Paso, Texas.)

WHAT requirements, if any, are there in the legal literature with regard to how the Torah should be taken out of the Ark (i.e., with which hand, etc.) and how should it be carried to the reading desk? The analogy suggested in the question with the *tefillin* is a helpful one. The Talmud is very specific with regard to the *tefillin*. The *tefillin shel yad* shall be put on the left arm of a right-handed person and on the right arm of a left-handed person (b. *Menachos* 37a ff.). Some such parallel is indeed implied in some of the later legal literature with regard to handling the Torah, as will be seen. Of course there is this basic difference between the *tefillin* and the Torah: the *tefillin* are required to be worn by each person, but no one is required to have the Torah with him constantly except, perhaps, the king (see Deuteronomy 17: 18, 19). The king is required to have the Torah with him at all times, but Scripture does not specify how this Torah should be handled. As for the average person who comes into contact with the Torah only occasionally, there are certainly no legal specifications (in Bible or Talmud) as to how he shall handle the Torah.

While it is true that neither the Bible nor the Talmud has any requirement as to how the Torah should be handled, some such requirement begins to appear very soon in post-Talmudic times. The *Tractate Soferim* 3:10, a Gaonic tractate, states that he who hands a *Sefer Torah* to another man should give it with his right hand and the recipient should take it with his right hand. This requirement, if it can actually be called a *requirement,* is based on the verse in Deuteronomy 33:2: "From His right hand, He gave them a fiery law," i.e., since, according to this poem, God gave the Torah with His right hand, we should always handle it with our right hand. Perhaps the next reference is in *Sefer Chassidim* (109) written in the Rhineland in the twelfth century, which quotes the statement in *Tractate Soferim* almost verbatim.

From this source the requirement of handling the Torah with the right hand found its way into the law gradually, apparently through the Ashkenazim. The classic Sephardic authorities do not mention it at all. Thus, there is no such requirement in the *Tur* (written by Jacob ben Asher in the fourteenth century in Spain) in *Orah Hayyim* 134, which would be the natural place to mention it since he speaks of taking out the Torah. Nor does Joseph Caro in his *Bes Joseph,* his great commentary on the *Tur,* make any reference to it. However, Moses Isserles of Cracow, in his commentary *Darche Moshe* to the *Tur,* quoting a Rhineland authority, Maharil (Jacob Moellin), says he should take the Torah with his right hand; but here he cites as a proof text, not the verse given in *Soferim* from Deuteronomy, that God gave the law with His right hand, but the verse from Song of Songs 2:6: "With his right hand doth he embrace me."

Likewise in the *Shulchan Aruch,* Joseph Caro himself makes no mention of which hand should take out the Torah from the Ark but, again, Isserles in his note does mention it. Furthermore, the latest authorities seem to bear in mind the analogy with the *tefillin.* Ephraim Z. Margolis of the last century, in his *Shaare Ephraim* (section 10) says that the man should take the Torah out with his right hand, but if he is left-handed, he should take it out with his left hand. The requirement of using the right hand (for average right-handed people) has become a fixed rule with Ashkenazim at least, and is to be found in the two latest authorities in discussing this *Shulchan Aruch* section, namely, the *Aruch ha-Shulchan* by Jehiel Epstein and the *Mishnah Berura* by the Chofetz Chaim.

Now, having taken it out with his right hand, should he rest it on his left shoulder or on his right shoulder? In this regard there is not even a semblance of a requirement. There are two hints, but they seem to be mutually contradictory. If Isserles (and Maharil, his source) quote the verse from the Song of Songs, "His right hand embraceth me," it would seem to imply that it should be the right hand which curls around the Torah and presumably the Torah then rests on the right shoulder. On the other hand, Dov Ber Reifman, in his classic work on the rules governing the Torah reading, *Shulchan ha-Keriah,* page 12, says that the man should indeed take it out with his right hand, but carry it against his heart (*k'neged libo*). This would imply that when you take it out with your right hand, you rest it on your left shoulder against the heart. This procedure would seem to be the natural one, but there is no clear requirement with regard to it.

To sum up, then, there is no definite requirement in the Talmud as to which hand should take out the Torah; but based upon the post-Talmudic treatise *Soferim,* the Ashkenazim gradually developed the rule that the right hand should always take it out of the Ark (except for a left-handed man). As to which shoulder it should rest against, only the vague reference of Reifman (*k'neged libo*) and perhaps, too, the convenience of handling seems to require that it should rest against the left shoulder.

10

WHEN EIGHTH DAY OF PASSOVER IS ON SABBATH

Since the Reform practice as to the length of the festivals is the same as the biblical and the Israeli, which Torah reading shall be used on the Sabbath of what would be the eighth day of Passover? What is the practice of Reform congregations in America?

THIS question has been asked a number of times, and answered by the writer as Chairman of the C.C.A.R. Committee on Responsa, so the answer may be deemed official, or as nearly official as any Conference responsum is. That is to say, it is meant for guidance and not for strict governance. Yet in general, it represents a fairly universal practice among our congregations.

The actual problem is this: On the holidays, the regular sequence of weekly readings (the *Sedras*) is suspended and a special holiday Torah reading is provided. When the holiday is over, the regular sequence of Torah *Sedras* resumes on the first Saturday after the holiday.

But if, as happens fairly often, the eighth day of Passover is on a Saturday, then in Israel, which considers the eighth day a regular non-festival Sabbath, the regular cycle of Torah reading resumes. Therefore Israel is one week ahead of the rest of the Jewish world in the Torah cycle. But not for long! Israel continues ahead until they come to the first double portion. On Pesach, which usually takes place on the *Sedra Tzav,* the dislocation continues for only two weeks, when the double portion *Sazria-Mezoro* comes. That week Israel just reads *Sazria* separately, and the next week

Mezoro separately, and thus the rest of world Jewry catches up with them.

This problem does not arise with regard to the ninth day of Succos because that cannot be on Sabbath.

Now, this solution (of Israel being ahead one week until the next double portion comes) works well because of the fact that the different schedule of readings occurs in different countries (although even in Israel it is still a problem for visitors who do not come there as permanent settlers, since they must follow their home schedule).

But the problem remains in the relationship between Reform and non-Reform congregations in America, England, etc. Here we are in the *same* country, and it is not convenient that for a number of weeks we should be in dislocation as to Torah reading with the rest of American Jewry. We have therefore arrived at the following practical solution: We simply reread on that Sabbath the special reading of the holiday that we read the day before, and take a Psalm as the supplementary reading, but the service that day is a regular Sabbath service. In this way, on the very next Sabbath we are in accord with all the Jews of our environment. The list of Torah readings at the back of the *Union Prayer Book Newly Revised* follows this solution of the problem.

11

A SEDER WITHOUT WINE

A blackberry wine has been advertised as "Kosher for Pesach." Since blackberries grow on bushes and not on vines, would it be proper to have that wine in the *Kiddush* cup when the blessing is invoked which specifically refers to the "fruit of the vine"? Or would it be necessary to use the wine that came from grapes specifically? (From Rabbi Bernard Perelmuter, Erie, Pennsylvania.)

ALL the Talmudic literature constantly praises wine (grape wine) as a symbol of joy and blessing and health and, of course, takes it for granted that grape wine is used for *Kiddush* on Sabbath, holidays, and the four cups for Passover. The first question is, therefore, whether it is possible or permissible to use any other wine but grape wine for the holidays and especially for the Seder.

Actually, they knew and mentioned a large variety of wines, some of which would hardly be called wine. Besides the various fortified and spiced wines, they speak also of raisin wine, which is apparently not fermented but boiled. After Talmudic times there is reference to wine made from pomegranates or from apples, which would really be our apple cider. (See *Yore Deah* 114:3, and the references for the earlier sources.)

Now the question is whether these variations of wine or pseudo-wine are usable for religious purposes. The first discussions concern the Sabbath. There is no question that on the Sabbath, substitutes for wine can be used, as is obvious from the fact that it is possible to make the *Kiddush* over bread or over whiskey. The law is clearly stated in the *Shulchan Aruch, Orah Hayyim* 272. In 272:8, while Joseph Caro himself says that there are "some who say" that we may not make *Kiddush* over boiled wine (i.e., non-fermented) and honeyed wine, nevertheless the weight of his own opinion is that we may make *Kiddush* on these. And so in 272:9, Isserles proposes the custom that if no wine is available, one may make *Kiddush* over bread, etc.

However, the law is generally stricter in demanding wine for the four cups of the Seder than it is for Kiddush on

Sabbath. For example, Solomon ha-Levi (in his responsa quoted by Lamperonti in *Pachad Yitzchok*) says that at the Seder you may use nothing but wine. However, this is an extreme opinion. An opposite opinion, which became the law, starts with Issac Alfasi at the end of *Pesachim*. He says that he who has no wine can make *Kiddush* over the *matzoh* (just as on Friday night over the bread). He describes the process as follows: The man makes the first of the two blessings over the *matzoh,* then lays his hand on the *matzoh* (in analogy to holding the wine cup) and after the *Kiddush* which he then recites, he makes the second blessing over the matzoh. Rabbenu Nissim in his commentary (*ad loc.*) says that Alfasi derived this from a Gaonic decision in the case of a man who was not permitted to drink wine. This decision finally became law as one can see in the *Shulchan Aruch, Orah Hayyim* 483, in which it is clearly stated that one can conduct the Seder without wine. Caro gives the law there clearly and Isserles adds that in our countries where we drink mead, we may use this or any other liquor if it is prevalent in the country.

So it is clear that if one does not have wine or one may not drink wine or, according to Isserles, if other liquors are the favorite drink of the community, one may use them for the Passover Seder. Of course, one may not recite the blessing "fruit of the vine" over such liquors, but the general blessing, "everything created by His word."

Now as to the actual status of this blackberry wine, since it is now clear that it is permissible. Which blessing should be recited over it? I consulted an expert in the wine business (M. O., of Pittsburgh) and he tells me that the blackberry in the blackberry wine is actually only a flavoring of the essence of blackberries, but that the bulk of blackberry wine is actually bland grape wine. Therefore this is exactly the situation with the various flavored wines mentioned in the Talmudic sources and may be used as a Passover wine, and the blessing over wine invoked. This latter might require a little more thought on the question of the "change of taste" from usual grape wine. If the general taste is like wine, then it is simply like the various spiced wines and it may be used for the Seder.

12

FROZEN ETROGIM

I have been successful in growing *Etrogim,* but due to the difference in seasons in this part of the world, they have come to fruit now. Would it be permissible to put them into deep freeze until Succoth? Equally, would it be permissible to re-use an Etrog which has been put into deep freeze after the Festival? (From Rabbi C. E. Cassell, Bulawayo, South Africa.)

This question is most interesting and is, I believe, much easier to answer nowadays than it would have been fifty years ago. In the last few years the development and the availability of deep-freezers have resulted in quite a good deal of rabbinic discussion which has found its way into the Responsa literature. The question is whether meat may be put into a deep-freezer and be kept for months. Since the questions involved with the deep-freezer and its use have so far been confined to the matter of freezing meat and using it months later, we ought to go into this question first and see if there are any analogies or principles developed which would aid us in the question which you ask about the *Etrog.*

About frozen meat, all they knew in the past was of meat that was accidentally frozen by the cold of the northern winter or had fallen into a river in winter during transportation. The question then arose about such frozen meat because of the rule in the *Shulchan Aruch* (*Yore Deah* 69:12) that meat which is kept three days without salting may not be boiled (but may be roasted), because after three days the blood is dried up in the veins and arteries and will not be drawn out any more by the salt. Isserles' note that follows is crucial to all later decisions. He says that we prohibit the use of such meat altogether (not even permitting roasting) because some may believe that boiling also is permitted. What, then, is the status of frozen meat? On the face of it, it should be prohibited because of the lapse of time without salting. In fact, Joseph Teomim (in the *Peri Megadim*) says that it should be absolutely prohibited because freezing has the effect of cooking.

But a later authority (still before the time of freezers and still speaking of meat frozen by accident, etc.) Jehiel Epstein in the authoritative code, *Aruch ha-Shulchan,* permits such frozen meat. He says the meat so frozen is in a state of suspension; it is like a stone and the blood does not rot or spoil it. His decision became the basis of the various permissions given recently for the use of the freezer, namely, that the meat becomes like stone, no spoiling occurs and, therefore, after thawing out it is like new, and may be salted and the blood drawn out thereby. This is virtually the decision of the latest authority, Moses Feinstein, in his *Responsa Igros Moshe* (*Yore Deah* 28). He says that Joseph Teomim's objection in the *Peri Megadim* that freezing is equivalent to cooking (and therefore the meat cannot be eaten since it is as if it were cooked without salting) applies only if the meat were frozen by direct contact with the ice and got wet; but if it is frozen hard and dry, it would be quite usable later. In other words, he follows the decision of Jehiel Epstein in the *Aruch ha-Shulchan.*

Now, what principles do we derive from this discussion of frozen meat which would apply to the frozen *Etrog?* One thing is sure, if the freezing is not done merely by putting it on ice, where water from melting ice would penetrate and spoil the *Etrog,* but if the *Etrog* is wrapped and frozen dry, then by analogy with the meat, it would be quite usable.

However, the main problem with regard to the suitability of an *Etrog* for ritual use is not quite the same as a problem with regard to meat, although it is really analogous to it. With meat the question is whether or not the freezing dries up the blood so that it can never be drawn out again. With an *Etrog* the liquid or the juice must not be drawn out but must remain in it for the *Etrog* to be usable. An *Etrog* that is dried up cannot be used. These laws are discussed in *Orah Hayyim* 648, though there are some authorities (see 648, 4) who it would permit even a dried *Etrog* if its outer form were intact and its inner seed chambers were intact. But in general the question of whether it was dried up or not is the crucial one. Therefore Isserles says (648, 1) that last year's *Etrog,* because it surely *must* be dried up, cannot be used. This he bases upon a Responsum of Maharil, 5. However the *Mogen David* questions this decision and says it depends upon whether it is really dried up or not (i.e., not merely upon the age of the *Etrog*). As to whether it is dried up or not, the *Shulchan Aruch* gives a definite and practical test: A needle and thread is run through the *Etrog* and if the thread is damp, the *Etrog* is Kosher.

Therefore, applying all this to your question, we would conclude as follows: First of all, you do not intend to keep these a whole year but only part of a year. Therefore even Isserles would not object to it. But even if you kept them a whole year, the rule of testing by needle and thread would still apply. Since modern freezing does not involve contact with ice, which on melting would give water to penetrate and spoil the *Etrog,* then we can say that as long as the *Etrog* keeps its shape and its beauty (because it has to be *hadar*) and as long as it keeps its moisture, it is usable.

13

BOWING AND KNEELING ON YOM KIPPUR

The congregation has an established custom of kneeling on Yom Kippur in the *Mussaf* (at the *olenu* and the High Priest's confession). Now it is considering abolishing the custom. To what extent would it be justified in doing so? (From Dr. Morris Goldstein, San Francisco, California.)

THE custom of prostrating during the *Seder Avodah* in the Yom Kippur *Mussaf* is derived from the practice described in the Mishnah (*Yoma* VI, 2) namely, that when the High Priest in his confessions on Yom Kippur mentioned the Ineffable Name of God, the people who stood in the courts of the Temple prostrated themselves and said, "Blessed be His glorious Name," etc. There is, however, no early mention of this prostration as a mandatory action after the Temple was destroyed and the High Priest's service was carried over into the Yom Kippur synagogue service. Even though the Talmud has many discussions as to prostration and deep bowing in many parts of the service (cf., for example, *Berachoth* 28b) nevertheless there is no mention of this specific prostration in the Yom Kippur service. In Babylon prostration, etc., was practiced more than in Palestine (where it was restricted because Christianity took it over; see Ginzberg's article on "Adoration" in the Jewish Encyclopedia). Nevertheless, I have found no statement in the *Responsa of the Geonim* requiring or even discussing this Yom Kippur prostration, even though the *Geonim* have considerable discussion about the *Seder Avodah* in the Yom Kippur service.

The earliest reference to such a prostration is (as far as I can trace) from the Rhineland in the twelfth century. Eliezer b. Joel Halevi (Raviah, Abi Ezri, to *Yom Kippur,* p. 197) speaks of the prostration in the Temple in Jerusalem and adds: "We do so also as a symbol ('*dugma*')." His pupil, Isaac Or Zorua (*Or Zorua, Hilchoth Yom ha-Kippurim*) repeats his teacher's statement.

That this custom did not achieve the status of a law can be seen from the fact that it was never regularized and clearly defined. For example, it is not quite clear who performs the prostration. Is it the cantor alone, or is it the people alone, or is it both?

Israel of Krems (*Haggahot Asheri* to the *Rosh* in *Berachoth,* chapter 4) speaks of the people merely bowing the head. Although it is not clear that he refers to Yom Kippur, yet immediately after that, he speaks of the cantor prostrating himself in the Yom Kippur *Avodah* service. Isaac Bar Sheshes (in his Responsa, 332) rebukes the cantor for leaving his place and moving before the Ark to prostrate himself. He does not mention the people. Jacob ben Asher in *Tur* (*Orah Hayyim* 621) merely quotes the *Raviah.* Joel Sirkes (*Bach — ad loc.*) says clearly that *only* the people must prostrate; and he rebukes the cantor for such prostration, explaining that the prostration is not *necessary,* but is "only a symbol."

In the *Shulchan Aruch* (*Orah Hayyim* 621), Isserles says: It is the custom to "fall upon the face" at this part of the service. Moses Meth, the pupil of Isserles' contemporary, Solomon Luria, speaks of this prostration as a regular custom (*Matteh Moshe,* 476). But Caro himself in this passage makes no mention of it at all. Of course the custom did spread among the Sephardim, as can be seen from the rebuke of Isaac Bar Sheshes to the cantor who prostrated himself. But if it were a fixed custom among the Sephardim, Caro would surely have mentioned it; and he does not do so.

Gaguine (in *Keser Shem Tov,* Vol. VI, p. 388) who gives the Sephardic customs, says it is a custom to do so, but that the Sephardic congregations in London and in Amsterdam did not observe it. There is no mention of the custom in the Sephardic *Abudraham,* nor in the Ashkenazic *Agur* or *Rokeach.*

Clearly, then, it was not considered to be an indispensable custom. Perhaps the reason was that neither the Talmud nor the *Geonim* require it or even speak of it. Besides, even the original custom in the Temple, of which this is a symbolic replica, is itself open to question. The *Jerushalmi* (*Yoma* III, 40d) says that only those worshipers prostrated who were near enough to the High Priest to hear him utter the Divine Name. The rest of the people in the Temple who could not hear him, but who saw those in front prostrate, merely said the formula, "Blessed be His Name," etc.

There is another consideration involved in the specific question asked, namely, that in this synagogue whose rabbi asks this question, the people actually knelt. Of course kneeling was practiced in the Bible, see Solomon (in Kings 8:54) and Ezra (in Ezra 9:6). However, kneeling has become associated with Christian worship and for that reason might be avoided, especially on Yom Kippur.

The conclusion to which the history and status of the custom would lead us is this: If the custom of prostration or deep bowing (rather than kneeling) is a beloved *minhag* in the congregation, there is enough custom in the past to justify its continuance. If, however, the congregation desires to abolish the observance, it well may do so, since the custom is not based upon the Talmud, was introduced merely as a symbol (*dugma*) and never attained the status of mandatory law; as Joel Sirkes said: "It is not necessary. It is merely a symbol."

14

SYNAGOGUE CONTRIBUTION FROM A CRIMINAL

A man known or reputed to be a gangster wishes to make a contribution to the Temple. Should his gift be accepted? The question may also arise as to whether a plaque be put up in appreciation of his gift, as is done with other generous donors. (From M.A.K.)

THERE is considerable discussion in the legal literature which relates to the question raised here. The chain of Halachic reasoning begins with the verse (in Deuteronomy 23:19): "Thou shalt not bring the hire of a harlot or the price of a dog into the house of the Lord thy God for any vow; for both these are an abomination. . . ." Aaron of

Barcelona, in his *Sefer ha-Chinuch,* explains the reason for the prohibition as follows: If a lamb is brought to the altar in the fulfillment of a vow, its purpose is to purify the heart, but if one brings a lamb which had been given as the hire of a harlot, it would bring back lascivious memories of the sin.

The law is carried over to the Mishnah (*Temura,* VI, 2) and thence to the Talmud (*Temura* 29a ff., *Baba Kama* 65b). In the Talmud the application of the law is generally restricted. There are opinions given, that the word "harlot" used in the verse applies only to sexual relations with a married woman (which could not be legitimized by marriage). Other opinions say that only the object itself (e.g., the lamb) may not be given. But if the object is changed (if it be converted into money) or if corn be given to the harlot and the corn is converted into flour, or olives into oil, then these converted objects are no longer unfit and may be brought to the Temple in payment of a vow. So Maimonides records this as the Law (*Hilchoth Issure Mizbeach,* IV, 14): "Only the object itself (i.e., the payment in its original form) is prohibited to be brought to the altar." The "hire of a harlot," etc., is the only "dirty money" mentioned in Scripture as prohibited as Temple gifts, and even these are restricted to the "hire" in its original form.

But there is a further and more important question involved here. The law as given in Bible and Talmud applies only to the Temple in Jerusalem and the altar, etc. Can it be legitimately extended to apply also to the synagogue?

There is considerable doubt about the justification of thus transferring and extending the old Temple restriction to the synagogue. The doubt is clearly expressed by the *Magen Avraham* (to *Orah Hayyim* 153:21). He says that the law refers only to the Temple, and that no classic decisor has extended it to apply to the synagogue except Jacob Weil. (I could not find the passage he refers to in the Responsa of Jacob Weil.) Therefore the *Magen Avraham* decides that (since there is doubt whether the prohibition really applies to the synagogue at all) all questions on the matter should be decided *l'kula,* i.e., permissively.

Magen Avraham's comment is in reference to the note of Moses Isserles (ad loc.) who does apply the law to the synagogue, and says that no sacred synagogue object or *Sefer Torah* can come from "the hire of a harlot." But he adds that money (if the gift is converted into money) may be used. As a matter of fact, the application of the Temple Law to the synagogue was made before Isserles (i.e., before the sixteenth century) by Rabbenu Yeruchem (of Provence, fourteenth century). In his *Toldoth Adam V'Chava* (Section *Chavah,* Path 23, part 1) he says that "the hire," etc., may not be used for a *Sefer Torah* or for synagogue lights, etc. But he also says (in reference to Temple times) that if a man gave money and she bought an animal, it *would* be permitted on the altar (because she did not give the object that she recieved).

So as far as the law is concerned, it is clear that as long as the man you refer to does not give the actual money (coins or gift) which changed hands in the prostitution transaction, it is not prohibited by the Halacha.

However, our present concern is not restricted to the letter of the law, even though it does have weight with us. We are concerned also with the moral effect upon the community if we accept such a gift. This is a delicate matter and must be carefully weighed. In my judgment you *should* accept the gift, because it is his obligation (a *mitzvah*) to support the synagogue and we have no right to prevent a sinner from performing a righteous act. For example, it is a *mitzvah* encumbent upon a *Cohen* to bless the people (in the Duchan). But suppose a *Cohen* has committed a grievous sin, should we allow him to bless the people? To which Maimonides says (*Hilchoth Tefilla* XV, 6) that he must perform the *mitzvah*. He says: "We may not tell a man to add to his sin by neglecting a *mitzvah*."

So it is in this case. He, as a Jew, has the duty to support the synagogue according to his means. We have no right to prevent him from doing his duty.

But as to putting up a plaque honoring him, that should not be done. Of course, in general, Jewish tradition favors recording and publicizing the names of donors in order to encourage other donors and also in order to prevent a specific gift-object being used or melted up for another purpose. (See Isserles, *Yore Deah* 249:13, and the whole discussion in *Recent Reform Responsa,* p. 203 ff.) Nevertheless, the putting up of a plaque would also be honoring him as a person, and such a man is not one whom the synagogue "delighteth to honor."

Yet even in this case, something constructive can be done. If he wishes to honor his parents or some other close relative, a plaque can be put up in their name and his name included as the donor. In this case, besides giving a gift to the synagogue, he is honoring his parents, which makes it a double *mitzvah*.

To sum up, the money itself is changed from its original form and all authorities agree that it is acceptable. As for the donor, it is his duty to support the Temple according to his means and we have no right to prevent him from doing his duty. As for a plaque, he should not be so honored in his own right, but if he wishes to have a plaque put up in memory of a close relative, such a plaque should be put up, and his name mentioned on it as the donor.

15

GAMBLING FOR THE BENEFIT OF THE SYNAGOGUE

The C.C.A.R. and the U.A.H.C. have passed resolutions opposed to gambling of all kinds sponsored by the synagogue. Have these resolutions so firm a foundation in Jewish legal and ethical tradition that the Rabbi and the Board of the Congregation should absolutely prohibit such method of raising money for the synagogue? (From Rabbi Paul H. Levenson, Fords, New Jersey.)

THE Central Conference and the Union do not have a governmental authority over the rabbis and the congregations. They are voluntary associations. Their resolutions, therefore, are primarily advisory and are meant to be of guidance and assistance to the rabbis and the congregations. Therefore it is quite justified to ask how strong a foundation in Jewish tradition there is or is not for these resolutions against any gambling sponsored by the congregation. Besides the question of the right to independent judgment on the part of rabbi and congregation respectively, the question itself has special importance nowadays, when increasing suggestions are being made for secular lotteries to be established to help finance local and state government.

When these questions come up as public questions, the rabbi and the congregation may well need to express an opinion in the name of the ethics of our religious tradition. Thus, the whole subject of public gambling, at least in relation to our religious institutions, deserves a fuller discussion than is available in encyclopedic articles.

The matter cannot be discussed entirely upon the basis of Jewish law, because changing sentiments are involved and have to be considered. For example, nowadays many Catholic churches in America receive considerable income from bingo games, and I am told that there are some Jewish congregations which follow that practice. More widespread than bingo games for the benefit of Jewish congregations in America is the use of lotteries for many types of Jewish social and philanthropic organizations. There is hardly a year in any large Jewish community in which automobiles or bonds are not raffled off. The fact that people are getting used to the idea as normal tends to give raffles and lotteries almost the status of an accepted custom; and an accepted custom, if it is not manifestly bad, has certain status in Jewish law. However, a distinction would naturally be considered between social or philanthropic organizations and the synagogue itself. The synagogue must be treated with special sanctity. It was this feeling that the sanctity of the synagogue itself should be especially protected against general laxity, which must be the motivation behind the resolutions referred to. What, then, is the opinion and the mood of Jewish tradition on this matter?

It is a manifest fact that gambling is not mentioned in the Bible itself. Evidently our people in Biblical times were free from that vice or it certainly would have been mentioned as a prohibited sin. Objections to gambling do not appear until the time of the Mishnah. Nevertheless, the Bible makes frequent use of the device of casting lots. For example, which of two goats should be used for which of the two sacrifices on Yom Kippur was determined by lot (see Leviticus 13:8 and also M. *Yoma* IV, 1). The land was divided among the tribes by lot. The various duties of the priests were distributed by lot (M. *Tamid* I, 2). In fact, the use of lots was sanctioned by the later law codes. The *Shulchan Aruch* in *Orah Hayyim* 322:6 says that the man may distribute the various portions of the meal by lot on the Sabbath to members of his household. This law goes back to the Mishnah, *Shabbas* XXIII, 2. However, if this casting of lots, which is permitted, results in one person gaining much more than another, then it is prohibited as gambling (*m'shum kuvya*). This is the subject of occasional discussion in the Responsa literature: Certain property belongs jointly to a few men. They may divide it by lot. This is legitimate, unless the casting of lots gives one of the men (the winner) a great advantage (see Jacob Reischer, *Shevus Yaacov,* II, 167). In other words, a difference must be made between the casting of lots and a lottery. Merely to determine who gets what, without any particular advantage but just to avoid disputes, is only a casting of lots and is permissible, but who shall win a special prize is *lottery* and is gambling.

If, then, a lottery which will result in some one or a certain few winning a special prize is to be considered gambling, we must now ask what is the attitude of the tradition to gambling. There is no question that gambling of various kinds finally spread among our people in post-Biblical times up to modern times and, therefore, in reaction to that fact, there is a great deal of material in the legal tradition on the subject. The original source of the laws is in

Mishnah *Sanhedrin,* III, 3, which lists those who are ineligible to give testimony in the Jewish courts, and at the beginning of the list, there are mentioned "those who play with dice and those who race pigeons." The Talmud takes this up in b. *Sanhedrin* 24 b. and 25 b., and gives as the reason for the ineligibility of such gamblers that they do not participate as they should in constructive social efforts (*b'yeshuvo shel olam*). From here on the law is carried over into the codes. Maimonides, in *Hilchos Gezela,* VII, 7, says the objection to gambling is that it is a form of robbery. So the *Shulchan Aruch* in *Choshen Mishpot* 370:2, gives this as a definite law. Some of the authorities (based upon a minority opinion in the Talmud) wish to confine the ineligibility (to testify) to those who have no occupation except gambling, but this exception remains only a side opinion.

The large amount of legal discussion which the literature contains is itself an evidence of how widespread the habit of gambling became. Frequently communities passed communal regulation against any sort of gambling in the community (i.e., even private gambling; see *Pachad Yitzchok,* s.v., *"Cherem"*). This practice of public prohibition by the community of all gambling naturally led to questions which are analogous to the one you are asking. When is the *cherem* applicable and when is it not applicable? When is it deemed properly ordained or improperly ordained and, therefore, invalid? What if a man from a community which does not have such a ruling visits a community which does have such a ruling; is he in duty bound to refrain from gambling during his visit? (See *Shevus Yaacov* II, 79; see also Reischer's full discussion of this matter in his commentary, *Chok Yaacov* to *Shulchan Aruch Orah Hayyim*

468). In addition to these communal decisions there are many instances of men disgusted with their own addiction to gambling, who take personal vows never to gamble again. This habit led to a series of legal questions as to whether such vows can be released by the proper authorities or not.

In spite of all this evidence that gambling was an urgent problem all through the Middle Ages, and the law and individuals struggled against it, I do not recall at the present any discussion of whether gambling would be acceptable if carried out for the benefit of the congregation. I have the impression that I once read such a responsum about a lottery and that the suggestion was indignantly rejected. But the fact that such discussions, if they have occurred, are very rare, would in itself indicate that it would hardly enter anybody's mind to think that it would be permissible.

While, then, there is no specific prohibition of a lottery in behalf of a synagogue, the whole mood of the Jewish struggle against gambling, even private gambling, makes it evident that such a proposal would be deemed flagrantly wrong. However, the Committee on Responsa of the Conference (Jacob Mann, Chairman) in the *Yearbook* Volume XLVI, page 126, cites a rather permissive opinion by the Rabbi of Modena, Ishmael Sacerdote (died 1811) in his *Zera Emeth,* Volume III, 144 (p. 171d). He gives this rather permissive opinion in an analogous situation: A man had become poor, but he possessed a *Sefer Torah* which he wanted to sell by a lottery, in order to support himself and his family. The rabbi agreed to it on the ground that this method of selling would not be a disgrace to the *Sefer Torah.* He even gave the man a letter to send out to prospective purchasers of the lottery tickets. To this opinion cited by the Conference, one can add another which Rabbi

Ishmael quotes, namely, that of Meir Eisenstadt in Hungary (*Panim Meiros,* III, 43). His case was very much like the one of the Rabbi Ishmael's: A man needed to provide a trousseau for his daughter and he wanted to sell a *Sefer Torah* by lottery. Eisenstadt agrees that this is no disgrace to the Torah. In fact, he says, it is an honor to the Torah to have people compete and want to pay a higher price for it. He says further that it is the custom in his part of the country for scribes, when they write the scroll of the Book of Esther, to sell it by lottery. However, there is a contrary opinion to these two, cited by the editor and pupil of Rabbi Ishmael. The contrary opinion is by Zvi Ashkenazi of Amsterdam, in his responsa *Chacham Zvi,* 123. He speaks of the custom in Amsterdam of selling a *Sefer Torah* by auction (i.e., by competitive bidding) and he objects to it strenuously.

But these isolated opinions which are not in agreement with each other are not sufficient to help decide the question before us. We must judge by the general mood of the law. Although the decisions of the Union and the Conference on this matter do not have (as we have mentioned) the prohibitory force of the medieval *cherem,* it does indeed represent the spirit of the Jewish tradition. As Jacob Reischer properly says, "The *cherem* against gambling is a public vow and 'a fence' to protect the commandments." Your congregation, therefore, is not *prohibited* and cannot be prohibited from conducting its "Las Vegas" night, but the spirit of tradition would urge them to refrain.

Some additional references for completeness' sake: Israel Mizrahi in his *Peri Ha-Aretz,* II, 16, decides that the Torah may be sold by a scribe by lottery, although he is concerned that his own teacher says that it may not be so sold. Joseph Messas in his *Mayim Chayim,* 78, also decides in favor of an indigent scribe, permitting him to sell the Torah by lottery.

Mordecai Roller in *Be'er Chaim Mordecai,* Volume I, 50, asked whether it is permitted to raise money for a synagogue by a dance, (i.e., men and women dancing together) forbids it based on the verse in Deuteronomy, "The hire of a harlot, etc." Kalman Zuckerman in *Minchas Ha-Komtez,* 9 and 10, refutes this on the usual ground that it means only the actual object given to the harlot (e.g., a lamb may not be brought to the altar).

16

AN UNWORTHY MAN CALLED TO TORAH

At the regular Sabbath service, it is the custom of the congregation to call up two men to recite the blessings over the Torah reading. One Sabbath morning after the service, an officer of the congregation protested the fact that a certain man had been called up to the Torah that day. He said that the man (who was a lawyer) did not have a good reputation in his professional career. Is it justified to debar a man from being called up to the Torah because his character is open to question? Or is his reputation or character irrelevant to his being called to perform this religious function? (From C.G.B., Pittsburgh, Pennsylvania.)

THE question asked is of considerable importance because the answer given to it might well be applied to various other religious functions for which people are called up to the pulpit. The subject has been discussed sporadically in the literature. Simon ben Zemach Duran (fourteenth-fifteenth century, *Tashbetz* II:261) was asked whether unmarried youths may be prohibited from reading the Torah, either because the honor of the Torah requires only mature married adults to be called or because an unmarried youth could not remain clean-minded. He answered that according to the law, a young man is permitted to be called up to the Torah, and adds that even sinners are not forbidden to be called to the Torah; but, nevertheless, if the congregation, in order to make "a fence against evil," desires to forbid certain groups to come up, the congregation is always permitted to do so.

Duran is cited in a recent volume of responsa, *Mispar ha-Sofer*, by Isaac Zvi Sofer (Jerusalem, 1961, Responsum 5) not with regard to the calling up of young unmarried men, but with regard to the more characteristically modern question as to whether a public violator of the Sabbath may be called up to the Torah. Sofer follows the decision of Duran, namely, that whatever be the actual rights of the individual in this matter, the congregation has, always, the right as a congregation to make decisions excluding sinners from being called up. He adds that many Hungarian congregations have long made such decisions as a "fence against evil-doers."

The difficulties involved in this question are reflected in the very wording of the dispute as it was presented to Simon ben Zemach Duran. Some of the disputants considered that what was involved was *kevode ha-Torah*, the honor due to the Torah, and therefore the dignity of the service. Other disputants insisted that to come up to the Torah reading was an obligation, a *mitzvah,* and therefore we have no right to keep a man from his religious duty.

The fact is that the legal literature never clearly defines

the true status of this function. For example, is being called up to the Torah to be deemed as a religious *duty,* incumbent upon every Jew, just as praying three times a day is a duty? If it is a duty, then it would not be possible to debar a man from it, and thus prevent him from performing a *mitzvah.* Maimonides says (*Hilchos Tefilla,* XV, 6) in a somewhat analogous situation, speaking of a priest who had sinned: "We do not tell a man to add to his sin by neglecting a *mitzvah.*"

But being called up to the Torah may not be a *mitzvah* at all. It may be a *right* that any Jew can claim and, therefore, could protest if he were not called up to the Torah after a long time. There is no doubt that many pious Jews consider this a right which they can demand, and object if they are not called up. The Talmud (*Berachos* 55a) says that if a man is given a Torah to read and does not read it, his life will be shortened. Therefore it is believed by some that to refuse to go up to the Torah shortens one's life (see *Yesode Yeshurun* II, 201). A Yemenite, some time ago in Israel, sued the officers of his congregation on the ground that they were prejudiced against him and had not called him up to the Torah for a long time. He was suing for what he called his rights as a Jew. Certainly many Jews have that feeling, whether it is so in the law. Then again, it may be neither a duty on a man's part which he must fulfill, nor a right which he may demand, but a privilege which the congregation confers. In that case, the congregation can bestow that privilege upon whomever it deems worthy and withold it from whomever it judges unworthy.

Since this basic definition of what the status of the ceremony is (duty, right, or privilege) has not been clarified in the law, the probabilities are that the status is vague and that it has the nature of all three of these possible classifications. It is necessary, therefore, to see to what extent it partakes of each.

Is it a duty, a *mitzvah,* incumbent upon every Jew, to be called up to the Torah? When a boy who is to be Bar Mitzvah is called up to the Torah, his father is required to recite the blessing (*boruch sh'petorani*). Now, clearly in this case, this is a religious *duty* incumbent upon the father. How could we possibly prevent him from performing this *mitzvah,* even if he were a notorious sinner? Yet, even in this case, it is to be observed that it is doubtful whether the blessing is really *required.* The requirement is found in a note by Isserles in *Orah Hayyim* 225:1, and even he is uncertain about it and, therefore, suggests that in reciting the blessing, the father should leave out God's name (a practice which is followed in the case of all blessings of dubious validity, so that God's name be not recited in vain). If, then, it is not, broadly speaking, a duty to go up to the Torah, is it a right which a Jew can claim? To some extent this may be so. Certainly a priest can count it as his right to be called up to the Torah first. The law frequently discusses who should be called up to the Torah, after the priest and the Levite have been called up for the first two portions: A bridegroom in the week of his marriage has precedence over a Bar Mitzvah; next, a father whose child is circumcised that week; then a mourner, on his *yahrzeit.* Are all these rights which a man can demand? The most that can be said is that they have become customary rights. The law does not make them firm rights, but a man can well be aggrieved if he is denied them. If, for example, someone gives a large sum of money for the privilege of being called up, the old congregations would certainly call him up, and no one of the categories above would feel that they had a right to dispute.

Certainly the calling up partakes, also, of the nature of a privilege because the congregation often calls up a man in order to honor him. It will call up the rabbi for the third portion, which is the first to which a non-priest or non-Levite can be called up. That honor is certainly involved in the Torah reading is clear from the statement in b. *Megilla* 23a, where it is said that while women may be called up as one of the seven on the Sabbath, we do not call up women because of "the dignity of the congregation" (*mipne kovode ha-tzibur*). Thus the dignity and the propriety of the situation involved is a significant consideration.

It is possible to decide the matter more closely than merely upon the vague fact that being called up to the Torah partakes somewhat of the nature of all three, a duty, a right, or a privilege. Ephraim Margolies, the famous scholar of Brody (1762–1828) wrote a book dealing specifically with the questions involved in the reading of the Torah (*Sha'are Ephraim,* many editions). In Section 1, paragraph 32, he discusses who should not be called up to the Torah. Most of this discussion is based chiefly upon two passages in the *Shulchan Aruch* which provide some material analogous to our problem. One in *Orah Hayyim* 128 deals with sinful priests and their rights to go up to bless the people; and the other in *Yore Deah,* 334 (also *Orah Hayyim* 55:11) speaks of a man who has been put under ban, as to whether he may be included in the *minyan,* etc. The implications of these two laws and their bearing on our question about calling an unworthy man up to the Torah have been rather fully explored in an interesting responsa-sequence. It is found in *Shetey Helechem* (331) by Moses Hagiz, a Palestinian rabbi who lived in Leghorn and Amsterdam (1671–1750).

The incident which evoked this series of responsa throws some light on the social conditions of the time. In one of the Sephardic congregations (Amsterdam or London) a man embezzled the money of the *chazan* and ran away with the *chazan's* wife. The guilty couple fled to Spain, but terrified by the Inquisition, they came to London. Meantime, the *chazan,* in poverty and anguish, died. The culprit in London was told by the *Chacham* to make a public confession of guilt. This he did in the syngagogue, in the presence of the congregation. Thereafter he was frequently called up to the Torah. One Yom Kippur, the brother of the dead *chazan* was in London and saw this man holding the Torah at *Kol Nidre*. He bitterly protested. He said that this man had not returned the embezzled money or made any attempt to do so; his repentance is, therefore, insincere, and such a scoundrel should not be called up to the Torah.

Although this was a quarrel within the Sephardic community, many Ashkenazic scholars were consulted, as well as the rabbis of Mantua, etc., and among the Ashkenazim were the famous scholars, Jacob Reischer of Metz (Shevus Jacob) and Jacob Emden of Altona. Between them, they dealt with the implications of the references to the sinful priest in *Orah Hayyim* and the excommunicated man in *Yore Deah*. Most of the opinions were to the effect that since the man had made no attempt to restore what he had stolen, his repentance is incomplete and, therefore, he should not be called up to the Torah. This would indicate the feeling, at least on the part of most of the scholars, that a non-repentant sinner should not be called up to the Torah. This opinion is generally based on the *Orah Hayyim* statement that if a priest has committed certain crucial sins, such as marrying a divorced woman, wilfully defiling himself by contact with the dead, then if he is not repentant, he is not permitted to bless the people.

Two of the scholars, one anonymous and the other Jacob Emden, say that this is a bad analogy. A priest, if he repents, may bless the people because blessing the people is a *mitzvah,* a commandment imposed upon him ("Thus shall ye bless," Numbers 6:23). Thus it is clear in the mind of these scholars that being called up to the Torah is *not* a commandment before which we may not put obstacles. As for the analogy with the law in *Yore Deah,* that a man who is under ban may not be counted to the *minyan,* Jacob Emden says that the law clearly states that only the man who has been officially put under ban is debarred. As long as a sinner has not been put officially under ban, he may still be counted to the *minyan.* This sinner in London has not been put under ban officially. Therefore he may still be counted to the *minyan.* Jacob Emden then adds that being called up to the Torah is less important than being counted to the *minyan.* Women and children, although they may not be counted to the *minyan,* may, nevertheless (according to the Talmud, *Megilla* 23a) be called up to the Torah. So it is conceivable that this wicked man in London could be excluded from the *minyan* and yet be called up to the Torah. But Jacob Emden says that since he was not put under ban, and since, anyhow, being called up to the Torah is not as strict a matter as being counted to a *minyan,* then it might be a kindness to let him be called to the Torah. This might help him towards righteousness. Besides, he adds, we "must not close the door in the face of the would-be repentant." In fact, Ephraim Margolies in his handbook says that if it is not definitely proved that a man is a sinner, we ought to allow him to be called up.

Ephraim Margolies goes into specific details about who should not be called up. A man who is known to have taken bribes should not be called up to the passage dealing with justice and laws; and a man whose wife neglects the mikvah, etc., should not be called up to the passage which deals with these matters. On fast days, a man who is not fasting is not called up to the Torah (*Shaare Ephraim* I, 17). The commentator, Shaare Rachamim (Sabbetai Lifschitz) bases an explanation of these selective restrictions upon the *P'ri Megadim* (Joseph Teomim) to *Orah Hayyim* 141, end of paragraph 8, in which he indicates that such a man would be bearing false witness to the passage being read. But in spite of these selective restrictions, where there would be a shocking contrast between the reading from Scripture and the character of the man called up, Margolies concludes that, in the spirit of Jacob Emden: "If we call him up and some indignant worshiper scolds him, the embarrassment may lead the sinner to full repentance." The commentator Shaare Rachamim to this passage in Margolies adds another leniency as follows: Although it is not permissible to call a blind man to the Torah, nevertheless we do call up blind people and illiterates because they do not read the Torah and we rely upon the reading by the official reader. Thus (he continues) we can call up sinners who should not be permitted to read the Torah (themselves) because nowadays we count on the reading by the official reader. (See also Jehiel Weinberg in *Seridey Esh,* II, as to Sabbath violators called to the Torah.)

We may therefore conclude as follows: While it is not clear in the law whether being called up is a duty, a right, or a privilege, the ceremony clearly partakes of each of these. A man of dubious reputation should not be called up for certain specific passages, where his character contradicts the reading. Nor, of course, should a notoriously evil man, as the one mentioned by Moses Hagiz, be allowed to shame the congregation by being called up to the Torah. But in general, in less heinous offenses, as long as the man has not been excluded or ostracized by the community, we should not "shut the door in his face." We should always consider the honor of the congregation, yet be lenient and avoid complete exclusion.

(Originally published in *Central Conference of American Rabbis Yearbook,* Vol. LXXII, 1962.)

17

BAR MITZVAH AT THE AGE OF TWELVE

A father in our congregation has a serious disease and his prospects are not good. His daughter was Bat Mitzvah at the age of twelve. In a year his son will be twelve and he would like to see his son Bar Mitzvah. I heard that there is a custom to make a boy Bar Mitzvah at the age of twelve if he is an orphan. Is the custom well founded? May I extend this custom to give this boy his Bar Mitzvah at the age of twelve, so that his father may have the joy of participating? (From Rabbi Leonard Winograd, Johnstown, Pennsylvania.)

HIRSHOWITZ, in *Ozar Minhagey Yeshurun,* says that it is the custom of the Sephardim in Jerusalem that an orphaned boy begins the laying of *tefillin* a whole year before his Bar

Mitzvah, in order to gain merit for his deceased father. The same custom is referred to by Yechiel Epstein in his authoritative work on the *Shulchan Aruch, Aruch ha-Shulchan* to *Orah Hayyim* 37. But he dismisses the idea rather contemptuously, saying, "It is a current idea among the common people that an orphan should begin putting on *tefillin* a year before. I do not know any reason for this notion, and it is not proper to do so."

A later authority, Wolf Leiter of Pittsburgh, in his *Bes David,* 41, though he knows of the dismissal of the custom by Epstein, nevertheless calls it "our custom," and explains it as follows, that since the orphan has no one to teach him and guide him, he needs a longer time to learn the mitzvos. In other words, Leiter considers the custom as acceptable. However, Hillel Posek in *Hillel Omer,* 18, quotes Leiter and opposes his acceptance of this custom and says that there should be no *tefillin* and no Bar Mitzvah before the age of thirteen.

Since there is, therefore, some disagreement as to the acceptability of the custom, it might help us to go back into the history of Bar Mitzvah, to see to what extent the date of Bar Mitzvah is actually fixed at thirteen.

The Ethics of the Fathers, chapter 5, says that thirteen is the age for *mitzvos,* but this statement is an Aggadic one, not a legal one, and not meant to fix the exact age for Bar Mitzvah any more than the age of eighteen, which the passage also mentions for marriage, is meant to be the compulsory age for marriage. The legal basis of the discussion on the age of Bar Mitzvah is the Talmud (b. *Succah,* 42a), in which we are told that if a boy knows enough to keep the *tefillin* from defilement, his father should get him *tefillin*.

On the basis of this statement, the discussion continues in

the *Tur (Orah Hayyim,* 37). There the law is repeated that any male child who can take care of them, should be given *tefillin* to wear. Joseph Caro *(Bes Joseph)* quotes the Ittur (Isaac ben Abba Mari of Provence) who says, that means when the child is thirteen. Caro refutes that and says it means any age that the child can take care of *tefillin* decently. However, Isserles *(Darche Moshe)* says that it should be at the age of thirteen. The discussion is carried over into the *Shulchan Aruch* (same reference), and Caro again says that the boy should be given *tefillin* at any age that he is able to keep them clean, and Isserles repeats that only at the age of thirteen should he be given *tefillin.*

It is clear that the discussion, in general, tends to divide up between Ashkenazim and Sephardim. Possibly in the Orient, boys mature sooner. At all events, it is a fact that in Morocco, boys put on *tefillin* at the age of twelve. (See article on "Bar Mitzvah" in Jewish Encyclopedia, Vol. II, p. 510, first column.)

In *L'Os u-Lezikaron* by Isaac Rifkind, New York, 1942, on page 19, he says the Sephardim precede the laying on of *tefillin* by a whole year till the boy is twelve and then they have a celebration.

Reb Isaac in Usha said that a man should struggle with the training of his son till the age of twelve *(Ketuboth,* 50).

Vows are examined after the person is twelve *(Nidda,* 45b).

Also see *Sofrim* edition Higger, chapter 18,7—From twelve years on he can lead in the service *(Sofrim,* 14:14).

Saadia in his *Siddur,* Jerusalem edition, p. 34, permits a boy of twelve who can put on *tefillin* to be counted in the *minyan.*

Benvenisti, *Sh'yarey Kenesses Hagdolah, Orah Hayyim,*

37 to *Bes Joseph*: "In these places we are accustomed to train a boy of twelve to *tefillin*."

Perhaps there is, also, another reason for the Sephardic custom of an earlier Bar Mitzvah (i.e., in certain countries). The *Mishnah Berurah* to *Orah Hayyim,* 55, Note 41, says that only the father is to be believed when he says the child is thirteen. Therefore when the father is dead, puberty is the test of maturity, based on *Kiddushin* 64a, *Tosfos,* s.v., *Ne-emon.*

Since the date of Bar Mitzvah thus seems to have considerable variation, and since even among us Ashkenazim there exists a debated custom of having an orphan put on *tefillin* a year earlier, what should be our attitude to this custom? Should we encourage it for all orphaned boys?

It would seem logical not to encourage this custom in general. First of all, the custom is debatable, as we have mentioned; but more importantly, it is to be noted that the custom does not mean that the boy should be *actually Bar Mitzvah* at the age of twelve, but only that he should put on *tefillin* a year earlier. Putting on *tefillin* a year earlier does not make the boy necessarily a religious adult (Bar Mitzvah). In fact, it is our general custom for all boys to begin putting on *tefillin* a month or two before their Bar Mizvah, but they do not become of age religiously until their actual Bar Mitzvah is past. Besides this legal consideration against a twelve year old Bar Mitzvah, it would not be psychologically wise to single out all orphaned children in this way. It is better that an orphan be treated just as other boys are and have his Bar Mitzvah at the regular time.

However, in exceptional cases, as in the one which you mention, there is enough in tradition to make the boy Bar Mitzvah (i.e., one boy, exceptionally) at the age of twelve.

While it is true that our custom merely speaks of putting on the *tefillin* at the age of twelve, the Moroccan Jews (as mentioned) actually have Bar Mitzvah at the age of twelve.

18

BLIND PERSON WITH DOG AT SERVICES

A graduate student from out of the city came to the local university. She asked for complimentary tickets for the High Holidays. When assured that she would be given them, she added that she is blind and cannot come without her seeing-eye dog. May she be admitted with the dog to the Holiday services?

THERE is a great deal of discussion and decision in the legal literature with regard to the duties and the exemptions of the blind. Therefore it would not be amiss at the outset to consider whether this blind person needs to come to the public services at all; whether she could not stay at home, for example, and read the services with a greater sense of security and therefore perhaps with greater concentration and devotion.

The laws about the blind are found in many parts of the Talmudic literature. For example, in the Talmud, in b. *Megilla* 24a, there is a discussion as to which parts of the service the blind may conduct. Rabbi Judah says that if it is a blind person who has never seen light (i.e., blind from birth) he cannot truthfully bless God as the Creator of Light, and therefore cannot officiate. Also a blind *Cohen* cannot bless the people. Leviticus 21:17 forbids any *Cohen* with any physical blemish to officiate as priest. There is also considerable discussion whether a blind person may be called up to the Torah. Yet it is evident that as the law developed, more and more participation is allowed to the blind. As for being called up to the Torah, it is now virtually a universally accepted custom to call them. All the basic arguments on this part of the question are summed up by Benjamin Slonick, pupil of Isserles, in his *Massas Binyomin,* 62. He ends with the conclusion that they *should be* called up to the Torah. (See also the various specific cases cited in this regard by Isaac Lamperoni in *Pachad Yitzchok,* s.v., "Suma.") The most extreme opinion forbidding the blind to participate was by Rabbi Judah mentioned above. In b. *Baba Kamma,* 87a, he makes a general prohibition or exemption when he says that "the blind are free from the observance of any of the commandments." This general exemption is discussed by Hezekiah Silva 17th century) in his commentary to the *Shulchan Aruch, P'ri Chadash,* to *Orah Hayyim,* 473 (near the end of the section) in which he virtually cancels the exemption enunciated by Rabbi Judah.

The most touching commentary on Rabbi Judah's blanket exemption occurs on the very page of the Talmud on which it is stated. Rabbi Joseph, who himself was blind, said that he rejoiced at that statement because, he said, "Although I was *not* commanded, nevertheless I have obeyed God's commandments." The spirit of this discussion and the mood of the law applies to this situation before us. This blind student could very easily say, "It will be much less trouble for me to pray at home." Nevertheless, she desires to pray with the congregation and in this, of course, she deserves our respect and every assistance.

But the question arises whether we can admit a dog into the service. Considering the general contempt which the biblical literature has for dogs (which is so unlike the present-day affection for them) one would think that to bring a dog into the house of God would contravene at least the mood of traditional literature. Yet, actually, this is not the case. The very question (or close to it) was asked of the well-known head of a Yeshiva in New York, Moses Feinstein. In his four-volume book of responsa, *Igros Moshe, I*, 45, he discusses the following case: A pious Jew who is blind and wants to worship with the congregation every day, asks permission to come to the synagogue with his seeing-eye dog. Feinstein gives permission for the blind man to come into the synagogue with the dog. His reasoning, based of course on the Talmud, is of some interest. It begins with the statement in the Palestinian Talmud, *Megilla* III, 3, in which it is said: "If a scholar comes with his donkey (for a night's lodging) admit him, and his animal, and his possessions into the synagogue." The passage refers to the discussion as to the propriety of using the synagogue as a lodging-place, and is further based upon the thought that scholars have a special right to the use of the synagogue. Now, argues Rabbi Feinstein, to come to the synagogue to worship is much more important than to come to lodge in the building, and a dog is no worse than a donkey, while to deprive this pious man who is blind of hearing *Kaddish* and *Kedusha* (which can only be recited with a *minyan*) would certainly be wrong. Therefore he decides that a blind man can come; but that he should sit by the door with his dog so as not to disturb the congregation. Of course, were this question asked of him (as it is asked of us) with regard to a woman, it is doubtful whether he would have given any permission, since a woman is not in duty bound to pray with the congregation at regular prayer. But to us, to whom the status of women is equal to that of men in all matters of worship, we must conclude that she certainly should in general be given permission to come.

However, what disturbed Rabbi Feinstein even in the case of the pious man, was that the dog may disturb the congregation. This certainly concerns us too. While it is true that these dogs are said to be so well-trained that they do not bark, nevertheless, a great hall filled with people on the High Holidays can easily be unnaturally exciting for the dog, and a disturbance from him would disturb a great congregation.

Therefore it would be better if she be asked not to bring the dog but that a member of the congregation be assigned to bring her to services, to sit by her during the services, and to bring her home after the services. The spirit of the statement of Rabbi Joseph quoted above, the nobility of the desire to worship God in public when she could easily find reasons not to do so, deserves every sympathetic help; and it should be a special privilege, a *mitzvah,* for a member of the congregation to take complete charge of her on that occasion. (See also Breisch; *Chelkas Yaàcov* III, 87.)

19

SEFER TORAH IN JAILS

The M. State Hospital for mental patients will have a chapel for Jewish patients. Someone stated that it is against Orthodox Judaism to have a Torah and an Ark in

this chapel; that it would be a "desecration of the Torah
to house it among mental patients." Is this objection
justified by Jewish legal tradition? (From Rabbi Harold
L. Gelfman, Macon, Georgia.)

IT is a principle in Jewish law that just as it is wrong to
permit that which is actually prohibited, so it is likewise
wrong to prohibit that which is actually permitted. The
legal literature constantly warns against adding prohibitions
which are not justified. If, therefore, the person who said
that it was "a desecration" to have the *Sefer Torah* in a
mental institution is a scholar, please ask him for the basis
of his opinion. I am not aware of any prohibition in the
legal literature based upon the fact that the sick patients are
insane and therefore no Torah may be housed among them.

These are sick people with various degrees of mental ill-
ness. The violent ones and those too deeply sunk inwardly
will certainly not be permitted to attend services by the
authorities. Those who will come to services are those who
have various degrees of mental disturbance and certainly
can understand the service, or part of it. The question is
whether sick people may have the Torah brought to them,
or whether they must wait until they are well to be able to
go to the synagogue and hear the Torah read there.

This question of the Torah being brought to the sick was
discussed as early as the sixteenth century by Meir of
Padua, who says in his Responsum 88 that the only objection to bringing the Torah to the sick is if it is brought there
on the day of the service merely for the purpose of the
service; but if it is brought there a day or two previously
and kept in an Ark, there is no objection at all. This has
been codified in the *Shulchan Aruch*. The *Shulchan Aruch*

in *Orah Hayyim* 135:14 discusses the matter and combines the question of the sick with people who are kept in jail. While Joseph Caro himself says that we do not bring the Torah to people in jail, Isserles gives the later law which we follow, namely, that if the Torah is brought there previously and kept in an Ark it is quite permitted (see, also, *Mogen Avraham, ad loc.*).

So it is clear that it is permitted to have a Torah prepared for the sick and for prisoners. But an additional question is involved in your question: During the week when services will not be held (or if they are held every day, then in the hours when the services are not held) the Torah would be in the charge of Gentiles. Is it permitted to put the Torah scroll in charge of the Gentile wardens all week? This question was discussed in great detail by Meir Arik, one of the great authorities of Galicia in the last generation, in his responsa *Imre Yosher,* II, 197:5. The question was asked by Rabbi Wolf Leiter of Pittsburgh. Rabbi Leiter was chaplain at the time at the Western Penitentiary on the outskirts of Pittsburgh. He had a Torah and an Ark in the chapel of the penitentiary, but asked the question of Meir Arik whether it was permissible to leave the Torah and the Ark under the care of Gentile wardens all week. Meir Arik connected this with the discussion in *Yore Deah* 291:2, whether a Jew moving out of a house in which a Christian will be the next tenant, may leave the mezuzah on the door (since it will now be under the care of a Gentile). Finally Meir Arik decided that if the Ark is well locked there is no objection to leaving the Torah under the care of a Gentile during the week.

So the law is clear: You may bring the Torah to the sick and to jails, especially if the Torah is kept there in an Ark.

The Ark, if adequately locked, may be left in the care of the Gentile wardens.

20

CONVERSION OF INFANTS

A Jewish couple from Colorado is adopting a Colorado infant child of a Gentile mother. The couple has moved to Massachusetts. Here the adoption cannot take place unless the social service agency involved (The Jewish Family and Child Service Agency of Denver) approves. The Jewish agency in Denver will not approve unless the child is first formally converted to Judaism. The questions, therefore, are as follows: According to Jewish law, can a Gentile child be converted unless the Gentile mother is also converted? What is the process of conversion? If a *mikveh* is to be used, cannot a more sanitary bathtub be used, since children are so susceptible to infection? (From Rabbi Bernard H. Bloom, Lexington, Massachusetts.)

FIRST of all, can a Gentile infant be converted without its mother being converted? The law stems from Talmud *Kesubos* 11a. There it says clearly that if a Gentile mother brings a child for conversion, the *Bes Din* converts the child. The Talmud does not state that the mother needs to be converted too. When the law is given in the *Shulchan Aruch, Yore Deah* 268:7, no mention is made of a requirement that the mother be converted also. In fact, the law seems clearly stated as to avoid any such requirement.

The law adds that the child can repudiate the conversion

when it grows up. This privilege of repudiation is questioned in an interesting way by Moses Sofer (*Yore Deah* 253; see *Pische Teshuva to Yore Deah* 268:7). He says that if the child's parents are converted with him, he can never repudiate the conversion. So aside from the question as to whether he may or may not repudiate, it is clear, at all events, that the parents need not be converted with him.

Now, as to the *process* of conversion, the Orthodox law requires dipping in the *mikveh*, both for boy and girl infants. You ask whether a clean bathtub might not serve as well as the (possibly non-hygienic) *mikveh*. This question can make sense only on the basis of the desire to satisfy Orthodox opinion. To satisfy the Orthodox, nothing but a dipping in the regular *mikveh* will serve. It is true that a Jewish scholar tried to devise some sort of hygienic home tank in place of the communal *mikveh*, and although he wrote a book on it ("The Secret of the Jew," Rabbi David Miller) nothing came of his suggestions. On the contrary, there is a movement in Orthodoxy in America to be stricter and stricter about the regulations of the *mikveh*. In fact, a recent immigrant, Rabbi Yom Tov Lippe Deutsch (Der Helmetzer) has been traveling through the country changing the *mikvehs* in city after city, on the ground that the former Orthodox *mikvehs* were not kosher enough. You can be sure that no bathtub will satisfy the Orthodox. As a matter of fact, I am sure they would not be satisfied even if you arranged for the communal *mikveh* to be used. In fact, there has been a recent Halachic discussion raising doubt as to whether the Orthodox community should even make the *mikveh* available to non-Orthodox rabbis.

In general, therefore, it should be abundantly clear that no approximation of Orthodox procedures will ever satisfy the Orthodox, and sometimes the very attempt to approximate these procedures awaken indignation among them. The *Bes Din* of the Chief Rabbi of the British Empire has recently issued a special pamphlet denouncing the Reform Congregation in London because it (the Reform Congregation) has a *Bes Din* to issue bills of divorce. The Orthodox *Bes Din* considers this attempt to resemble Orthodoxy as a conscious deception of the community.

The most intelligent procedure, therefore, is to take for granted (which, of course, we must) that the Jewish social service authorities will not presume to raise any doubts that we Reform Jews are a legitimate form of Judaism and that our procedures are legitimately Jewish. We must never permit this to be questioned by any communal Jewish organization. In this matter of conversion of infants, we have a very definite and official Conference attitude, and it is stated in the official report on Marriage and Intermarriage, as follows:

"With regard to infants, the declaration of the parents to raise them as Jews shall be deemed as sufficient for conversion. This could apply, for example, to adopted children. This decision is in line with the traditional procedure in which, according to the Talmud, the parents bring young children (the Talmud speaks of children younger than the age of three) to be converted, and the Talmud comments that although an infant cannot give its consent, it is permissible to *benefit* somebody without his consent (or presence). On the same page the Talmud also speaks of a father bringing his children for conversion, and says that the children will be satisfied with the action of their father. If the parents therefore will make a declaration to the rabbi that it is their intention to raise the child as a Jew, the child may, for the sake of impressive formality, be recorded in the Cradle-Roll of the religious school and thus be considered converted."

There may be some objection to our Conference procedure of the conversion of infants, on the grounds that a child attending our school may, nevertheless, join the religion of his mother and decide to be a Christian. However, the same objection could apply to the Orthodox procedure, since according to the law, an infant converted by *mikveh,* etc., has the right to repudiate later. The complication attendant upon such repudiation affects Orthodox law too. In the responsum of Moses Sofer referred to above, *Yore Deah* 253 discusses the question: How can we make a blessing over the immersion of this child when the child may yet some day repudiate the whole procedure? Will not that be a vain blessing? Moses Sofer says that we need not be concerned with the future contingency. This applies to our conversion too. Yet our education lasting over many years is more likely to have a permanent influence than a ceremony performed in infancy.

Therefore, in the case that you mention, the procedure should be as follows: The parents must promise to raise the child as a Jew. You record the child on the Cradle-Roll of the Congregation, and that is sufficient to fulfill our Reform procedure.

21

EXPULSION OF MEMBER FROM THE CONGREGATION

Is it in accordance with the spirit of Jewish tradition for a congregation to provide in its by-laws for the expulsion of a member? The proposed by-law is as follows:

SUSPENSION AND EXPULSION

I. For Financial cause . . .

II. For Other Causes. The Board shall have the authority to remove, expel, or suspend any member in the interest of the general welfare of the congregation. Such action on the part of the Board shall be preceded by notification by certified mail to the party concerned at least two (2) weeks prior to a meeting of the Board, and the party involved may request a hearing before the Board.

THE question which is asked is of great delicacy because of the long and complex history of the legal instruments for the exclusion of a Jew from the Jewish community. The various instruments of exclusion, the ban, the excommunication, well-known as instruments of discipline in the Catholic Church, were from early days instruments of discipline in Judaism (*niddui* and *cherem*) and even have a Biblical root. When Ezra wished to summon the entire community to a special assembly, the proclamation was accompanied with this threat of penalty (Ezra 10:8): "Whosoever came not within three days, according to the counsel of the princes and the elders, all his substance should be forfeited and himself separated from the congregation of the captivity." In other words, merely for absenting himself from this assembly, the man was "separated from the congregation."

The Talmud, in *Berachos* 19a, mentions twenty-four causes for which a person may be excommunicated. These are not enumerated in the Talmud, but all the twenty-four are given in Maimonides' *Yad*, (*Hilchos Talmud Torah* VI:14) and also in the *Shulchan Aruch, Yore Deah* 334:43. Among these causes for excommunication would be some of the motivations akin to the suggestions for expulsion in your proposed by-laws; for example, he who despises the head of the congregation or insults his neighbor, or refuses to accept the decisions of the congregation, or who uses the name of God in vain; in other words, a troublemaker.

In the Middle Ages, the ban was used to enforce the various decisions of the community. Many of them were financial decisions. It is doubtful whether the isolated, struggling, Jewish communities could have maintained themselves without this instrument of exclusion to help enforce their regulations.

However, this instrument, so indispensable for communal continuity, was used in the last centuries as an instrument against all liberalism and modernization of Judaism, and so was particularly disliked by liberals. For the use of the ban by rabbinical authorities against liberal tendencies, see particularly the end of Wiesner's *Der Bann*. We may say, in general, that the use of the traditional (and once indispensable) instrument of exclusion should be distasteful to any modern Reform congregation and should be sparingly used, if at all. The instrument of expulsion, if the congregation feels it is necessary for its self-protection, should be hedged in with many safeguards. Let us, therefore, go a little more deeply into the traditional provisions with regard to the exclusion of people from the community, and see which might possibly be applicable or acceptable today.

There are obvious differences between what your congregation desires to do and what was done in the past in the matter of exclusion. In one way, what you intend to do by excluding a man from membership is equivalent to what was done in some of the provisions of the traditional ban. The man could not be counted in the *minyan* for the service and could not even participate in the joint grace after meals, etc. (*Yore Deah* 334:10).

However, there were certain important differences. First of all, what you are doing is, from one point of view, much more serious. The old excommunication presumably lasts only thirty days (*Yore Deah* 334:13), and you mean to exclude the person permanently from participating in congregational affairs. On the other hand, what you are doing is much less serious than what was done in the past. In the Middle Ages, when these laws were most frequently applied, the community was identical with the congregation. When a man was excluded, he was excluded from the entire community. Here you are excluding him only from one separate organization, and he can still join other congregations. Furthermore, the old excommunication forbade anybody except his immediate family from doing business with him or even from conversing with him. You are merely removing him from membership and not isolating him personally.

However, there is one element about the old laws of exclusion which is important to notice. Every ban was presumed to last for thirty days only, unless there was ground for its renewal. Furthermore, there was a method provided for the immediate lifting of the ban at any time (see *Yore Deah* 334:13). Therefore, if there would be any objection to your proposed by-law, it would be as follows:

1. The old laws contained an earlier stage, *"nezifah,"* which means "rebuke." Sometimes a man was put under "rebuke" and needed no further discipline. Your by-laws do have the statement that a man should receive two weeks prior notification by mail, but that is hardly enough. There should be a preliminary punishment, such as suspension, which might be as effective as the old "rebuke," and may make the final expulsion unnecessary.

2. Since the Jewish law puts a time limit on the exclusion and makes provisions for reinstatement, your by-laws should do likewise and make provision for a man applying for readmittance.

In general, we would conclude as follows: Since the exclusion is only from one congregation and not from the community, you have the right to determine who shall cease to be a member. Your membership committee which has the unquestioned right to determine who shall become a member in the first place, should also have the right to determine who shall cease to be a member, especially since the expulsion is only from one congregation and not from the entire community. However, since Jewish law has certain safeguards, you should surround the by-law with the two traditional safeguards mentioned; first, a preliminary suspension and, also, if the punishment of expulsion is carried out, there must be an opportunity for reinstatement.

(Originally published in *Central Conference of American Rabbis Yearbook,* Vol. LXXIV, 1964.)

22

PRE-CONVERTS PARTICIPATING IN SERVICES

Women who are under instruction to become converts have the various religious ceremonies explained to them. Before the process of conversion is completed, may they, for the purpose of learning, light the Sabbath candles and recite the blessing over them? (From Chaplain Hirshel L. Jaffe, Travis AFB, California.)

THE main objection is the question of "a blessing in vain," (*beracha l'vatala*). When a blessing is not required and is nevertheless recited, it is, in a sense, using the name of God in vain. Is the Gentile, while still a Gentile, able to say, "Who has commanded *us* to light the Sabbath lights," and to use the name of God in such a blessing? The answer to this question depends upon whether Gentiles, while still Gentiles (i.e., "Children of Noah") are in duty bound to keep the Sabbath. Clearly the Sabbath is not one of the seven commandments which "Sons of Noah," i.e., Gentiles, are in duty bound to observe. In fact, there is a rather harsh Aggadic saying to the effect that a Gentile who observes the Sabbath does not deserve to live (*Sanhedrin* 58b). However, this statement, being Aggadic, is not to be taken too seriously. They also say, for example, in *Berachos* 4b that he who transgresses the words of the sages deserves death. The stern expression in *Sanhedrin* simply indicates that the rabbis disapproved of the Gentile observing the Sabbath since he is not commanded to do so. Since that is the case, we may take this to be an objection to having these candidates for conversion (while they are still Gentiles) recite the blessing. It would be a *beracha l'vatala.*

Yet aside from the question of *beracha l'vatala,* there is basically no objection in general to a Gentile reciting blessings. What objection there does exist is to a Samaritan reciting a blessing (*Berachos* VIII:8). The reason is that the Samaritan was suspected of praying to Mount Gerizim. When the *Tosefta* repeats this law (*Berachos* V:21) it says that when a Gentile (i.e., not a Samaritan) blesses, using God's name, we say "Amen" after his blessing. So this law is carried all the way through the literature and is found actually codified in the *Shulchan Aruch, Orah Hayyim* 215:2, where it is clearly said that we do not answer "Amen" after a blessing of a Samaritan, etc.; to which Isserles says that after a Gentile, we may say "Amen" if we have heard the whole blessing. Therefore, except for the consideration of "a blessing in vain," there is no real objection to a Gentile reciting the blessing.

There is, of course, a fairly simple way out of the objection against the violation involved in *beracha l'vatala.* This is illustrated by the decision of Moses Isserles to *Orah Hayyim* 225:2, where there is some doubt as to the validity of the blessing to be recited by the father at the son's Bar Mitzvah. Here, there is danger of a *beracha l'vatala* if, after all, the blessing is really not required. Therefore Isserles solves the problem by having the blessing recited, leaving out the words, "O Lord, our God, King of the universe." This is the method that the rabbis often follow when they are uncertain as to whether the blessing is required or not. They have the blessing recited without using the Name of God, or as they say, *"b'li Shem u-malchus,"* because the real objection to the "wasted" blessing is using the name of God in vain. When you leave out the name of God, the objection to reciting the blessing virtually vanishes.

There is, perhaps, another consideration which might lead you to allow the woman to recite the blessing. We train children in preparation for their observance of the commandments which they will not be in duty bound to observe until they are thirteen, and certainly we teach them to recite the blessings which will be required six months later. Of course, there is some weakness in this argument, namely, that according to many authorities, any young child who can take good care of *tefillin* is already in duty bound to put them on. Also, according to the Talmud, *Megilla* 23a, even minors may be called up to the Torah. However, to us, to whom Bar Mitzvah begins actually at thirteen, there is certainly a fairly strong analogy in letting children under training pronounce the blessings before they are legally due.

To sum up: The objection to these candidates reciting the Friday evening blessing is that the Sabbath is not one of the commandments incumbent upon Gentiles and, therefore, a blessing recited by them over the Sabbath lights would be "a blessing in vain." However, in general, Gentiles may recite the blessings and we may recite "Amen" after them. When there is doubt about the validity of the blessing, we can leave out the name of God. Since, however, this would shorten the blessing, too, and not constitute an adequate training, we may rely upon the analogy of the training of pre-Bar Mitzvah boys and allow these candidates to recite the blessing.

23

GENTILE STEPFATHER AT BAR MITZVAH

The following question has been asked a number of times: A Jewish woman divorced from a Jewish husband, remarries an unconverted Christian. Her son by her first marriage is being Bar Mitzvah. The Christian stepfather has adopted the child and has been truly a father to the boy. It seems wrong to keep him from participating as father in the Bar Mitzvah ceremony of the son. What may or may not a Christian stepfather do in the ceremony?

FIRST of all, he can certainly be called to the Torah, since the Bible is sacred to Jews and Christians alike, but the question would be whether he can sincerely recite the blessings over the Torah. We should not require him to pronounce words which he does not believe and thus make of the blessing an insincere formality. The blessings over the Torah say, "Who has chosen us among all people and given us His law." This refers to the people of Israel. If he were a convert to Judaism, he could count himself as a member of a family of Israel and recite the blessings as if he were of Jewish descent (see Maimonides' answer to Obadiah, the proselyte, *Treasury of Responsa*, page 28). But this stepfather is not a Jew by religion and so he cannot truthfully recite the blessing. We might perhaps write out a special blessing for him somewhat as follows:

"Praised be Thou, Lord our God, King of the universe, Who has given His sacred law unto all His children that we may learn, observe, and serve Him in righteousness."

However, the father is also expected to recite the special blessing at the Bar Mitzvah, *baruch sheptorani*. This blessing involves a problem. Although there are alternate explanations of the meaning of this blessing, it is generally understood to mean, "Now I am rid of the responsibility for this person's obedience to the law." Who had had the responsibility until now? The authorities would agree that it was the boy's natural father. The fact that the father and mother had been divorced does not excuse the natural father from the responsibilities of teaching his child the Torah, etc. If, therefore, the natural father were present, it would be he who should recite the blessing, *baruch sheptorani*.

But if the father is not present, as may well be the case, and the Gentile father, who is legally the adopted father, is the only father participating in the Bar Mitzvah ceremony, who shall then recite this particular blessing? A Gentile is a *ben Noach* and has special commandments incumbent upon him. But clearly the commandment to teach his son the Torah and to keep him obedient to the *mitzvos* is no part of the duty of the Gentile. It is not one of the seven commandments incumbent upon the sons of Noah. Therefore for him to say this blessing would be a mockery. What can be done in these circumstances without offending decent, well-intentioned people?

First of all, we may consider that his blessing is not indispensable. Joseph Caro does not even mention such a blessing. Moses Isserles who suggests the blessing (see *Orah Hayyim* 225:2) has considerable doubt as to the validity of the blessing and therefore recommends, as is done in all cases of such doubt as to the validity of a blessing, that the blessing be recited without including God's name, because there is the danger of using God's name in vain; and in this case the danger derives from the fact that the blessing is of dubious validity. Hence, in these special circumstances, we may well omit the blessing entirely. There is another procedure which we might follow. When, for example, a boy has not been circumcised, either because his father was not available or if he were negligent, the *Bes Din* has the obligation to circumcise the child in *loco parentis*. A similar circumstance exists with regard to the redemption of a first born son. If the father is not available, the grandfather is eligible to perform the ceremony in *loco parentis*. Therefore, in this case, where the adoptive stepfather is a Christian who cannot sincerely recite this special blessing, the grandfather may be called upon to pronounce it, or the rabbi himself as the *Bes Din* may recite it.

24

HALLOWEEN MASKS

Is it contrary to the mood of Jewish legal tradition for Jewish children to dress up in disguises and costumes on Halloween and to go "trick or treating" on that day? (From Rabbi Jack Segal, Far Rockaway, New York.)

HALLOWEEN, which is now a play-night for children, was originally one of the special saint's days in the Christian church. Actually, it is older than Christianity and according to the Encyclopedia Britannica, it was a pre-Christian Druidic observance in England and Ireland and, in fact, the giving of nuts and apples, etc., which was made part of

Halloween, was taken from the Roman festival in honor of the harvest goddess Pomona. The Christian Church, as it did with a number of heathen festivals (since it could not wean the people away from their favorite pagan folk festival), embodied it in the Christian calendar as All Saints' Day; and the eve before, All Hallows Eve (when, in pagan times, fires were lighted) is now Halloween, with its pumpkin illumination, etc. But as far as we are concerned, it has come down as a date in the Christian religious year.

The first question we should ask is this: To what extent may Jews participate in a folk festival which has vague religious connotations? There is a perfect parallel to the question of Halloween in the Gentile observation of New Year's Day. New Year's Day also has (or had been given by the early Church) a Christian religious connotation. It is celebrated in the Church as the Feast of the Circumcision, being the eighth day after the birth of Jesus (Christmas). Should this Christian redefinition of an old festival render the day too specifically Christian for us to participate in it, by sending greetings and gifts to our Christian neighbors? Certainly it is, basically, forbidden to Jews to participate in Christian festivals. Would New Year's Day and the almost perfect parallel, Halloween, be therefore forbidden to Jews, as far as participation in them is concerned? This very question is discussed by one of the greatest late medieval authorities, Israel Isserlein, in his Responsa collection *Terumas ha Deshen*, 195. (In the East European edition, this resposum is out of the regular order and is printed in the back of the book.) He says there is no objection to sending gifts to Gentiles on this festival. Of course, the Jew who is scrupulous will try to send his gifts, not precisely on that very day, but the day before; but if the day before happens to be

Shabbas, there is no real objection to sending it on the very day itself, because (he says) it is not really a day of worship, but a day of good luck, etc. So we may conclude as to Halloween which has long ceased to be Christian in any religious sense, that there is no real objection to Jewish children participating in it.

But now we must ask the second question: Is the costuming and the "trick or treating" contrary to the spirit of the Jewish tradition? Actually, there is a biblical basis upon which objection could well be raised. The Bible, in Deuteronomy 22:5, clearly prohibits men from putting on women's garments and women from putting on men's garments. The purpose of the prohibition is to guard against immorality, so that a woman disguised as a man or a man disguised as a woman should not stay long in the company of the other sex. This biblical prohibition is cited frequently in such questions as whether a man may dye his beard, since the dyeing of hair is deemed to be a woman's procedure. It is also cited in discussions about Purim, where people costumed in various ways and wore masks.

The full discussion of this question is found in the last responsum of Judah Minz, the great Rabbi of Padua in the sixteenth century. He cites a whole string of authorities, and says that he and his famous predecessors observed this masking and costuming and merrymaking all their lives in their various communities and never raised any objection to it. Clearly there is no objection to it, or they would have objected. Then he adds an interesting comment which is very close to our "trick or treat." The students, as part of the hilarity of Purim, would snatch food; and he says, "This custom should not be considered 'gezel' (i.e., robbery) but is part of the fun of the occasion."

So we may conclude on the basis of the spirit of tradition that neither the fact that Halloween has a vague Christian association, nor the masking or costuming or the taking of food, etc., give any ground for prohibiting Jewish children from participating in the Halloween costuming, disguising, or "trick or treating."

25

LAYMEN CONDUCTING A CONVERSION

An Indian Gentile girl in Bombay desires to convert to Judaism. She has presented herself as a candidate for conversion to our Reform congregation in Bombay (a congregation of the *Bene Israel*). The congregation has no rabbi at present and they have asked whether laymen are eligible to perform the ceremony of conversion.

THE *Shulchan Aruch* in *Yore Deah* 268:3 says that a conversion must be conducted by a court of three "eligible to judge." The question which concerns us is what is meant by this phrase. Of course, "eligible to judge" can mean simply that the judges are not relatives. See Perisha to the *Tur* who quotes the Mordecai as the source of this explanation. However, there is a much more fundamental question involved as to the nature of the court.

In Mishnaic and Talmudic times there were two classes of courts, those that dealt with religious and criminal matters and those that dealt with adjudicating civil disputes. The courts that dealt with religious and criminal matters were generally the fixed courts and were composed of men who were formally ordained (*musmachim*). Since ordination in the old classic sense could take place only in Palestine, then those who conducted such courts in Babylon had a somewhat different status, but one which amounted to the same thing. They were called "*mumchim*," literally "skilled men." It meant, actually, official appointees of the Exilarch. "*Musmachim*" in Palestine and "*mumchim*" in Babylon could also judge civil matters; but civil matters could legally be judged by amateurs if the two parties in dispute selected them and were content with each other's selection.

In post-Talmudic times official ordination (or in Babylon, official appointment) has ceased. Our present "*semicha*" is merely the use of an old name; it is actually only a license to teach, although it uses the formula "he may judge." Modern rabbis considered that their right to judge in certain cases, which in the past required official judges, inheres in the fact that they are agents of the judges of the past. Now our question really amounts to this: Is conversion one of those religious functions which in the past would require official judges and therefore now require "ordained" rabbis who are deemed to be their direct agents, or is it rather akin in status to such civil matters which even in the past could be adjudicated by laymen?

The fullest discussion of the question of conversion is found in the Talmud in *Yevamos* 46 and 47. The Talmud concludes at the bottom of 46b that the incident described on that page proves that a court of three is required for conversion. Then it raises but rejects the supposition that the court must be composed of *mumchim*, learned officials. However, although *mumchim* were not required for conversion in those days, it nevertheless may be that nowadays scholars (*talmiday chachomim*) may nevertheless be required and that ordinary laymen are ineligible. There are certain functions which for various reasons came to be restricted to scholars (therefore generally rabbis), for example, matters of marriage or divorce, or matters of releasing vows, etc. Is conversion to be considered such a matter which today must be left to scholars (i.e., rabbis)?

The Talmud in *Kiddushin* 62a and 62b gives a discussion which begins with the question of heave offering, starting with the statement that a man may not give heave offering from fruit that is still unharvested for fruit that is already harvested. It then moves to a discussion of whether a man may say to a woman, "I hereby marry you, the marriage to take effect after I have become (or after you have become) a proselyte." Then the discussion continues as follows: "But surely to become a proselyte is within his power to achieve" (and therefore the marriage proposal would be valid) and the Talmud answers, "No; it is not necessarily within his power to achieve because a proselyte needs three people because the word '*mishpot*' is used with regard to it, as with civil cases which require three." Then the Talmud says, "How does he know that he will be able to find three who will assemble to convert him?" Rashi simply explains this as saying he may not find three Israelites to gather to go through with the process.

It is clear from this discussion and Rashi's commentary that any three Israelites are authorized to perform the conversion, and the *Tosfos* to the place addresses itself exactly to this question and comes to the same conclusion, and quotes Rabbi Nathaniel to the same effect, that conversion does not require trained and official personnel.

Benjamin Zeev (sixteenth century) in his Responsa I, 72, quotes the responsum of Isaac the son of Samuel to the effect that conversion is valid even if conducted by three *hedyotos* (i.e., three ordinary unlearned laymen). Benjamin Zeev concludes with the general statement that in matters of conversion, we ought to follow the line of leniency and therefore should, if necessary, allow three ordinary men to conduct the conversion, lest we "lock the doors in the face of converts." The phrase is from *Tosfos, Yebamos* 47a. However, Zvi Hirsch Chayes of Zolkiev, who lived about a hundred years ago, says that it is preferable that the three men be scholars. See his Notes to the Talmud to *Sabbath* 46b (the Notes are to be found at the back of the large Vilna edition.)

Benjamin Zeev's general principle that in matters of conversion we should be lenient rather than too strict is revealed in the summary of the law as found in the *Shulchan Aruch, Yore Deah* 268. There we are told that while a court of three is required, nevertheless if a person is converted before two, the conversion is valid as a *fait accompli* (*B'di-eved*), although not as a preferred procedure. So, too, while the whole conversion process must be consciously directed with full understanding of the implications, nevertheless a formal bathing for some other purpose than conversion can be considered valid for conversion as a *fait accompli*. All these opinions are based upon earlier legal decisions. Besides the clear evidence of the preference for leniency in this matter, the *Shulchan Aruch* also reveals the uncertainty as to the types of judges required. Whereas in 268:3 it merely says "three men who are eligible to judge," i.e., not relatives, nevertheless when the words of admonition are repeated after the ritual bath (in 268:1) Isserles adds to the statement that it must be scholars who give him the final instruction. However, the *Shulchan Aruch* in

268:12 sums it up by saying that if he were circumcised and bathed in the presence of three *hedyotos* (i.e., three average men) he is fully a *ger*.

Ben Zion Uziel, the late Chief Sephardic Rabbi, in his very last book of Responsa *Mishpote Uziel, Even Hoezer* 13, p. 54, Jerusalem, 1964 says: "It is the Halacha, as we learn from the words of the Rambam, that the reception of proselytes does not require a *Bes Din* of skilled men, but even with three ordinary men (*hedyotos*) it is quite sufficient."

In brief, the general mood of leniency has led the majority of the authorities cited and the *Shulchan Aruch* itself to conclude that any three laymen can legally conduct the conversion. However, since the people are of the Bene Israel, this woman and her husband (after she has been converted and married) may move to Israel, and since the Orthodox rabbinate in Israel generally refuses to accept conversion by a Reform rabbi on the ground that the requisite bathing has not been performed, it would be advisable to have three men send in a woman with her to the *mikveh* to have her fulfill this ritual requirement.

26

CIRCUMCISION OF CHILD OF UNMARRIED MOTHER

What has tradition said about the circumcision of the child born out of wedlock, where no father can be present and there is no relative of the father's family available? (From Judge J.W.P., New York City.)

IN general the Jewish law is that the duty to have a child circumcised is encumbent upon the father of the child. But suppose for some reason the father of the child neglects this duty, or suppose he is in another country. The duty, then, devolves upon the *Beth Din* to have the child circumcised. If the *Beth Din* for some reason neglects this, then the sin of neglect falls upon the person himself when he grows up. When he grows up, he is in duty bound then to arrange for his circumcision (see *Shulchan Aruch, Yore Deah* 261).

Of course, if the father is not Jewish, the duty of having his son circumcised cannot devolve upon him. A Gentile is not obligated to obey Jewish law (except, of course, the seven commandments of the "Sons of Noah"). Hence, clearly, a child must be circumcised at the order of the *Beth Din*. If the mother, however, is Gentile and the father Jewish, the child, as in all mixed relationships, follows the status of the mother and is a Gentile child and does not need to be circumcised at all.

It is to be noted that a mother has no obligation at all to arrange for the circumcision of the child (see Isserles to *Yore Deah* 261). Therefore if the mother does nothing at all about it, there can be no complaint against her. She is not obligated at all.

As for the question whether a child born out of wedlock must be circumcised, that, too, is clear. The *Shulchan Aruch, Yore Deah* 265:4, speaks of the duty of circumcising an illegitimate child (*mamzer*) and the normal blessings are all recited over him, except the final prayer of well-wishing. The commentator Shach says that this is because we have no desire that such should increase among us. Also it is required that it shall be announced that such a child is illegitimate. (These restrictions date back to Jacob Moellin

[Maharil], in Mainz, fourteenth century). They must have had many such problems in those riotous days of persecution in the Rhineland.

However, it must be understood that the term "illegitimate child" (*mamzer*) does not apply to the average child born out of wedlock. Such a child is not a *mamzer*, unless the mother is married to some other man, or unless the father and the mother are of forbidden degrees of consanguinity. So there is no question that the child born out of wedlock must be circumcised and that if the father cannot do so, it is the duty of the *Bes Din*.

Most of the children with whom you deal are not children of married women by some man other than their husband, and generally not of people of forbidden degrees of consanguinity. They are certainly not *mamzerim* and even if they were, they would have to be circumcised if the mother is Jewish.

If the *Bes Din* has the duty of circumcising the child of a Jewish mother, who, then, is the *Bes Din* under present circumstances? It would be the rabbinate or the community; in other words, your organization would be deemed to have the obligation to see that the child is circumcised. If, therefore, the child is circumcised in the hospital, or if later the adoptive parents have the child circumcised, your organization has done its duty.

27

ANESTHETIC FOR CIRCUMCISION

A physician performing a circumcision insisted upon using an anesthetic "to prevent fuss and bother with the
baby crying, etc." Should this be permitted or even encouraged from the point of view of Jewish legal tradition?
(From Rabbi Michael Goulston, Lancaster, England.)

THIS question has been asked a number of times in recent
years when the use of anesthetics (even for minor surgery)
has come into general use. The question is asked usually
with regard to adult converts. Sometimes a convert will not
consent to circumcision unless an anesthetic be used. In one
case the circumstances were reversed and the convert insisted that no anesthetic be used because he wanted to feel
pain, since he considered the pain to be sacrificial. Sometimes it is asked with regard to children. A Jewish child had
not been circumcised in infancy (for reasons of ill health).
Now at the age of five, he is to be circumcised and the
mother insists that a local anesthetic be used. Out of these
various cases a general attitude has emerged as to the use of
anesthetics in circumcisions for adults and for children.

The first discussion of the question was by Meir Arik, the
great Galician authority in the past generation. In his Responsa *Imre Yosher,* II, 140, he decides definitely in the
negative. His arguments are worth notice because they reveal the general mood of the authorities of the time to all
new suggestions which may effect the ceremonial laws. He
calls attention to the Talmudic debate (in *Kiddushin* 21b)
which deals with the piercing of the ear of a Hebrew slave
who refuses to be set free. The Talmud there speaks of

"sahm" (an anesthetic medicine). This proves, he said, that the Talmud was well acquainted with such medicines. Yet since the Talmud does not mention the use of anesthetic medicines in circumcision, it clearly was opposed to their use. Furthermore, he says that the Midrash (Genesis *Rabba* 47:9) tells that Abraham was in pain because of his circumcision, and it was for that pain that God gave him additional reward. Then he concludes with a general statement in the nature of a warning, namely, that we have never used anesthetics in the past and God forbid that we should introduce any novelties.

This firm and indignant negative is not shared by the majority of the scholars who have dealt with the question. For example, Bezalel Shafran (Responsa *Rabaz* 125) refutes the prohibitory opinion found in the book *Sefer ha-Bris,* in which it was insisted that the circumcised must be awake, since the fulfillments of commandments require conscious intention (*kavvana*). Shafran proves that a child may be asleep during the operation and that fact would not impair the legal validity of the circumcision.

The strongest opinion in favor of the use of anesthetics comes from the famous Rabbi of Kishinev, Judah Lev Zirelsohn (who was martyred by the Nazis). It was he who dealt with the question of the five-year-old boy mentioned above. In his *Ma'arche Lev,* 53, after reviewing various arguments, he comes to the general conclusion that the Torah *nowhere requires pain* in the circumcision, and therefore he agrees in the case mentioned to the use of anesthetics.

Gedalia Felder of Toronto, who has done yeoman service in collecting and organizing the Law and Customs in his four-volume work *Yesodey Yeshurun,* has now written a special work on adoption, conversion, etc. In this work (*Nachalas Z'vi*, p. 57) he summarizes the various opinions on this question and also refutes the negative opinion of Meir Arik.

In the light of the above, we may conclude that there is no objection to anesthetics. The law does not insist upon pain in the fulfillment of this commandment. However, to this extent Meir Arik is correct, that we should not introduce novelties unless there is a good reason for them. If the child is likely to be naturally asleep during the operation (as often happens) the law does not require that he be wakened (cf. the opinion of Bezalel Shafran). However, if the operation is done by a doctor and he insists that an anesthetic be used, then we assume that he has a good reason for it and we should not raise any objections. In general, *we* should not institute the use of anesthetics as a regular procedure, but should permit them when the surgeon or the parent ask that they be used.

The inquirer subsequently asked about the popular idea that the wine which is (sometimes) given the infant during circumcision is for the purpose of allaying the pain of circumcision.

It is customary for the *mohel* to give a drop or a touch of wine with his finger tip after the two blessings, when the phrase from Ezekiel is used, "Live in thy blood." This *custom* is mentioned by Joseph Caro in the *Shulchan Aruch* (*Yore Deah* 265:2). Of all the classic commentators, only the Spaniard, Abudraham, gives an explanation; but his explanation has to do with the sinful Israelites being given to drink the water into which their Golden Calf had been ground. A later commentator tries to connect it with the word "live" in the Ezekiel quotation, and attempts to have the drop of wine symbolize eternal life.

These explanations are obviously forced. One may say that no explanation is given for the drop of wine. Nowadays they sometimes give the child a bit of cloth or cake soaked in wine. This would lend itself to the notion that it was for the purpose of allaying pain. But the texts only speak of a "drop" or a finger touch. This could hardly have any pain-allaying effect and, therefore, this could not be the reason.

For completeness' sake, it might be added that another taste of wine is sometimes given the child on fast-days at the blessing. The *mohel* recites the blessing but since it is a fast-day, he may not taste the wine. Therefore (in order that the blessing not be a "vain blessing") a taste of the wine is given to the child (cf. Isserles to *Yore Deah* 265:4, *Orah Hayyim* 621:3). But Abudraham quotes Ibn Gayyat and Maimonides, who object to the practice and who prefer that on fast-days the wine blessing be omitted entirely. There is a wide variance in the *minhagim* about this practice. Some say: Give it to the *sandek* to taste. Some say: Give it to young boys present to taste. Some say: Give it to the mother (*Mishna Berura,* The *"Chofetz Chaim"* to 621) and some say: Give it to the child. For a fuller discussion see *Eduth L'Yisroel* by Jacob Werdiger (Bnai Brak, 1963) page 127, 3.

The present custom of giving the child a wine-soaked object to suck and which leads to the notion of allaying pain, is not authentic. Only a drop was used and of this no pain alleviation is either mentioned or is possible.

(Originally published in *Central Conference of American Rabbis Yearbook,* Vol. LXXVI, 1966.)

28

BAR MITZVAH FOR UNCIRCUMCISED

If a boy is uncircumised, may he be permitted to be Bar
Mitzvah, and what is the practice in Reform synagogues
in America on this matter? (From A.Z., Paris, France.)

IT happens occasionally that an Orthodox rabbi will refuse
Bar Mitzvah to the son of a woman who had been converted to Judaism by a Reform rabbi. The reason for his
refusal has some relationship to our question. Since this
woman was not taken to the *mikveh,* the Orthodox rabbi
considers her conversion invalid. Therefore she is not a
Jewess and her child is not a Jew. It is obvious that if a boy
is not authentically a Jew, he cannot be Bar Mitzvah, because non-Jews are obligated only to the seven commandments of Noah.

The question therefore is: Is this uncircumcised boy
about whom you ask a Jew, or is he not? There is no basis
for saying that he is not a Jew. The *Shulchan Aruch* (in
Yore Deah 261) says it is the duty of a father to have his
son circumcised. If the father fails to do so, it is the duty of
the community (the *Bes Din*) to do it. If the *Bes Din* fails
to do so, the duty reposes on the boy himself when he grows
up; and if he does not have himself circumcised, then he has
committed a sin and will be punished at the hands of
heaven (*chayov koreth*). Obviously, if he were not a Jew
and uncircumcised this commandment of circumcision
would not be encumbent upon him. No one doubts that the
boy is a Jew. Since he is a Jew, you have no right to keep
him from Bar Mitzvah.

The late Yehiel Weinberg, one of the great Orthodox authorities of our time, and until the Nazi holocaust head of the Orthodox seminary in Berlin, makes it absolutely clear that a child born of Jewish parents is not to be considered "*orel*," (uncircumcised in the religious sense). He is to be considered fully Jewish even if the circumcision is not fulfilled due to some physical cause which excuses the non-fulfillment of the commandment, such as hemophilia, etc.

He explains this in a discussion with Rabbi Benet of Goblantze, Hungary, who had argued that a man who comes to be a proselyte and has diabetes and so cannot be safely circumcised, that such a man may be converted merely by the ritual bath. Weinberg says that this Gentile cannot be a proselyte without the circumcision because circumcision is an indispensable ritual of entrance into Judaism, but with Jews circumcision is not a ritual of entrance but is a commandment that must be fulfilled. Therefore a Jewish child is Jewish even if the commandment is not fulfilled.

His words are clear: "The basic distinction between a Jew and a Gentile who comes to be converted is that in a case of a Jew, the laws concerning an *orel*, an uncircumcised, are (merely) an outgrowth of the obligation of the commandment (i.e., and not an indispensable pre-condition to his being Jewish), for the child is of the seed of Abraham, our father, and is therefore included in the covenant which God made with the father of our people, except only that he is in duty bound to renew that covenant through the commandment of circumcision; therefore, he (i.e., a Jewish child) who is freed from the commandment (e.g., through hemophilia) is not to be classified as an "*orel*." However, with a Gentile, etc. . . . circumcision is not a commandment to him because he is not commanded, but with him (the candidate for conversion) it is an indispensable requirement of his very entrance into Judaism." (See the *Festschrift* in honor of Leo Jung, Hebrew section, pp. 28-29.)

However, a *Beth Din* (i.e., a rabbi or a community) has the right to make special prohibitory laws in times of emergency (*l'migdar milsa*). If, for example, there was in Paris at this time a growing habit of parents to refuse to have their children circumcised, you would have the right to protect the community in this emergency by refusing to give this boy Bar Mitzvah. But if there is no such emergency, you have no such right. If I am not mistaken, a Hungarian community refused burial in the cemetery to uncircumcised men. It was at the time of a radical anti-Orthodox movement in Hungary.

This boy's not being circumcised may be nobody's fault. It may be that his brothers were hemophiliacs and therefore, according to law, he may be free from having to be circumcised altogether during certain drastic stages of this sickness. Or there may be some other reason. By the way, if the father is dead, the duty of circumcision is not incumbent upon the mother at all. So if he is the son of a widow, his mother has committed no sin.

It is your duty to persuade the family to have the boy circumcised; but whether they do or not, he is a Jew if his mother is Jewish, and he has the right to Bar Mitzvah.

You ask about Reform practice in America. I do not know of any Reform congregation that would refuse such a boy Bar Mitzvah.

29

CONVERTING A GENTILE MOTHER WHOSE CHILDREN REMAIN CHRISTIAN

A Gentile woman has been married to a Jew for twenty-five years. They have three grown-up children, all three Christian. The youngest, a son now fifteen, also Christian, still lives at home. The woman, active in our Sisterhood work, now wishes to convert to Judaism. Should she be accepted for training and conversion? (From Rabbi Seymour M. Rosen, Margate City, New Jersey.)

THE reason for asking the question is that her children, especially the son who lives at home, will remain Christian. But there is a previous question frequently asked in the legal literature: May a Gentile woman married to a Jew (of course by a non-Jewish marriage ceremony) be Jewishly married to the Jew she has lived with?

The Law in general objects to such a conversion and marriage. The first objection is based upon the "insincerity" of the conversion. A conversion must not be made if there is suspicion that the purpose of it is to marry a Jew. A conversion must be out of pure conviction of the truth of Judaism, and not for any ulterior purpose, such as marriage to a Jew. That is why the Orthodox rabbinate is generally reluctant to accept proselytes these days, since it is obvious that the purpose is marriage to a Jew. Here it is clear that her marriage to the Jew is a consideration in her petition for conversion; therefore the conversion is questionable. The question of sincerity is also in the mind of the questioner, since she has no objection to her son who lives with her remaining a Christian.

But there is a second objection which applies more specifically to the case in question. The Mishna (*Yevamos* II, 8) says that if a man is suspected of living with a Gentile woman, he may never marry her (i.e., if she be converted) because such a marriage would confirm the suspicion.

As to these objections to her conversion, first that it is in relation to marriage and not purely out of conviction, and second that it is a case of a Jew living with a Gentile, both of these objections have been losing their force in recent decisions. For example, Jehiel Weinberg, the authority of the Berlin Orthodox Hildersheimer Seminary (and the successor to David Hoffmann) decides in almost precisely the case here in question, to permit the conversion and Jewish marriage (cf. *Seridey Esh* III, 50). The reasons are practical: First you cannot really say that the purpose of the conversion is in order to marry a Jew, since she feels that she is already legally married to him; and secondly it is meaningless to discuss "suspicion" since it is an open, publicly known fact that they have been living together. So as far as the two "classic" objections to this conversion, they need no longer be considered as applicable.

There remains only the last question, whether the fact that her fifteen year old son is to remain a Christian, is not a proof of insincerity on her part. As to this, it may be said that if her boy were still an infant and she, therefore, could make the decision as to his religion, it could be expected that she should raise the infant as a Jew. But a boy of fifteen must make his own decisions and she can hardly be responsible for them.

The fact that this boy and her other two children, both adults, are Christians, has no bearing on her conversion. According to Jewish law a convert is considered to be a "new born child," i.e., (technically) no longer related to her family (*Yebamoth* 22a).

She may therefore be converted and remarried in a Jewish marriage. The remarriage, of course, should be a simple, private ceremony so as not to occasion any derogatory implications against the children.

30

THE C.C.A.R. AND "ETHIOPIAN HEBREW" CONGREGATIONS

The struggle of the American Negro for justice and improved opportunities has raised again the question of the relationship of Judaism (through its organized bodies) to those Negro congregations in Harlem (and perhaps elsewhere) who declare themselves to be Jews. Some of the members of these congregations, or perhaps most of them, observe the Sabbath, the Jewish holidays, have their children circumcised and Bar Mitzvah. What is their status with regard to being Jews? (From Rabbi Morris N. Kertzer, Larchmont, New York, in behalf of the Ad Hoc Committee on Negro Jews of the Central Conference of American Rabbis.)

THE question is complicated, involving both theoretical and practical questions. First it must be made clear that Judaism is not a racial religion, neither in the smaller sense, meaning common descent, nor in the wider sense, meaning that it is confined to members of the white race. Of course, basically, Jews are of common descent. Nevertheless anyone who converts to Judaism is deemed to have become not only a member of the religion but also to have been adopted as a member of a family. In his famous answer to Obadiah the proselyte, Maimonides was asked by Obadiah whether in his prayers he may say, "God of *our* fathers Who has sanctified *us* by His commandments," etc. Maimonides answered, "You must say all of these as they are. You must not change a single word but just as a born Israelite prays and blesses, so must you bless and pray, whether you are praying privately or are the cantor of the congregation." The reason that Maimonides says that (since there *is* some doubt on the matter; see M. *Bikkurim* I:4) is that the proselyte is deemed to be of the family of Abraham our father, as we are; and he adds, "Let not your genealogy be deprecated in your sight. If we (born Jews) trace our genealogy to Abraham, Isaac and Jacob, you are related to Him Who created the world. As it is said in Isaiah 44:5, one will say, 'I am the Lord's.' (Maimonides means that this refers to the proselytes.) Another will call himself in the name of Jacob."

This general principle that proselytes join not only the religion but the family, might be considered as bearing upon the racial question. Precisely because the proselyte becomes not only a co-religionist but a member of a family, one might say that he should be a member of a race that can be easily embodied into the family. If Judaism were merely a church, it would make no difference whether a co-religionist is of one race or another, but since it is also a family, it might be reasoned that the converts should be more strictly screened and be of the type with regard to race that would fit into the family. Because of this possible argument it is necessary now to take up the question whether there is any sense of race color distinction in Judaism, i.e., in the larger sense of race, black, white or yellow. I have discussed the matter fully in *"Recent Reform Responsa,"* Number 16 and I cite part of that statement.

"Nowhere does the Bible prohibit the admixture of races. Ezekiel, speaking to the Children of Israel in Chapter 16, verse 3, says: The Amorite was thy father and thy mother was a Hittite. So, too, with regard to the vast mixed multitude which came out of Egypt. While this mixed multitude is sometimes deprecated as the source of sinfulness, there is no statement that I remember to the effect that the descendants of the Twelve Tribes kept from intermarrying with the mixed multitude.

Thus there is no sensitiveness in the historic tradition against the possibility of our being a mixed race. Furthermore, there is no statement in the law forbidding marriage between the members of different races, provided they become Jewish by conversion. There is, in fact, one important responsum which by eloquent silence indicates that there is absolutely no objection to intermarriage on the basis of race. I refer to the Responsa of David ben Zimri in his volume IV, 219, and volume VII, 9. The question involved a Falasha woman. In fact she is referred to plainly as a Cushite woman, therefore black-skinned. She is now in Cairo among white Jews. Her white master wants to marry her. The question involved is whether we shall accept or reject her claim that her original Cushite husband was killed in a raid in Abyssinia (and she is a widow, eligible to marry her master). But there is not the slightest question raised in the responsum about her skin color. Clearly, there *was* no objection on that ground."

Now the third question that arises is this: Do these Negroes claim to be Jews? Do they, for example, claim to have been converted? If, for example, three or four of their leaders were themselves duly converted and were competent to perform conversion, they (the congregation) might be considered as having been properly converted to Judaism. It would be difficult to prove a claim on the part of their leaders that they were properly converted to Judaism. Nevertheless this very question has received considerable discussion in Jewish law, namely, that if a person claims to be converted to Judaism before a certain *Beth Din*, do we or do we not accept his claim? In general such claims are accepted. The following are the relevant sources, indicating the tendency to accept unprovable claims of having been converted:

Asher ben Yehiel in the *"Piskey Harosh"* (to *Yevamos*) 4:34, 35, sums up the law to his time when he says: If a man claims that he was converted before a certain court, he must bring proof (since a court's actions are susceptible of proof); but all the proof that is needed is merely for people to say, "We have heard that he was converted." Further, if a man says he was converted privately, he has to take the ritual bath before marrying a Jewess, but his sons are held to be Jewish. To *Tur, Yore Deah* 368, Joel Sirkes (Bach) says: "At all events, it is our custom to believe the man's claims and even to marry him to a Jewess." Then Joel Sirkes proceeds to explain away partially the objections of Maimonides against believing the man. Joel Sirkes' statement is cited with approval by Sabbetai Cohen (*Shach,* to *Shulchan Aruch, Yore Deah* 368:10 and 11). Sirkes to the *Tur* also quotes the well-known legal authority, Moses of Coucy, in his *S'Mag,* who says: "This occurs every day. Strangers come (and claim to be Jews). We do not bother to investigate. We drink wine with them and eat meat from their slaughtering." This general tendency of the law to accept the claim of a man that he is a Jew is reflected in a recent responsum by Isaac ben Aryeh Rudnik (*S'de Yitzchok*) London, 1961. The case with which he deals is that of a soldier who came to England from overseas, who claimed to be a Jew, married a Jewess; then his wife left him and lived with another man. Rabbi Rudnik decided that the marriage to the soldier who said he was a Jew is valid enough as Jewish marriage to require a Jewish divorce (*get*).

But all this applies to the claim of an *individual* to having been converted and with regard to him the law, as we have seen, is lenient. But when it is a group which makes such a claim, the question is much more complicated. The very fact that the group would make such a claim would tend to raise suspicions about them rather than add credence to their claim. The reason is that if they claim to be Jewish, then the question of the validity of their divorces over the past generations becomes a vital question, certainly in the eyes of Orthodox scholars. If they claim to be Jews but if, also, their divorces over past generations are questionable, then the whole group cannot be admitted into Judaism because of the suspicion of *mamzerus* (*chashash mamzerus*). Since the divorces are invalid, a woman remarried after receiving an invalid divorce is still deemed to be the wife of her first husband and, therefore, the children from her second "marriage" are illegitimate. This is exactly the bitter problem facing the B'nai Israel of India in the State of Israel today; and this, too, was one of the chief grounds cited by those scholars in the past who wished to keep the Karaites at a distance.

Of course this argument of general illegitimacy in such a

group because of the dubiety of their divorces in the past is not a strong argument in our Reform movement in America, inasmuch as we do remarry Jews who have not received a Jewish *get*; and so the argument of the suspicion of illegitimacy could be raised against our community if someone had the nerve to do so. At all events, since we accept the validity of civil divorce, this traditional argument against admitting a whole group which claims to be Jewish has comparatively no force for us.

However, we have a much more general concern about this group from the standpoint of Jewish legal tradition. There is no provision in Jewish tradition for the acceptance of entire groups as proselytes. In fact, the tradition is against it. For example, they did not consider the masses who joined Judaism in the time of Esther and Mordecai or at the time of the triumphs of David and Solomon (b. *Yevamos* 24b) as being true proselytes. Conversion requires careful examination of the sincerity of the *individual*. Therefore it is contrary to the mood of Jewish tradition to accept any group, as a group. It is immaterial whether the group is white, black or yellow. These Negroes belonging to the congregations we are discussing are welcome as individuals to be converted to Judaism.

Whether or not we should make an effort to invite them to conversion is another matter. That depends on whether or not the Conference agrees with the spirit of the resolution passed at the last Union Biennial in San Francisco urging active work towards proselytization. I was opposed to the resolution and am still opposed to the effort at active proselytizing. However many members of the Conference are in favor of it; but this is a matter which the Conference must decide, whether actively to seek converts or not. In either event the race of these people makes no difference and any one of them who decides to convert to Judaism is acceptable as far as his race is concerned. The individual rabbi would then have to decide whether on other grounds the candidate merits conversion. If, then, the Conference decides in favor of active proselytizing, there is no objection in Jewish law against issuing to them a general invitation to come and be converted. If the Conference decides against such active proselytizing of any group, then the law still remains that individuals, whatever be their race, are eligible for conversion to Judaism and to become part of the Jewish family.

To summarize this discussion, there is no race distinction in Judaism. Unprovable claims of individuals to have been formerly converted are generally accepted, but whole groups who make that claim are open to suspicion with regard to the traditional marriage laws. In general Jewish tradition is opposed to mass conversion. Each conversion must be decided individually. So with regard to the Negroes in Harlem who claim to be Jewish, each one of them is eligible to be a candidate for conversion. Whether or not they should be encouraged to become converted depends on whether or not the Conference is in favor of active proselytizing in general.

31

SURGICAL TRANSPLANTS

What is the attitude of the Jewish legal tradition to the growing surgical practice of transplanting parts of a dead body into that of a living person?

IT should go without saying that Jewish tradition and feeling would be absolutely opposed to hastening the death of a potential donor by even one second, in order that the organ to be transplanted into another body be in good condition. Nothing must be done to hasten the death of the dying. This scrupulousness about preserving the last few moments of life is also the concern of modern medicine. There are serious discussions today among doctors, especially with regard to obtaining organs for transplanting without delay, as to exactly when the potential donor is to be considered actually dead. At first the rule was, when the heart stopped beating; now they are considering a further test, when the brain stops functioning. As the discussion in medical circles continues, they will devise more and even stricter tests.

As far as deciding when the potential donor is actually dead, modern scientific opinions are much stricter than Jewish tradition. The controversy arose a century ago as to whether the Jewish law of immediate burial was too hasty an action or not. Various governments in central Europe decreed that there must be a delay of three days before the burial. The great Hungarian authority, Moses Sofer, defended the Jewish custom of immediate burial (on the same day) and said that our traditional judgment, embodied in the knowledge of the *Chevra Kadisha,* was sufficient proof of death (see his responsum, *"Chasam Sofer," Yore Deah* 338). Let us therefore say at the outset that, at least according to the spirit of Jewish law, the stricter the test as to the time of death which physicians will arrive at, the better it is. We therefore agree with the strict judgments of modern medicine that the patient must be absolutely dead.

But it is from this point on that the real problem begins. Is it morally or legally permissible to take away parts of the body of the dead, and is it further permissible to insert such parts into a living body? The problem is difficult, first of all, because transplanting of organs is an entirely new surgical procedure and, therefore, there could be no direct parallel or discussion of such a procedure in the older literature. Whatever opinion is arrived at on this matter must be *derived* as the underlying ethical principle behind related discussions in the literature.

There is a second and more direct difficulty in analyzing this question. When we begin to study the ethical implications of related ideas in the Talmud and in the writings of later scholars, we discover that the relevant basic principles seem to be mutually contradictory. Since this fact constitutes an initial difficulty, let us consider it first.

There is a general principle as to healing and the materials used for healing which, on the face of it, is so general as to make all further discussion of this problem unnecessary. The Talmud says (*Pesachim* 25a): "We may use any material for healing except that which is connected with idolatry, immorality and bloodshed." These are the three cardinal sins to avoid, for which a person must be willing to undergo martyrdom. But aside from three such sources of healing methods or materials, any material or any method would be permitted. Maimonides, himself a great physician, makes this Talmudic statement even clearer. He says (*Hilchos Yesodey Torah,* 5:6):

> "He who is sick and in danger of death, and the physician tells him that he can be cured by a certain object or material which is forbidden by the Torah, he must obey the physician and be cured."

This is codified as a law in the *Shulchan Aruch, Yore Deah* 155:3.

Considering this general permission to use anything we

need, no further discussion would seem to be necessary, except for the fact that the body of the dead has a special sacredness in Jewish law. There is a general principle that the body of the dead may not be used for the benefit of the living (*mayss ossur b'hana'ah,* based on *Sanhedrin* 47b). If the two principles are taken together, the general permissiveness would then need to be restated as follows: We may use all materials except those involved in the three cardinal sins mentioned above and *except, also,* the body of the dead.

But this apparent prohibition of using parts of the body of the dead depends upon a closer definition of the word *hana'ah* (benefit). Later scholars understand the word *hana'ah,* "benefit," to mean really not "general benefit," but rather "satisfaction," in the sense chiefly of the satisfaction of food. Therefore they speak of materials taken into the body in other ways than by the way of eating, and they call such absorption of material (other than eating) "not in the way of benefit, or satisfaction," (*lo k'derech hana'aso*). For example, the eating of blood is forbidden, but taking a blood *infusion* by means of the veins is described as not by way of *hana'ah* or satisfaction, and therefore is permitted. Thus the question of getting *hana'ah* (satisfaction) from the body of the dead depends now on whether it is taken as medicine by way of food. If the parts of the body of the dead are taken "not by the way of satisfaction" (*derech hana'ah*) but inserted into the body in another way, the law forbidding "benefit" from the dead is usually much more permissively interpreted.

There is another phase of the principle that the dead may not be used for the benefit or satisfaction of the living. That has to do with the distinction between Jewish dead and Gentile dead. In general we are in duty bound to heal the

sick, bury the dead, comfort the mourners of Gentiles, just
as we do with the bodies of Jewish dead (b. *Gittin* 60a).
But with regard to the Jewish dead, Jewish law adds certain
special regulations. For example, a *Cohen* may not be in
the same building with the Jewish dead because he may not
defile himself except for his own relatives. There are detailed burial requirements as to washing, shrouds, etc.,
which are required for the Jewish dead. These extra requirements do not apply to the Gentile dead. We are, of
course, in duty bound to bury and console, but neither Gentiles nor we are required to obey these additional minutiae
of Jewish burial laws. It is sufficient if Gentile dead are
respectfully buried and their mourners consoled.

There seems to be no Christian objection to such use of
the bodies of the dead. But there is a debate in Jewish law
as to whether the body of the Gentile dead may or may not
be used for the benefit of the living. The *Shulchan Aruch,
Yore Deah* 349, is inclined to the belief that the body of the
Gentile dead may not be so used, but the majority of opinion inclines to the side that such bodies may be used for the
benefit of the living (see the authorities marshalled by
Moses Feinstein, *Igros Moshe, Y.D.* 229, 230). Since, therefore, the majority of the available bodies as sources of organs for transplant are Gentile bodies, this detail of the
doubt as to whether "benefit for the living" may come from
the body of the dead does not have heavy weight.

There is, of course, a third consideration and that is the
duty of burying the whole body of the dead. This duty is the
source of the basic objection of Orthodox authorities to
autopsy. Therefore the question now is whether a part of a
body which is inserted into a living body is still to be considered part of the dead, which must be buried, or rather is
it now a part of a living body?

All, or almost all, of these rather complex considerations and apparent contradictions which needed to be harmonized are discussed in the Talmud and its early commentators, but of course they have no definite statement about the actual consuming or using the body of the dead for the healing of the living. Such an actual use for healing begins to appear in the literature in later centuries.

One of the strangest discussions of the use of the dead medically for the healing of the living, is found in the responsa of David ibn Zimri (Egypt, 1479-1589). He is asked a question which seems bizarre to us, who no longer are aware of medieval popular medical superstitions. It seems that mummies from the ancient Egyptian tombs were in David ibn Zimri's time a regular article of commerce. They were sold for medical purposes. People would actually eat those mummies to heal certain diseases. He is asked whether it is permitted to get benefit (*hana'ah* or satisfaction) from these bodies of the dead (Responsa *Radbaz,* III, 548). He states the general principle that one may not have *hana'ah* from the flesh of the dead (based on *Avodah Zara* 29b). Then he says that these bodies, embalmed so long ago with various chemicals, are no longer human flesh but are now another product. The ancient embalming preserved merely the outlines of the features but transformed the flesh into something else entirely. Furthermore, he says, these were once the bodies of the ancient Egyptians and, of course, here the law is less strict than the laws about "benefit" from the Jewish dead.

As far as I am aware, there is no other discussion in the responsa of the use of parts of a dead body for healing. There are some references to the use of tanned skin, but that was not for medical purposes. But in our time there are two detailed discussions of precisely our problem. They are by Moses Feinstein of New York, who may well be considered the prime Orthodox author of responsa (although, indeed, some extreme Chassidim recently denounced him for an allegedly liberal opinion with regard to artificial insemination). Moses Feinstein in his *Igros Moshe, Yore Deah,* has two successive responsa on the subject (229 and 230). These responsa, although only four or five years old, do not yet know of heart and liver transplants, but the author already knows of bone transplants and that is sufficient for him to marshal all the relevant opinions.

He discusses, as was indicated above, the exact definition of the term *hana'ah,* benefit, and explains it as literally meaning "satisfaction of food." Hence that which is taken into the body not by way of food (i.e., not by mouth) is to be considered more leniently. Furthermore, he speaks of the fact that most bodies available for organs are Gentile and therefore the stricter prohibitions do not apply to them. Finally he comes to a conclusion which is vital to the whole discussion, that when a part of a body is taken by a surgeon and put into a living body, it becomes part of a living body. Its status as part of the dead which needs to be buried is now void (*botul*).

There is a confirmation of the permissive opinion of Feinstein in the responsa of Nahum Kornmehl, published in 1966 in New York, *Teferes Zvi,* 75. His explanation is really charming. He says with regard to the prohibition of *hana'ah* from the dead in transplants that when the operation occurs there is certainly no *hana'ah* for the patient, only misery for days. The *hana'ah* comes when the transplant comes to life and becomes part of his body. But now it is alive and therefore this has nothing to do with benefit from the dead.

To sum up the discussion: The exceptional nature and

rights of the dead body do not stand in the way of the use of parts of the body for healing of another body. The part taken is not taken into the living body as food. Hence it is not considered *derech hana'ah*. The part becomes integrated into a living body and therefore the requirement of its burial has lapsed. Therefore the general principle first stated remains unimpugned, that "we may heal with any of the prohibited materials mentioned in Scripture." This is especially true, as Maimonides indicates, because the patients about to receive these implants are actually in danger of death, and for such patients any possible help is permitted by Jewish tradition.

(Originally submitted to the *Central Conference of American Rabbis,* 1968.)

32

GREETING MOURNERS

What is the basis of the tradition that when people come to call upon mourners they may not greet them (with the usual greeting of *"Sholom aleichem"*)? (From W.J., Pittsburgh, Pennsylvania.)

IN general there are many circumstances under which the greeting of "Peace" may not be exchanged. One set of circumstances applies to unclean places such as privies and bath houses where people are naked. In such places one may not teach nor study the Torah nor give the greeting of

"Peace." (See b. *Sabbath* 10b top and *Shulchan Aruch, Orah Hayyim,* especially 84.) The objection to greeting there is that *Sholom* is considered to be one of the many names of God which may not be uttered in unclean places. This is based on Rashi's comment to the verse in Judges 6:24 where Gideon called the name of the altar which he built *Adonoi Sholom* and Rashi (not in his Biblical commentary but in the Talmud, *Sabbath* 10b) explains that he addressed God by the name *Sholom.*

There would be some question whether this objection would apply today; at least the question is raised by Isserles in *Yore Deah,* 385, where the laws are given concerning a mourner not being permitted to greet with the standard greeting. He says that some are lenient in this matter because our *"sholom"* greeting is not the same as it was in those days. (See Be'er Hetev who quotes Joseph Caro to the effect that our greeting is like "Good morning" and is no longer an invocation of the Name of God.) This is supported indirectly by the law in *Orah Hayyim* 89:2 where it is stated that when the time comes for the daily morning prayer a man may not walk by the house of his neighbor and greet him with *"Sholom"* because that is one of the Names of God, but he may say to him, "Good morning."

A second reason against greeting with the classic greeting is not based upon the uncleanness of certain places which makes it improper to mention the Name of God there (i.e., *Sholom*) but rather that people in suffering may be considered under God's rebuke and therefore it would be inappropriate to ask them whether they are at peace. This basis for prohibition is found first in Mishnah *Taanis,* Chapter I:7, where the law is that if the various periods of fasts have gone and still no rain has fallen, people stop business, building, marriages and the greeting of "Peace" between man and his neighbor, and the Mishnah adds: "Like people under God's rebuke." (See *Tosfos Yom Tov, ad. loc.*)

Thus, also, as in the fast days for lack of rain, on the Ninth of Av it is prohibited really to greet with the greeting of "Peace." If unlettered people greet, it is permitted to answer; but that is all (*Orah Hayyim* 554:20).

This second motive might be called psychological. It would be unkind to ask a person (on fast days or in mourning), "Are you at peace?" The second motive (the psychological one) seems to be the dominant reason in the prohibition against greeting the mourner with the greetings of "Peace."

There is also a third explanation (somewhat less direct) of the reason for the omission of the "*Sholom*" greeting which is based upon *Mo'ed Koton* 15a. There the verse from Ezekiel 24:17 is quoted in which God tells Ezekiel "to mourn silently," which Rashi explains as meaning that he, Ezekiel, the mourner, should not greet anybody (see also *Tosfos, ad loc.*).

It would be useful to trace the law from its beginnings. The chief source of the law is in *Mo'ed Koton,* 21b, where a number of *boraitas* are cited as to this prohibition. These various forms of the prohibition are carried over into the post-Talmudic tractate *Semachos* (ed. Higger, Chapter VI) then quoted in full by the eleventh century Spanish teacher, Isaac ibn Gayyat, *Shaarey Simcha,* page 53, and then finally in the *Shulchan Aruch, Yore Deah* 385, where a whole section is devoted to it.

A consideration of the Talmudic foundation of the law in *Mo'ed Koton* 21b shows that the prohibition was primarily incumbent upon the mourner. It is he who is "under God's rebuke" and therefore the first three days of the seven, he may not greet and he may not answer if greeted. In fact, he may hardly speak and dismisses the consoling friend with a nod. After the first three days he still may not greet, but he may answer someone's greetings. After thirty days he may greet and answer, unless he is mourning for his father and mother; then the prohibition remains somewhat in effect for a year.

Hai Gaon (*Ozar Hageonim Berachos,* page 38) speaking of avoiding greetings of *sholom* before prayer, says that instead of "*Sholom*" we should greet with "Good morning;" but that the real objection is not the word of greeting but the bowing (*keriah*) which should be avoided. This decision is repeated in the medieval code *Orchos Chayim* (*Hilchoth Tefilla* 14).

As mentioned above, Isserles speaks of the fact that people are not too strict about the prohibition of greeting because our greeting is no longer an invocation of God's Name. (cf. *Be'er Hetev to Yore Deah* 385, end of paragraph 2.) In the latest authoritative code, *Aruch Ha-Schulchan,* Yehiel Epstein, says that nowadays people are not too strict about it, perhaps for the reason mentioned by Isserles. Furthermore, the prohibition is primarily incumbent upon the mourner himself, and if greeted after the first three days, he may respond. Also, the Talmud in *Mo'ed Koton* cites Rabbi Akiba who responded to the greeting when he was in mourning because a large group came and one must not affront a group. Moreover, on the Sabbath he may give and answer the greeting if that is the local custom. (Cf. *Rosh* to *mo'ed Koton* III, 38, based on *Jerushalmi Ber.* II, 7.) Rabbi Oshaya came to a certain place and he saw mourners on the Sabbath and said: "I do not know your local custom, but according to my custom, I give you the greeting of '*Sholom*'." At all events the real objection is against using God's name, *Sholom.* Our greetings of "Good evening" or "How do you do" are certainly less objection-able to the law. The law is firmly based on the Talmud and is in the *Shulchan Aruch,* but for the reasons mentioned, it is less and less strictly observed.

33

MEMORIAL LIGHTS IN THE HOME

Is the memorial light which is kindled in the house of the deceased during *shivah* a well established observance? What are the rules and customs which govern it? (From Louis J. Freehof, San Francisco, California.)

THERE is a Biblical verse and also a Talmudic statement which have been cited as a basis for the custom of lighting a seven-day memorial light in the house of the deceased. The Biblical verse is in Proverbs 20:27: "The candle (or the "light") of the Lord is the soul of man." The Talmudic statement is in the final request of Rabbi Judah the Prince (b. *Ket.* 103a). He asked that after his death the light should be kept burning, the table should remain set, and the bed remain arranged.

However, if we follow through the development of the legal literature, we find that none of the classic legal authorities based any fixed requirement upon this verse or on this statement in the Talmud. In fact, the custom of the home *shivah* light is not mentioned at all in any of the basic codes.

An evidence that the custom was not prevalent even in the sixteenth century in the times of Moses Isserles, can be seen from the fact that although Isserles is careful to record all worthy customs (*minhagim*) he does not mention this custom at all. In *Orah Hayyim* 610:4, he speaks of lighting a candle in memory of the dead on Yom Kippur in the synagogue, but he does not mention the custom of a home memorial light at all. Nor does he mention such a custom in *Yore Deah* in the section dealing with the observances in the house of the deceased. Moses of Przmyzl in the next generation, who collected all the proper customs in his work *Matteh Moshe*, does not mention this home custom either.

Just when the custom arose it is hard to determine. All such folk customs develop "underground," as it were, and then suddenly appear. Tekuchinski, in his recent work, *Gesher Ha-Chayim* (Vol. I, Chapter 20, p. 194) gives as his authority for the custom, "the later teachers" (*ha-acharonim*).

By the seventeenth century there is a full discussion of the custom in the responsa *Nachlas Shiva*, 73 (by Samuel b. David Halevi of Poland and Germany, 1625-1681). After that the custom is mentioned in many of the later legal works. Nathan Landau (*Kenaf Renana* II, 37 *Yore Deah*) speaks of it. So does Solomon Haas in *Kerem Shelomo* to *Yore Deah*, 399. So, also, Greenwald in *Kol Bo Al Avelus*, p. 361 and Note 20, and Hirshowitz, *Ozar Kol Minhage Jeshurun*, p. 305.

These later scholars seem to grope around for a justification for the custom. Of course they cite the verse in Proverbs and the dying request of Rabbi Judah. Obviously Rabbi Judah did not mean that a light should be kindled at his death, but that after his death everything should remain as it was in his lifetime: his table, his bed and his light. They also find some support in the *Maavor Yabbok,* the compendium on death by Aaron Berachia ben Moses of Modena, the Italian cabbalist (died 1639). He compares the body of man to the tallow of the candle and his soul to the flame. They also find some hint in the *Zohar (Chaye Soroh)* where the candle that burned in Sarah's tent (during her lifetime) was evidence of the presence of the *shechina.* Nevertheless, they cannot, nor do they attempt to find any chain of legal authorities for the custom.

Since, clearly, the custom is hardly more than two centuries old, these later legal authorities have not yet had time to iron out all the irregularities in the observance and to arrive at a clear and a definite series of rules for it. Samuel b. David Halevi (*Nachlas Shiva,* 17th century) sets down the first rule, namely, that the candle must be lit as soon as the person dies and burn for seven days. Even if he dies on a holiday and therefore the *shivah* is postponed till after the holiday, the lighting must not be postponed till after the holiday when the *shivah* begins, but must be kindled at once and burn for seven days.

Solomon Haas (in *Kerem Shelomo*) repeats that it must be lit the first seven days after the death, and adds that it can only be lit in the place where the man dies; i.e., if the relatives sit *shivah* in another place (or in another city) then they may not kindle the seven-day light at all.

However, this restriction is not confirmed by Nathan Landau (*Kenaf Renana*). He says that the light must be lit wherever the mourners sit *shivah.* Finally, Tekuchinski, in *Gesher Ha-Chayim* (Vol. I, p. 198), brings some order into the observance by a sort of compromise, and this compromise can be considered to be the present custom. The light must be kindled for the first seven days after the death (i.e., whether actual sitting of *shivah* is postponed by the holiday or not). Even if a man dies the day before the holiday and the onset of the holiday voids the *shivah* altogether, nevertheless the light must burn for seven days, even though they do not sit *shivah* for more than an hour. Preferably the light must be kindled in the place where he died, but if he died elsewhere (as in a hospital) it must be kindled where the family sits *shivah*.

To sum up: The custom is not more than about two centuries old. There is no firm basis for it in the law, but it has become a well established observance, and its mode of observance is generally as given by Tekuchinski and cited above.

34

THE ALIGNMENT OF GRAVES

The graves in the cemetery are aligned in the same direction. Is this a requirement of Jewish law? Suppose the shape of a new, unused parcel of land makes it convenient to align the graves in another direction; would this be permitted? (From Louis J. Freehof, San Francisco, California.)

THE alignment of graves in any predetermined direction, such as North to South or East to West, etc., is not a requirement of Jewish law. In *Yore Deah* 362, where a discussion of grave-alignment would properly belong, the commentary *Pis-che Teshuva* discusses the matter, but the *Shulchan Aruch* itself has not the slightest mention of it.

This is a negative proof, but there is also a more positive one which is cited by the great Hungarian authority, Moses Sofer, in a discussion of the matter in his responsa (*Yore Deah* 332). He calls attention to the geometrical discussion of the burial cave in the Talmud (*Baba Bathra* 101 ff.). The question at issue in the Talmud was: How many graves could be dug in that cave? By the debate (and the illustrations) it was evident that they dug the graves into the walls of the cave in *all* directions. Thus, for example, if the cave ran from East to West, the grave dug into the back wall ran from East to West (continuing the axis of the cave). Those graves which were dug in the long side walls ran from North to South (and South to North); and those which were dug in the corners, ran diagonally Northwest to Southeast, etc. Thus it is clear (as Moses Sofer correctly argues) that the Talmud has no restrictions at all as to the directions of graves.

Yet, while it is evident that the Talmud has no requirement of grave alignment, nevertheless the custom in Europe (at least) in the Middle Ages developed into a definite preference for aligning the graves in each cemetery in one direction. This can be seen from the large responsum of David Oppenheimer (1664-1733), the famous Rabbi of Prague, in his responsum which is published at the end of the responsa volume of *Yair Chaim Bachrach* (*Chavos Yair*). The problem discussed in this responsum is as follows: An excavation was going on for some building. During the digging for the foundations, human bones were discovered and the question was whether these were bones of Jewish dead. If they were the bones of Jewish dead, then a

Cohen could not enter the completed building. David Oppenheimer gives the inquirer the following test to use: If the graves are helter-skelter, they cannot be graves of the Jewish dead because the graves of Jews are always aligned in orderly fashion. The same rule of alignment is revealed in the question asked of Yekuthiel Enzil of Przmyzl; it is in his Responsa 37. Again, a house was being built and bones were discovered, and the question was were they bones of Jewish dead or not. The questioner was sure they were Jewish dead because they were aligned in orderly fashion.

Thus in ancient Palestine, they buried in any direction, depending on the layout of the burial caves; but in the Diaspora (at least in Europe where they did not bury in caves) they laid out the graves in orderly fashion. Just why the custom rose to align the graves in orderly fashion in Europe seems fairly clear: First, as we have mentioned, because they no longer buried in caves where they would use the walls and the corners. Secondly, because, as indicated in a number of the relevant responsa, they were buried as we pray, towards Jerusalem. A further reason gradually developed, that the direction of the body should in itself express the faith in the resurrection of the dead; namely, that when the Messiah comes and the dead will rise, they will be facing in the right direction for the journey, without delay, to the Holy Land.

While the faith in resurrection was clearly a determining factor, nevertheless it did not dictate precisely the direction in which the body must lie. After all, the body was laid on its back, facing upward. What, then would be the direction toward Jerusalem? For that reason, perhaps many customs of varying alignment arose. Another complication which led to a confusion of customs was the belief that only in

Palestine would the dead rise from their graves and walk. But outside of Palestine there would be tunnels (*m'chillos*) along which they would roll to the Holy Land. One can see the differing customs by considering the question and response in the various responsa that discuss the matter. The questioner will mention that the burial custom in his city is North to South, and the respondent will say that in his city the custom is from East to West, or vice versa. Sometimes the custom had nothing to do with the cardinal points of the compass, but the dead were laid in the cemetery with their feet pointing to the cemetery gate, (i.e., to be ready to march when the Messiah gives the signal). Therefore Moses Sofer, in his well known responsum on the matter, when he permits a congregation to change direction of grave alignment for practical reasons (the shape of the land, etc.) suggests that another gateway might be opened in another wall so that the feet of the people buried in the new direction be pointed to the exit gate.

Out of all these difficulties various customs arose. Most of the important references to these customs are cited by Greenwald in his *Kol Bo,* p. 177-8. Perhaps the most frequent one is that the lines of the *rows* were North to South Therefore each grave in these lines was East to West, and in that grave the body was laid with its feet to the East and its head to the West (so that when he rose on his feet in Messiah's time, he would be facing East). Another custom, almost as prevalent (judging by the questions asked) was that the rows were East and West and therefore the bodies lay North and South. In fact, one scholar, Elazar Lev of Ungvar, in his *Pekudoth Elazar* 123, makes a novel suggestion: that all the graves on one side of the cemetery gate be arranged in one direction, and those on the other side of the gate be arranged in the opposite direction; all this, in order to fulfill (when Messiah comes) the Talmudic dictum that all our "turnings should be to the right."

The very multiplicity of customs (East-West or North-South or towards the gate) would itself be an indication that we are not dealing here with a matter of law. If it were a matter of law, the scholars would have finally arrived at a definite decision after all these centuries. It is only local custom which is permitted to remain so vague and varied, since it is generally accepted that local customs, if they are not absurd in themselves, should always be tolerated and even respected. Further evidence that this is merely a matter of custom is the fact cited by Greenwald, of two great rabbis, Maharil and Abraham of Prostitz, who specifically asked that they be buried in a different direction from the other people in the cemetery. If the grave alignment were really a matter of law, they certainly would not have violated it for personal reasons. However, Abraham Isaac Glick (in *Yad Yitzchok,* Vol. III, 83) warns against breaking the alignment (whichever the local alignment may be) when burying the body of an average person. If a *famous* person is buried in irregular alignment, it is assumed that he had a valid reason for it; but if an average person is so buried, people may later imagine that he or she was purposely buried in irregular alignment because of some sin which he or she committed. This would constitute an injustice to the dead. Therefore Abraham Glick suggests, in the case of a woman who was buried from South to North instead of from North to South as the rest of the bodies were buried, that her tombstone be placed in conformity with the other tombstones so that people visiting the cemetery may not misjudge her in the future.

While it might seem desirable to shift the tombstone on an individual grave to adjust the alignment, the need for alignment is not so serious as to justify disturbing the body. Chaim Yeruchem in his *Birchas Chaim,* II:3, says that since the alignment is based upon varying customs, we may not disinter a body which was buried out of alignment in order to rebury it in accordance with the direction of the other bodies in the cemetery.

All these variations indicate that we are dealing here with customs which vary from locality to locality; yet whatever the local custom is, it should generally be conformed with and the dead buried in alignment, unless some highly honored man requests a variation for himself.

The final question which we must ask is this: If, for example, the local custom is to bury North to South and the cemetery has a long, narrow, unused piece of land in which it is only possible to arrange the new graves East to West, may the community vary its own local custom and bury, now, in a new direction? This is precisely the question which came before the great Hungarian authority, Moses Sofer (cited above). He mentions the variations in custom which we have recorded and says in general that the custom is not so firmly grounded that if there is a good reason for changing, a change may not be permitted. In fact, he says (rather playfully) that one can go to the Holy Land either directly South to the Mediterranean and then turn East; or go directly East to Constantinople. So in general the alignment directions are not important and they may be changed. More directly than this, Abraham Isaac Glick, in the responsum cited above, says forthrightly there is no source in the Talmud or the authorities (*Poskim*) determining the direction of the alignment of graves.

To sum up: In Mishnah and Talmud, they clearly buried in all directions, since they speak of graves dug in the walls of caves. In Europe the custom of alignment arose; but because of the various difficulties mentioned above (the body lying on its back, etc.) local customs vary as to what should be the proper alignment, some North to South, some East to West, and some merely with the feet pointing to the exit gate. The authorities are clear that no firm law is involved here and, therefore, alignment may be varied for any substantial reason.

35

THE FIRST GRAVE IN THE CEMETERY

Some people object to having their deceased relatives buried as the first body in a new cemetery. Is there any basis in tradition for such an apprehension? (From M.S., Flint, Michigan.)

THE legal tradition exhibits considerable sensitiveness as to the honor of the dead in relation to the place of their burial. Thus a righteous man may not be buried next to a wicked man, and not even next to a partially wicked man. Therefore, if there were any deprecation to the dead in being the first buried in a new cemetery, then surely that fact would have been specifically mentioned. Nor can one say that they may not have mentioned the fact because they had no special occasion to refer to it. As a matter of fact, there was plenty of occasion to refer to such a supposed deprecation of the dead, because there are many long responsa on the matter of new cemeteries. Yet in not one of them have I seen any reference to such an idea. They could well have said if a righteous man died, a place should still be found for him in the old cemetery, and that a still-born infant should be buried first, etc. But they did not. This argumentation *ex silentio* is a strong evidence that it never entered the minds of the authorities that there could be any objection or shame in such a burial.

On the contrary, there is some indication that there was a special status and worth in the first burial. At least one authority holds that the transaction of the purchase of the new cemetery should not be completed until there is a body ready to be buried in it. This is the opinion of Joseph Sinzheim, cited in *Sha'agas Aryeh* (New Series, 17). This opinion is also cited by Maharam Shick in his Responsa (*Yore Deah* 357). Furthermore, there are opinions that the first burial is a worthy spiritual protection to the new cemetery, since certain authorities believe that a new cemetery requires a special watchman (*shomer*) until the first burial. After that it is safe (cited by Eliezer Deutsch in his *Peri Hasodeh,* III, 81). So it is evident that according to the above opinions, a special honor or status is implied in the first burial.

Incidentally, most authorities disagree with the opinions that the completion of the purchase must await the first burial, or that a *shomer* is needed for the new cemetery until the first burial takes place. Yet the very fact that these opinions exist certainly indicates, at least, that there was no disgrace to a family if their deceased was first to be buried.

This fear is therefore purely folkloristic and has no roots

in Jewish law or established custom. It might be worthwhile to speculate how the fear arose. Perhaps it was an outcome of the fact that the dedication of a new cemetery was bound to create a certain feeling of foreboding in the community, in that it was a provision for so many dead in the future. So one authority felt it involved an invoking of misfortune, "opening one's mouth to Satan," (*al tivtach pe l'satan*). Hence the ritual of dedication prescribed fasting (at least on the part of the *Chevrah Kadisha*) and the giving of redemptive charity. Perhaps this solemn mood of apprehension led some families to desire to disassociate themselves from initiating the new cemetery with *their* family.

But this is only speculative. Be that as it may, the clear fact is that there is not the slightest implication of dishonor or danger to a family if one of its number is the first to be buried in the new cemetery.

For the sake of completeness, I will add the main references to the responsa which deal with new cemeteries. They are:

Eliezer Deutsch (*Peri Ha-Sodeh*, III, 81)

Moses Shick (*Maharam Shick, Yore Deah*, 357)

Isaac Schmelkes (*Bes Yitzchok*, II, *Yore Deah*, 156)

Joseph Schwartz (*Ginze Yoseph*, 86)

Chaim Halberstam (*Der Zansar, Divre Chayim, Yore Deah*, 135)

Aryeh Lev of Metz (*Sha'agas Aryeh*, II, 17)

Chaim Medini (*S'de Chemed, Maareches Avelus*, 82)

J. Greenwald (*Kol Bo Avelus*, 82, p. 163 ff.)

36

A TOMBSTONE IN ABSENCE OF THE BODY
(CENOTAPH)

A group of former immigrants from Central Europe feel the need to visit the graves of their parents, as is traditional. But the parents and other close relatives were murdered during the Nazi period, and there is no possible way of finding their graves, if indeed there are any graves. Their question, therefore, is this: May they (in the Jewish cemetery of Milwaukee, where they live) set up a tombstone where they can visit, and count it as a grave of their parents and other dear ones who have perished?

JEWISH burial and mourning traditions have frequently needed adjustment to the uncertain circumstances of the Jewish life in the Old World. Some of the adjustments made in the law and the customs prove the flexibility of the tradition in providing for the emotional needs of mourning families when the circumstances of the death are unusual. Most of the questions which needed adjustment concern the problem of mourning: When should *shiva* begin? When should *Yahrzeit* be observed in the case when a deceased man's body is no longer to be found; or, indeed, in cases when there can no longer be any proof that the person is actually dead?

The classical decision was made in the twelfth century in the Rhineland by Isaac Or Zorua of Vienna, who said that the moment the family gives up hope, that moment of despair, shall be counted as the moment of death, and mourning, etc., shall begin from that date (*Or Zorua,* II, *Hilchos Avelus* 424; see also *Yore Deah* 375:6). This indicates at least the willingness of the tradition to adjust itself to the emotional needs of mourners when violence or accident creates the exceptional circumstances that make the body unavailable for burial.

However, the specific question asked here concerns the permissibility of setting up a tombstone in the absence of the body. As far as I know, this question has never come up in the legal literature. It is strange that it has not come up. If the question was frequently asked, "May we say Kaddish if the body was never found," they could easily have also asked, "May we put up a tombstone if the body was never found." It would be interesting to speculate as to why this natural question was *not* asked. It may be because the historic Jewish cemeteries in the Rhineland and in Prague, etc., were so crowded with tombstones that it was often difficult to find a place for those who were actually buried there, much less for those whose bodies were not laid to rest there.

Nowadays the question arises often. Bodies are frequently lost at sea or in airplane accidents and are never recovered. The American Military, in cemeteries overseas, have a stone on which is inscribed the names of those missing, and therefore not buried, in the cemetery. In London there is a "cenotaph" right in the middle of one of the main streets, in honor of soldiers who are buried elsewhere or who are missing.

Thus, while there is no discussion in the legal literature about setting up a tombstone where there is no body buried, there is nevertheless a great deal of discussion about tombstones in general, and part of this complex discussion has some relevance here. There is a long debate, going back to the beginnings of Jewish law in the Talmud, as to whether tombstones are meant to be for the honor of the dead or (also) for the benefit of the living. What would be involved in the discussion was whether survivors may dispose of tombstones in case bodies are moved. The whole discussion was summed up in both the *Tur* and the *Shulchan Aruch, Yore Deah* 364. Also there is a handy summary of the debate in the responsa of Abraham Isaac Glick, *Yad Yitzchok,* III:38 (published in Satmar, 1908). What is relevant to our question is that there is a growing body of opinion that the tombstones are also for the benefit of the *living*. As is said in the above mentioned responsum, the tombstone is for the purpose of directing the survivors to where they can go and pray.

This side of the discussion, that the purpose of the tombstone is also to benefit the survivors spiritually, was used in the one responsum which actually deals with almost the same question that you ask. Ephraim Oshry, now rabbi in New York, was, during the Nazi period, in the Kovno concentration ghetto to which Jews were sent from all over Europe. The Nazis destroyed and plowed over the Jewish cemeteries in the neighborhood. A man came to Rabbi Oshry after the liberation with the following question: Since it is now impossible to locate the graves of his parents and he was accustomed to go to the graves of his parents to pray, what shall he do? Rabbi Oshry advised (responsum *M'Mamakim,* I:28) that he set up a tombstone anywhere in the cemetery, and that will be an appropriate memorial where he can pray. Oshry uses the argument that tombstones are for the benefit of the living, and also calls attention to the fact that we put up memorials (even memorial plaques with the names of the deceased) in many synagogues and schools, far away from where the bodies are buried.

Rabbi Oshry has recently published a second volume of *M'Mamakim,* in which he returns to the problem in an interesting and rather touching way: The stones from the Jewish cemeteries had been taken during the Nazi occupation and used as paving stones in certain towns. The question was, how could Jewish people walk on such paving stones, the inscriptions on which were still legible? He urges that efforts be made to buy those stones, and since the graves to which they belong can no longer be located, since the centuries are plowed up, the tombstones should be set up anywhere in a Jewish cemetery (*M'Mamakim,* II:20).

Let us, therefore, sum up the situation in Jewish tradition: From the earliest medieval days, adjustments were made (with regard to mourning) when bodies could not be found. With regard to the tombstones, one body of opinion is that they are put up for the spiritual benefit of the living. On the basis of the above, Rabbi Oshry decided that tombstones may be put up, even when the bodies can no longer be located. Therefore, on the basis of the above, a group of you who wish to do so, should set up a tombstone with the inscription of the names that you wish to remember. There can be two or three such stones, perhaps classified according to the cemeteries where they might have been buried had they died normally. Your members from Frankfurt could put up one stone, with all their names recorded, etc. You are free to make one or many stones, as you wish.

The inscription can be easily worked out. It is suggested that you have the usual five Hebrew letters, *tav, nun, zadek, bez, heh,* which are appropriate because they say, "May their souls be bound up in eternal life." This can be followed, in English, with: "To the unforgettable memory of our martyred dear ones," and the list of names. All this is justified on the basis of Jewish law and tradition.

(Originally published in *Central Conference of American Rabbis Yearbook,* Vol. LXXIV, 1964.)

37

MOTHER'S ASHES IN SON'S GRAVE

A mother in the United States has made provision in her will to be cremated, and that her ashes be buried in her son's grave in Venezuela. She has communicated with the congregation in Venezuela, but they informed her that they would be willing to put a stone urn containing the ashes upon the top of the grave (or in a niche above ground cut into the tombstone). But they would not bury the ashes and would not open the grave. Are there any precedents or reasons in the Halachic literature which might convince them to accede to this mother's request? (Asked by Rabbi Robert I. Kahn, Houston, Texas.)

THIS, of course, is not a question for guidance as to our own practice, since we already have an established custom of cutting a small space in a grave to bury ashes of a relative. The question is primarily for information as to the traditional Halacha, asked in the hope of convincing the Venezuelan congregation to grant this woman's request.

As for the burial of the ashes of cremation, I have already discussed this in a previous letter to you. But now I will add the opinion of some Orthodox authorities permitting the burial of such ashes. The chief opinions *against* such burial were collected by Rabbi Lerner in his book, *Chaye Olam.* But, as I mentioned previously, Elijah Benamozegh, Rabbi of Leghorn, in his *Ya'aney Vo-esh,* said that while it is against Orthodox law to cremate, nevertheless, it is a *duty* to bury the ashes. Now I add the following: Enoch Ehrentreu, in *Cheker Halacha,* permits the burial of the ashes, as does also Simon Deutsch, in *Or Ho-emes,* who said also that ashes were buried in the Frankfurt cemetery at the express direction of Azriel Hildesheimer, the leader of German Orthodoxy. See also David Hoffman (*Melamed L'ho-il,* Yore Deah, 113) who says that while it is not obligatory to bury the ashes, it is not forbidden to do so.

Now as to the refusal of the Venezuelan congregation to open the grave: In this matter they rest on firm traditional authority but, even so, there are strong Orthodox opinions permitting the opening of graves under certain special circumstances. (A full discussion of the question is to be found in *Pis-che Teshuva* to *Yore Deah* 363:7 and in Greenwald, *Kol Bo Al Avelus,* p. 217 ff.) The law seems clear that graves, once they are filled up, should not be opened again (*Yore Deah* 363:7). This law is based primarily upon a decision in a specific case, made by Rabbi Akiba in b. *Baba Bathra* 154a. Some property had been sold and the seller died. Relatives claimed that the deceased was a minor, so could not legally have sold the property. They wanted to exhume the body to prove their case. Rabbi Akiba forbade this and said: "You are forbidden to show his ugliness," (*l'navlo*) i.e., to shame the deceased by looking at the ugly decay of his body.

But this prohibition of Rabbi Akiba forbids only the uncovering of the body, but does not forbid any opening of the grave which would not reach or disturb the body at all. To forbid the opening of the grave altogether, an additional principle was invoked: namely, that the very disturbing of the grave brings to the consciousness of the deceased (the dead having awareness) a fear that he is being subjected to punishment (*cherdas ha-din*). This idea is somehow based on the statement of the ghost of Samuel to Saul at Endor: "Why hast thou disturbed and troubled me?" (I Samuel 28:15) and on the statement of Job (3:13): "Then I shall sleep (in death) and be at peace."

Yet, though the law in the *Shulchan Aruch,* thus based, seems clear and definite, nevertheless in the very same section of the *Shulchan Aruch* (*Yore Deah* 363:1) we are told that a body may be removed from its grave in order to be buried in the burial place of the family (363:1). Thus it is clear that there is at least *this* exception to the general prohibition. In fact, there are many more exceptions which will now be listed.

David Oppenheimer, rabbi of Prague, in his large responsum at the end of Bachrach's *Chavos Yair,* cites a decision of Rabbi Gerson of Metz (the author of *Avodas Ha-Gershuni*) in the following case: Two brothers were buried hastily and it was remembered that they were buried without the required shrouds. May the graves be opened in order to provide the shrouds? Rabbi Gerson said that the grave of the older brother, who was over twenty-one, may not be opened because the "judgment" and, therefore, the "fear of judgment" (*cherdas ha-din*) only applies after the age of twenty. Therefore the younger brother, who was under this age, may have his grave opened for the shroud. Also, Jacob Reischer, rabbi of Metz (*Shevus Yaacov* II, 113) answered a pathetic question from the city of Brussels. Some ghouls had dug up some graves in the Jewish cemetery, stolen the shrouds and thrown the bodies on the ground. Some relatives feared (because of a dream in which the dead appeared to them) that other bodies were treated in the same way. Jacob Reischer gave permission to dig up those graves to make sure.

Another reason for some authorities permitting exhumation was in order to free a woman from the state of being an *agunah.* A woman suspected that it was her husband whose body was buried in another city. She said that he had carried certain proofs upon his body (in his wallet, etc.) of his identity. She wanted the body examined for this proof, so that she could be declared a widow and be free to remarry. Ezekiel Katzenellenbogen (in *Kenneses Yecheschel, Even Hoezer,* 46) at the very top of column "b" on page 57, permits such examination. So did Eleazar Fleckeles cited in *Shivas Zion,* 64. Fleckeles later changed his mind about his decision when he thought that this body was probably not of the husband and, therefore, it would be wrong to disturb the body of a stranger to no purpose. There are indeed prohibitory opinions in all these cases cited, but it is important that great Orthodox authorities permitted exhumation for certain reasons which appeared sufficient for them.

But there is a more general consideration for allowing the granting of this woman's request. It was the well-established custom in many of the old world Jewish communities to bury one body above the other. There were great rabbis in these communities who would have objected, had there been any objection, to opening a grave for a sufficiently good reason, particularly to bury another body. Of course, it was understood that they did not dig far enough to disturb the first body. How near could they get to the first body without violating the law? See *Kol Bo* by Greenwald, p. 179, where he states the generally accepted rule that where bodies are buried side by side there must be a partition of six hand-breadths; where bodies are buried one above the other (and therefore the partition, being compressed, would not fall away) three hand-breadths are sufficient. It is therefore an unquestioned practice to dig into a grave to within three hand-breadths of the previous body in order to perform a second burial.

This is, perhaps, a solution of the problem which will satisfy both the congregation and the woman who is making the request. This solution is based upon a decision of one of the strictest rabbinical authorities of the past generation, the Orthodox Rabbi of Muncacz, Eliezer Shapiro ("Der Muncaczer"). In his responsa, *Minchas Eliezer,* IV, 4, he reports the following question: A scholar had provided in his will that his writings be buried in his grave with him. For some reason, at the time of his burial, they had neglected to carry out his request. May they now open the grave to bury the writings of this scholar with him, as he had requested? Eliezer Shapiro mentions all the classic reasons for not opening the grave, but says that the space *underneath* the *tombstone* can be considered part of the grave and yet that space may be fully excavated to provide a place for the scholar's writings.

On the basis of opinion of this strictest of Hungarian Orthodox rabbis, the Venezuela congregation can dig a space *underneath* the tombstone for the urn or box of ashes. This would not be a violation of disturbing the grave and yet would be part of the grave. You might suggest this solution.

38

REMOVING A TOMBSTONE

A stonemason sold a tombstone to a Jewish family. The tombstone was set upon the grave. Now the stonemason claims that the tombstone was not paid for (completely) and he wants to take the stone back into his possession. The question asked is: May a Jewish cemetery permit a tombstone to be removed from a grave after it has been set? (From S.W. and C. G. B.)

THE civil law may, perhaps, permit the mason to recover his property; but even so, I am certain a civil court would take into consideration the customs and traditions of the cemetery in which the tombstone was set. If, for example, an analysis of the laws and customs of Jewish cemeteries would reveal a strong objection towards removing the tombstone, then stonemasons should be informed of that and would understand that this would be one of the risks that they would take, and might want to adjust their prices accordingly. In any case, it is important for us to be clear about Jewish law and custom as to removing the tombstone, not only in order that in fairness stonemasons should know beforehand what the situation is, but also in case the family cannot pay, the Jewish cemetery might want to make some financial adjustment with the stonemason, so that the tombstone not be removed; provided, of course, Jewish law and custom is actually against its removal.

The basic law goes back to the Talmud, b. *Sanhedrin* 47b, where the law is, in general, that a grave cannot be used for the benefit of the living; i.e., that the living cannot profit from a grave, as for example, to sell what grows on the earth of a grave, or to use its earth to spread upon one's field. The Talmud discusses which sort of grave and which part of a grave may be used for a living person's financial benefit and which may not. The part of this question which concerns us directly is whether the tombstone (*matzeva*) is an essential part of the grave and, therefore, comes under the general prohibition that the living may not get any financial benefit from it.

The overwhelming weight of opinion is that the tombstone is an essential part of the grave. For example, in the *Tur, Yore Deah* 348, where the law is stated that a man's heirs are compelled to pay for his burial, it is added that they must also pay for his tombstone. The author of the *Tur* bases this on the opinion of his father, Asher ben Yehiel. So, also, Israel of Krems, in his notes to the compendium of Asher ben Yehiel to *Moed Katan,* Ch. 3: 79 says that our graves cannot be used for the benefit of the living, and he adds that whatever is done for the needs of the dead and for the honor of the dead is forbidden to be of benefit to the living. Therefore it is forbidden to sell a broken tombstone and even to lean upon a tombstone. Israel of Krems quotes this from the great Rhineland authority, Isaac Or Zoruah. The statement of Asher ben Yehiel that the tombstone is an essential part of the grave and that, therefore, the sons must be compelled to pay for a tombstone is repeated as law in the *Shulchan Aruch, Yore Deah* 348. Nevertheless, in *Tur, Yore Deah* 364, Asher ben Yehiel is quoted as saying that the tombstone is not an essential part of the grave and therefore he would permit sitting on it, etc. But in this opinion he is a minority; against him are Isaiah of Trani and Rabbenu Yeruchim and the Or Zoruah, as quoted above. Later authorities explain away Asher ben Yehiel's unusually permissive point of view, and say that what he meant was that a stone which is set as a marker at some distance from the grave itself is not deemed to be an essential part of the grave; but with regard to the stone that is right on the grave, he would agree with the other authorities that it is an essential part of the grave and must not be used for the financial benefit of the living.

This is the basic tendency of the law, but there are a number of interesting variations due to special circumstances or, at least, there are some interesting cases that reveal some variation. For example, David ben Zimri, rabbi in Egypt in the sixteenth century, in his *Responsa* II:741, deals with the following case: When bodies of Jews were disinterred from the graveyard in Cairo for reburial in the Holy Land, Arabs would steal the tombstones, chisel out the names and sell them to Jews for use on graves. May the Jews buy these stones? He answers that of course a *Jew* may not sell a tombstone from a Jewish grave for use on another Jewish grave. He may, perhaps, *give* it for use on another Jewish grave, free of charge. But he may have no financial benefit from a tombstone. As for the direct question, he might be inclined to permit purchasing these used tombstones, except that the Arabs' habit of stealing Jewish tombstones is increasing and therefore he urges all Jews to use new tombstones.

Another case cited in the *Pische Teshuva* (From Azulai, *Birche Joseph*) is as follows: A widow put a small stone on her husband's grave. Later she found that she could afford a larger stone. May she return the smaller stone for credit on the larger stone? The answer is: No; she may not get any financial benefit from a tombstone. Interesting variations occur. Menachem Azariah of Fano (Italy 1548-1620) in his Responsum 56, tells of a case in which the cemetery was filled up with a thick layer of earth in order to bury new dead over the old graves, as was frequently done. The tombstone on one of the nether graves was thus covered over completely and, of course, its inscription could not be read. May the relatives of the deceased sell it? He answered they may do so since it is useless; but they must use the money to improve the grave.

The question of tombstones came up in the last century in a sort of wholesale fashion. Every now and then, with the expansion of the East European cities, the lord of the manor, or the other authorities, would demand that the Jews clear out the cemetery. The problem arose at once, what to do with the tombstones. The question arose on a grand scale, as one can see from a number of contemporary responsa from the last century. In Budapest, the old cemetery had to be cleared of graves, and there were sixty-two thousand old tombstones piled up in heaps. May these stones be sold? The question was asked of many leading authorities at the time. Their answers were all in line with the general tenor of the law. Sholom Mordecai Schwadron (II, 122) the great Galician authority, said that the stones may be sold, but the money used only for communal purposes, to improve the cemetery, care for the sick, etc. But even this restricted permission created doubts in his own mind; so, he said, he would not decide that even this restricted use should be made of the tombstones unless all the rabbis of Budapest agreed with him. Eliezer Deutsch of Bonyhad was also asked the same question. He was still more careful than Sholom Mordecai Schwadron. He said that only such tombstones as were put down at the expense of the community may now be used by the community, but tombstones put by private families on private graves cannot be used for any other purpose. One more example: Moses Taubes, in his *Responsa Chaim Shel Shalom* (II:104) was asked this question: A temporary wooden marker was placed at the grave. Now it was supplanted by a permanent stone tombstone. May the temporary wooden marker be used for other graves, etc.? He answered yes, because it was meant to be temporary and was not specifically applied to this grave, so it could be used for other graves. But a tombstone, not meant as temporary and meant specifically for a certain grave cannot be used for any sort of financial benefit (or even for any other grave).

So through all these various instances, the line of the law is clear. One or perhaps two authorities would be lenient about reuse of the tombstone, but the overwhelming weight of authority is that it is an essential part of a grave, and even if it were broken up, it could not be sold for profit. Some would permit the stone to be used for another grave, but then only as a gift and not to be sold for money. Some would even prohibit its use at all for another grave. So if this mason took the stone back, it is doubtful whether any Jewish family would buy that stone for use on its own family grave. But the important element is that the tendency of the law is that the tombstones should not be moved from the grave on which it was set.

In addition to the prohibition of any benefit (and even in many cases, reuse of a tombstone, and therefore removal) there is the strong disapproval in the law against disturbing the grave. This is too well known to go into at this time, but it is evident that taking out the tombstone, the way they are deeply set nowadays, would be a definite disturbance of the grave and as such should not be permitted.

What, then, should the Jewish cemetery do in the case which is being discussed? First it is important, for the sake of the tombstone masons, that they know that once a tombstone is set, it cannot be permitted to be removed. Secondly, if the tombstone-setter insists upon a legal effort to recover the stone, the cemetery authorities, together with the family, should try to arrive at some compromise; but the stone should not be disturbed.

39

BURIAL OF NON-JEWS IN JEWISH CEMETERY

The question of whether a Gentile wife or children of a mixed marriage may be buried in our cemeteries was answered for the Conference by Dr. Kaufman Kohler in

1914 (and reprinted in the Rabbi's Manual). The answer, although it is substantially correct, needs some rediscussion and development. In recent years we have been getting many more and slightly different inquiries on the matter. For example, may the Christian father of an unconverted Gentile married to a Jew be buried in Jewish cemetery? The status of the Jewish cemetery in the Jewish legal tradition, and the permissibility of burying non-Jews in it, needs a fuller discussion than has been hitherto available to the Conference.

LET us first consider the actual status of the cemetery as a sacred possession and trust of the Jewish community. It becomes clear at once that the cemetery does not have a legal status equal to that of the synagogue or the school. With regard to a synagogue or school, each community is compelled by Jewish law to provide them (see *Shulchan Aruch, Orah Hayyim* 150:1; *Yore Deah* 245:4, note of Isserles). "The people of the community 'compel each other' (*kofin zeh es zeh*) to build a synagogue . . . to establish a school." There is no such requirement anywhere in the law that a community *must* have a cemetery. As a matter of fact, while many a small community in Europe had, of course, its own *minyan* and provided for the instruction of its children, it did not have a cemetery of its own, but transported its dead to some other and larger city. A cemetery is, therefore, not one of the institutions imposed by Jewish law upon each Jewish community.

The reason for this difference in legal status between a cemetery on the one hand and synagogue and school on the other, is perhaps due to historical reasons. In Palestine, where the foundation of the law developed, people were generally buried in privately owned caves, etc., and therefore it remains an ideal in Jewish law that it is better for a man to be buried in his own property (*b'soch shelo*; b. *Baba Bathra*, 102a). When, therefore, communal cemeteries developed, mainly in Babylon where the alluvial soil made rock-cave burial impossible, there was no strong basis for requiring each community to have a cemetery. Though, of course, there is discussion about it, as to where it should be located, how far from the city, etc. (*M. Baba Bathra* II, 9; *Shulchan Aruch, Choshen Mishpot* 155:23), actually, the Mishnah does not say "cemetery," but simply, "graves."

Of course, over the centuries the communal cemetery became a precious possession and sacred trust of the Jewish community, but its sanctity is based primarily on *minhag*. Since the basic Palestinian experience was individual burial on a man's own property, we can see why the law is so meticulous about the rights of the individual grave and has no clear statement about the sanctity of the entire cemetery. The law is extremely careful to protect the individual grave. Thus it is asked: May the earth dug out from it be used by the living? May one even have the minor benefit of resting by leaning on the tombstone? May anyone benefit from the trees that draw their sustenance through their roots from the graves? There are scores of discussions on the sanctity of the individual grave, generally summed up in the principle that a grave may not be used for any living person's benefit. Even broken pieces of a tombstone are *osur b'hano'oh*. But there is no evidence that, for example, the unused quarter of the cemetery is in this sense sacredly and inalienably the possession of the dead. Dr. Kohler is quite right in saying that our cemeteries are not consecrated in their entirety, as are the Catholic cemeteries, but each grave is sacred by itself. Of course, it must be stated that in recent years there have developed ceremonies accompanying the opening of a new cemetery, and the rabbis, chiefly the Hungarian rabbis of the last generation (Moses Schick, *Yore Deah* 357; Eliezer Deutsch, *Peri Hasodeh* III, 81; Joseph Schwartz, *Ginze Yosef* 86) speak of it as a good custom. Mostly the ceremony involves the *Chevra Kadisha* fasting on that day and thinking thoughts of repentance, primarily in order to avert the evil omen of suddenly providing for a large and new amount of Jewish burials. It is almost like inviting Satan to bring evil (*al tiftach pe l'satan*). But this penitential fasting by the *Chevra Kadisha,* which at all events is not a widespread custom, can hardly be considered a formal consecration of a cemetery in its entirety.

Since, therefore, the communal cemetery has no firm rootage in basic Jewish law, but has a strong hold in Jewish custom and affection, the authorities find great difficulty in proving legally that a Jewish cemetery must be exclusively a Jewish cemetery. People feel, of course, that it should be such, but it is hard to prove that the law requires it to be such. Two rabbis of the last century tried valiantly (and rather pathetically) to prove that the cemetery should be only Jewish and sharply separated. One was Eliezer Shapiro of Muncacz (*Minchas Eliezer* II, 41) and the other was Eliezer Deutsch of Bonyhad (Dudae Ha-Sodeh, 66). Shapiro embarrassingly tried to base the reason for keeping Christian bodies separate from Jewish bodies on the Talmudic dictum: "We do not bury the wicked next to the righteous" (b. *Sanhedrin* 47a). This analogy has already been used by Joel Sirkes (*Bach* to *Yore Deah* 151) who says simply that even a wicked fellow Jew is not buried next to a righteous one; so it certainly is not proper to bury a non-Jew next to a Jew. Eliezer Deutsch tried to base the prohibition on a sort of cabbalistic classification of souls.

In the eighties, there was considerable Halachic discussion of this whole question. A rather original article on the matter was written by Meir Friedmann (*Bes Talmud*, IV, 3). He concludes that the burying of non-Jews in the same cemetery as Jews was actually a regular practice in the time of the Mishnah. The line of argument is of interest. Primarily it is based upon the Mishnah, *Gittin* V, 8: "We do not hinder the poor of Gentiles from gleaning the corner of the field," etc. On this, Mishnah in the Babylonian Talmud (the *Boraita* in *Gittin* 61a) says: "We sustain the poor of non-Jews, comfort their mourners, and bury their dead with the dead of Israel." The Jerushalmi, in the same chapter (*Gittin* 47c) adds some significant details as follows: "In a city where there are Gentiles and Jews, we establish Jewish and Gentile officials who will collect for charity from Gentiles and Jews," and then it continues more or less as in the Talmud, "and we sustain the poor, bury the dead," etc.

From this Friedmann concludes that there was joint social service. As for the separateness in burial, as implied in the dictum, "We do not bury the righteous by the wicked," etc., he gives the following explanation: The well-to-do were buried in their own caves, with niches dug in the cave. The prohibition, "We do not bury the wicked," etc., meant, "We do not bury them together in the same *cave*," since it is the same enclosure. But for the poor they also had separate and distinct graves in a cemetery (much like ours) and since each grave was separate with the proper partition, it was there that the cooperative social service authorities buried Jews and Christians, i.e., each in his own grave, but in the same cemetery. Meir Friedmann's famous colleague, Isaac Hirsch Weiss, agrees with this conclusion and says that Rashi's restrictive comment (to the *Boraita* in *Gittin* 61a) that "with" does not mean "in the same cemetery," is an unjustified restriction based upon the presupposition that the *Boraita* cannot mean what it clearly does mean. It is of interest that Joel Sirkes (to the *Tur, Yore Deah* 151) says that while Rashi means that Jews and non-Jews should not be buried side by side as a general practice, Rashi admits, according to Sirkes, that if a body of a slain Gentile is found, he may be buried in the same courtyard with Jews.

Friedmann's article, endorsed by Weiss, evoked a response from an Orthodox scholar, Eliezer (Louis) Hausdorff. He published a booklet on this subject (*Responsum with Regard to the Burial of a Non-Jew in the Jewish Cemetery,* Leipzig, 1884). He attacks all of Friedmann's conclusions, yet makes an interesting statement which is of concern to our discussion. He says (and in this he is clearly correct) that the dictum, "We do not bury the righteous by the wicked," etc., which is used as the basis of the argument against burial of Jews and Gentiles side by side, is not at all a matter of law. It is only a matter of feeling with regard to the dignity of the dead. A community has no right to bury a wicked person next to a departed person of good reputation, inasmuch as we are sure that if the departed worthy person had in his lifetime known that this wicked person would be buried next to him, he would have objected. Therefore, out of respect for all the dead whose sensitiveness in lifetime we may assume, we do not bury such people side by side, who worthy people would have felt, so far as they personally were concerned, should not be at their side. But Hausdorff continues that where the *communal* cemetery is not involved, this makes no difference. If a man is buried on his own property, he has the right to say that he does not care who is buried by his side; and on his own property, he may bury whom he wishes. There is no actual legal prohibition involved.

So it is clear that even in a vigorous, polemical article by an Orthodox writer, it is difficult to prove legally that we may not bury a Christian near a Jewish grave; but of course, again, Jewish feelings require that the Jewish cemetery should remain Jewish.

This being the state of the law, what are our present day feelings in the matter, and what should our attitude be to this question? Of course it is obvious that it is not a simple matter to speak of "our" feelings. The feelings of a mixed family that wants to have the deceased of their family buried side by side, are not the same as the feelings of other members of the congregation who have not this type of family bond. But, in general, even as a Jewish religious community, we do have a certain moral duty with regard to burial of non-Jewish dead. As the Talmud says (*Gittin* 61a): "We feed the poor of non-Jews, comfort their mourners, and bury their dead with the Jewish dead 'for the sake of peace.' " Although Rashi (as we have said) immediately explains the word "with" to mean not "in" Jewish cemeteries, but "as" we would bury Jewish dead, at least it is clear that being concerned with their burial when needed, certainly remains a religious duty with us. More than that, the consensus of opinion in Jewish law is that one may say Kaddish for a Gentile relative (see *Recent Reform Responsa*). Aaron Walkin, rabbi of Pinsk-Karlin, in a responsum written in 1933 (*Z'kan Aharon* II, 87) says a proselyte may say Kaddish for a Gentile father, and Abraham Zvi Klein, rabbi in Hungary in the past century, in *Beerot Avraham* 11, says that if a Christian woman gives a gift to the synagogue, there is no prohibition against the *Chevra Kadisha* recording her name and reciting *el mole rachamim* for her.

In the light of the above, the practical decisions to which the Conference had come in the past ought to be continued, and somewhat elaborated as follows: If a man owns a lot in our cemetery and he wishes his Gentile spouse or their children buried in his lot, we should not object. Even if one of her parents is to be buried in that lot, we should permit it. The Jewish owner's lot is to be considered *b'soch shelo,* his property, and he does not object to his Gentile relative being buried near where he himself will be buried.

The overwhelming number of such requests will come from a mixed family which wants to be buried side by side. But if it is a question of a single grave, not in a family plot, the situation is different. A Jew may object to a Gentile who is a stranger being buried next to his parent or other close relative. Here, then, where there is no family bond between the Jew and the Gentile, we have no right to force the burial of a Christian next to the grave of a Jew (in spite of the argument of Friedmann mentioned above). Therefore, for a single grave (not in a family plot) the cemetery may set aside a small section for such infrequent requests. This section of single graves for Gentile relatives would then be no different from a municipal cemetery (frequent in Europe) in which there is a Jewish section, a Gentile section, side by side.

Since the exclusive Jewishness of the Jewish cemetery is rooted deeply in Jewish sentiment, if not in formal Jewish law, any Christian service held in it awakens protest on the part of our people, as many of us have discovered. Such protests have come from "the most liberal," who objected to a Christological service conducted near the graves of their parents. The best solution, therefore, is the one that is generally followed. The Christian minister conducts the service in the funeral chapel or the home. The rabbi conducts the service in the Jewish cemetery; since at all events it is our duty to participate, if needed, in the burial of a non-Jew, as stated above. If it is unavoidable that the Christian minister officiate in the Jewish cemetery, then he must either use our Manual or just selections from the Psalms, etc. Certainly no Christian type of tombstone must ever be permitted in a Jewish cemetery.

In essence, it may be said that the point of view consistently followed by the Conference and now developed more fully, is based upon the following considerations: The communal (or congregational) cemetery has an honored status rooted in custom but not in law, except insofar as custom becomes law (*minhag yisroel Torah hu*). There is a special and older status for a man's own lot (*b'soch shelo*). Also, we have a moral obligation to be concerned, when needed, with funerals of non-Jews. Kaddish and *el mole rachamim* may be said for them, especially when there is a special relationship or situation involved. Close Gentile relatives, therefore, may at the request of the family be buried in the family plot; but as to single graves in a row, the congregation should not, on its own initiative, bury Jews and unrelated Gentiles side by side. Whatever service is conducted by a Christian minister in the home or funeral chapel does not concern us, but the services in the cemetery should always be a Jewish service.

(Originally published in *Central Conference of American Rabbis* 1968.)

40

TRANSFER OF JEW TO CHRISTIAN CEMETERY

A Jewish man was married to a Catholic woman, who remained a Catholic. They have a child who has been raised as a Catholic and is a Catholic. The man died a number of years ago and he was buried in the Jewish cemetery in the plot of his family. His Catholic widow lives in a suburb. She is considering asking permission to have the body of her Jewish husband disinterred from his family plot in the Jewish cemetery, in order to have him buried in a Catholic cemetery in the neighborhood in which she lives. Is such disinterment permissible in Jewish law or custom? (From Vigdor W. Kavaler, Pittsburgh, Pennsylvania.)

THE laws of the Commonwealth of Pennsylvania (and possibly of other states also) give to a widow the right to determine in which cemetery her husband should be buried. This widow, four years ago, had decided that her husband, being Jewish, should be buried as a Jew in the Jewish cemetery and in the plot of his family in that cemetery. Now she has changed her mind and is thinking of having his body disinterred and reburied in a Catholic cemetery. Upon inquiry from a prominent lawyer, I have ascertained that the law is as yet not quite clear as to whether this legal right of a widow to determine the cemetery in which her husband should be buried is her lifelong right and that, therefore, she may decide to disinter him and move him as often as she pleases; or whether, on the other hand, having once exercised her right at the time of his death and having buried him in one place, her authority over the body has now ceased. Whichever way the law is, or will be decided at some later time, it is certain that the courts will take into consideration the regulations and laws of the cemetery in which he is now buried. The following recent court decision in Pennsylvania makes clear the necessity for a statement of Jewish law and tradition in the matter:

1. The rights of the surviving spouse and next of kin to control the disposition of the remains of the

members of their family have been recognized in this Commonwealth. The paramount right is in the surviving husband or widow.

2. The reinterment involving the removal of the body to another locality is based upon a different rule of law, wherein the presumption is against a change or removal and will be permitted only in rare circumstances. It is a privilege to be accorded by a Court of Equity in the exercise of a sound and wise discretion.

The interest of the public is expressed in its public policy and the presumption is against removal.

3. Where restrictions are present, the court will give them due weight when not violative of the civil law.

It is therefore with regard to the regulations and laws of the Jewish cemetery that the following answer is directed. As a general principle, Jewish law and custom strongly object to any disinterment at all. The body, once buried, must be left undisturbed. This is clear in the *Shulchan Aruch, Yore Deah* 363, which is headed: "The prohibition of removing the dead or his bones from their place." The first paragraph states the law as follows: "We may not move the dead or the bones, neither from one honored grave to another, nor even from a less honored grave to a more honored grave, and certainly not from an honored grave to a less honored grave." The basic objection is, however, modified by certain special exceptions. If, for example, the body has been buried in one cemetery with the clearly announced intention of later removing it to another cemetery, such disinterment would be permitted. Or it is permitted to move the body to a grave in the plot where his family is buried if the body had been buried in a separate grave, as the *Shulchan Aruch* says, "It is pleasing to a man to rest with his ancestors." It is also permitted to move a body if it is now in some neglected place where the body might carelessly be disturbed. Such a body may be disinterred in order to be moved to a cemetery which is protected. It is always permitted to disinter a body in order to rebury it in the sacred soil of Palestine. Likewise, the great authority, Z'vi Ashkenazi, cited in the *Pis-che Teshuva* to this passage, declares that it is to the honor of the dead to be disinterred from a Gentile cemetery to a Jewish cemetery.

All these are specific exceptions to the firm general principle forbidding disinterment. Certainly, since it is deemed an honor for a Jew to be buried in a Jewish cemetery, it would not be permissible to remove him from a Jewish cemetery in order to be buried in a Gentile cemetery. Furthermore, since it is particularly "honorable" in a Jewish cemetery for a man "to rest with his fathers," and since this man is already buried in the family plot "with his fathers," it is certainly prohibited to disinter him, even to rebury him in some other Jewish cemetery. Therefore the request of the widow to move her husband from the family plot to a Christian cemetery is contrary both to the spirit and the letter of Jewish law and custom and cannot be permitted.

41

BURIAL OF A PET ANIMAL

A young husband and his pet dog were killed in an accident. His widow wanted to inter the dog with him or in a separate grave near him. Is it permissible to bury a dog in a Jewish cemetery? (From P.S.B.)

No question of this sort was ever asked in any of the traditional Jewish legal literature; and it is certain that if such a question had been asked, it would have been dismissed with derision. However, the fact that such a question is asked and perhaps will be asked frequently nowadays, indicates a widespread change of sentiment which deserves, for that reason alone, serious consideration.

In the last few centuries in the western world, there has spread through all branches of the population a great love for dogs. They are deeply beloved as comrades or as recipients for genuine affection. There are series of moving pictures in which the central hero is a dog. There are numerous novels in which the leading character is a dog. The American novelist, John Steinbeck, in his recent book of travels around America, calls his book *Travels with Charley* and Charley is his dog. Because of this great modern affection for dogs there are hundreds of enthusiastic breeding societies, a great development of medical care for dogs, special dog-caterers who bring the balanced dog food daily, and special cemeteries for their burial. I do not know what the rules are with regard to burying them in general human cemeteries, but it is absolutely certain that in states where such burial would be permitted, many people would bury dogs in their family plots.

But clearly the mere interment of a dog will not satisfy the strong modern emotion. There are ministers of certain denomination who give public blessings to hunting dogs. It is therefore to be assumed that certain ministers may well have been asked, or have even acceded to a request to officiate with a religious service at the burial of a dog. How could they logically refuse if they bless dogs at the beginning of their hunting enterprises? What, then, would we as rabbis do if we were actually asked to officiate at the burial of a dog? All this could be a possible consequence of our permitting their burial in a human cemetery.

Obviously this present affection for dogs represents a drastic reversal of the sentiments of the biblical and the Jewish past. When one considers the biblical references to dogs, one realizes that they all voice an utter contempt for that animal. In Deuteronomy 23:19, in discussing disgusting things which may not be brought into the house of God, there is coupled in one sentence, "the hire of a harlot and the price of a dog." When Goliath wanted to indicate his contempt of David, he said: "Am I, then, a dog that you come against me with sticks?" (I Samuel 17:43). Hazael says to Elijah (II Kings 8:13): "Is thy servant a dog?" How low a dog was reckoned can be seen when Ecclesiastes sought to express how utterly worthless was a dead hero (9:4): "Even a living dog is better than a dead lion."

Why this strong anti-dog sentiment pervades Scripture deserves serious study, but whatever its real cause is, it is clear that there is not a single pet dog in all of Scripture. The dogs are looked upon, as were the wild dogs in Constantinople, as nasty, scavenging beasts.

Upon this basis, there are certain decisions in Jewish law with regard to dogs. The Mishnah (*Baba Kama* 7:7) says definitely that a man shall not raise a dog unless he keeps it chained. The later scholars in the Talmud and in the *Shulchan Aruch* modify the text and speak of "an evil dog"; I suppose we would say "a fierce dog." So the Talmud in b. *Shabbas* 63a says: "He who raises an evil dog in his house, keeps mercy from his household and breaks the reverence for God." Also in *Baba Kama* 80a, the subject is taken up. Rabbi Ismael suggests some types of dogs that can be raised. It is not clear from Rashi whether he means village dogs, where they can run free, or small dogs. Maimonides (*Yad Hilchoth Nizke Mammon* V, 9) says that dogs may not be raised unless kept chained, and adds (on the basis of *Baba Kama* 82a) that the rabbis said, "Cursed is the man who raises dogs, because they dó damage." So the *Shulchan Aruch* (*Choshen Mishpot* 409) codifies it as a law that it is prohibited to raise dogs unless kept chained. But Isserles (showing, perhaps, the beginning of a change of sentiment) says that the people nowadays raise dogs anyhow, and that we might as well bow to their actions. In other words, he implies that the prohibition has become passé.

Therefore, it is clear that there is a powerful clash of opposite sentiment between modern feelings towards dogs and that of the traditional past.

To the aversion for dogs in the past, we must add the sense of reverential honor given to the cemetery, which was considered *bes olom*, "the house of eternity," and which was in the care of the most devoted men of the medieval community, "The Holy Society," the *Chevra Kadisha*. It is, then, clear that the very suggestion of burying a dog in the sacred cemetery would bring nothing but horror. Therefore no such discussion is found in any of the literature.

We must, therefore, conclude the following: There is no explicit legal prohibition against burying a pet in the cemetery because the question did not come up. The question could not come up because the very thought would be too horrid to contemplate. To them the dogs were too contemptible and the cemetery too holy. Therefore, while modern sentiment has changed perhaps for the better with regard to these animals, the whole mood of tradition is against such action.

42

MASS BURIALS

A chaplain is about to participate in a discussion under military auspices of the question of mass burial, and asks whether there had been any responsa written during the war on this question by our Responsa Committee. (From Chaplain Aryeh Lev, New York City.)

THERE has been no such responsum. While it is true that there were mass burials during the war, particularly when airplanes crashed on Pacific islands and left nothing there but fragments of bodies; and while, therefore, there was some discussion in our Chaplaincy Commission about them, nevertheless we concluded at that time not to write a formal responsum on the question. Our reasons were, first, because the body of a Jewish soldier killed in this way was to be considered equivalent to a *mays mitsvoh,* who must be buried where he fell and who, according to the law, "acquires" the land where his body was found, and that is his proper burial place. Secondly, if under war conditions any Jewish chaplain was asked to participate in such burial, he was under military orders, and in war time it was felt that he simply should obey, because even if the bodies were *all* of Gentile soldiers, it was part of his duty to bury them if called upon to do so.

However, now that we are under peacetime conditions, we can go into the subject more fully, especially since in the discussion panel that is about to be held, the authorities have the right to learn what our attitude is to such events, should they occur. They can very well occur since planes occasionally crash, or if, God forbid, there should be atomic hostilities and quick mass burials would then be necessary.

Tragically enough, it happens that precedents on the question of mass burial have now come up in Jewish legal literature since the war ended. The first one is described in the Responsa *M'ma'amakim* by Ephraim Oshry, and the other in the Responsa *M'gay Ha-Haregah,* by Simon Ephrati. The questions are discussed in *M'ma'amakim,* p. 131 ff., and in *M'gay Ha-Haregah,* p. 66 ff. These two discussions deal with many of the problems involved in our question, but it would be better for our purposes if we dealt with the questions systematically in accordance with the problems as they concern us. There are the following religio-legal questions involved in the type of mass burial which might occur under military circumstances.

1. Is it a religious duty, a *mitzvah,* to bury scattered limbs or parts of a body?

2. Does the burial of broken parts of the body constitute the official burial according to Jewish law, after which regular mourning must begin, and from the date of which Yahrzeit is fixed?

3. Is it permissible to bury the broken remains of a large number of individuals, helter-skelter in one grave?

4. Is it permissible to bury these broken remnants with broken remnants of non-Jewish soldiers? In other words, can the chaplain, in conscience, participate in such a "mixed" burial ceremony?

As to whether we are in duty bound to bury fragments of a body. There is no doubt that there is indeed such a duty incumbent upon us. Of course a distinction must be made between burial of an amputated limb of a living person and the burial of a limb of a dead person. As for the burial of a limb of a living person, there is no mandatory *mitzvah* of burial involved. If such a limb is buried, it is only for convenience. If, however, the limb from a living person is preserved in a bone bank, that also would be permitted. (See the earlier responsum by our Committee on this subject.) As to the custom in Talmudic times of burying the limbs so as to protect priests from defilement, (*Kesubos,* 20b and *Rashi*) note especially the responsum of Jacob Reischer, "*Shevus Jaacov,*" II, 101. As for the burial of the scattered limbs of the dead, the law goes back to the later tractate *Semachos* II, 10, where it speaks of the dead being discovered with scattered limbs and the limbs gathered and buried. This is clarified as law in the *Shulchan Aruch, Yore Deah* 374, 2, in the case of a priest who may defile his priestly sanctity with the burial of a *mays mitzvoh*. If he finds a body with limbs missing, he must search for the missing limbs (i.e., this is part of his duty). There is, however, disagreement in the law whether very small fragments of a body ("as much as a barley seed or an olive") must be searched for. Some authorities believe that even the smallest amount of a dead body must be buried. See, for example, *Minchas Hinuch,* 537. But this is an unsettled question in the law. There is no doubt that *larger* parts of the body must be buried. Moses Sofer, in *Responsa Yore Deah,* 353, says, "It makes no difference whether it be a complete body or an incomplete body; it must be buried."

Now as to the second question, whether the burial of, let us say, a few bones of a Jewish soldier is sufficient to make

it official burial, permitting the wife to be remarried, mark-
ing the time of mourning, etc. In this regard the law is
clearly in the negative, and it goes back to *Semachos* II, 10,
which states that mourning begins only if it is the head and
the bulk of the body or, according to one authority, the
head and the backbone. That much of the body is the mini-
mum sufficient to provide identification, and regular mourning may then ensue. However, the bereaved family, while it
cannot count on the burial of one or two scattered limbs as
permitting mourning, remarriage, etc., has another ground
for the permission. According to the law developed early,
mostly in the Rhineland, the family can begin regular
mourning over a body that is lost when they despair
(*mishenishyoashu*) of getting the body for burial. This law
is repeated frequently in the Rhineland authorities, such as
Or Zeruah, Mordecai, etc. Perhaps the most accessible
statement of the law is in Asher ben Yehiel's compendium
to the Talmud, to *Moed Katan* (56). Of course, ever since
the decision by Isaac Elkanan Spector (*Eyn Yitzchok,
Even Hoezer,* 19) the official statement of the government
that the man is dead, not merely that he is missing, is acceptable in Jewish law, and the notification from the government to that effect can be equivalent to "despair"
(*mishenishyoashu*). Of course, if in the mass burial there is
enough of the body for identification, "the head and the
spine," etc., then of course, mourning begins from the time
of burial, provided it had not begun sooner. In that case, it
does not need to be resumed. But if there are only a few
unidentifiable limbs, then the mourning dates from the
"despair" occasioned by the government notification.

Is it permitted in Jewish law to bury the bodies of a
number of Jews in one grave? The Law, in general, is very
strict that each body (except small children, who may be

buried with their parents, Yore Deah 362:2) should have its own space; and careful regulations determine how many handbreadths there shall be between grave and grave. However, when the flesh has gone and nothing is left but bones, the great Hungarian authority, Moses Sofer, in the responsum cited, declares that these bones do not require their own separate space. Nevertheless, the question comes up whether the bones of many dead should be buried helter-skelter together, or kept as separate as possible. This again is a matter of dispute in the law. Moses Sofer and others believe that the bones should be kept apart as much as possible. But the Egyptian authority, David ben Zimri, in his *Responsa* II, 611, comes to the opposite decision. (Incidentally, the whole discussion comes up in Jewish law when it is necessary to transfer, en masse, bones from an old cemetery which, for example, are being taken away by the government, and moved to the new cemetery.) David ben Zimri says, "We come to the conclusion that even if the bones of many of the dead are all mixed up together, we need not be concerned with that fact since the matter (i.e., the reburial into a safe cemetery) is for the honor of the dead, and the general rule is that whatever is for their honor, is permitted."

While Moses Sofer and others are opposed to mixing the bones of various bodies, their reasoning would apply only to circumstances in peacetime or whenever each set of bones lies separately in its own grave. But if the bones are found lying already scattered in a field, or in a bomb crater, there is no doubt that Moses Sofer would agree with David ben Zimri that the burial of them, even mixed together, is for "the honor of the dead," and therefore permitted. In fact, it is upon this basis (the separate bones could no longer be recognized) that Ephraim Oshry buried in one common grave (*kever achim*) the bones of Jews which they found on funeral pyres after the Germans retreated from Kovno. It is clear, then, that it is not contrary to Jewish law under the special circumstances which concern us, to bury the various bones together.

The final question is whether a Jewish chaplain can conscientiously officiate at the burial of the bones of Jewish soldiers when they are mixed up with the bones of non-Jewish soldiers. When we consider the efforts made by Jewish communities to maintain separate Jewish cemeteries, and to bring Jewish bodies to Jewish burial in a Jewish cemetery, it would seem at first blush that to bury deliberately Jewish bodies together with Christian bodies would be contrary to the spirit of Jewish legal tradition. However, the following considerations must be borne in mind: First of all, if it is wartime, we have always followed the practice of burying the Jewish boys in the general military cemetery, content with the Star of David marker to show that it is a Jewish grave. Here, too, in the mixed burial, we would have a Star of David among the other markers. Secondly, we must consider that these Jewish bodies are "*mays mitzvoh*" and, according to the Law, "acquire" the place where they have fallen and are to be buried there. Therefore, the Jewish soldiers have the right to be buried in that place, whoever else is buried there.

Of course, in a joint service, the Jewish chaplain is officiating also over the burial of the bodies of Christian soldiers; but this he is in duty bound to do, not only according to his military duty, but according to the Talmudic dictum: "We sustain the poor of non-Jews, comfort their mourning, and bury their dead." (*Gittin* 61a). We have a duty to bury the dead of Gentiles if there is no one else to do it. Note that Rashi says: "We engage in their (the Gentiles') burial, if they are found slain among Jewish slain." Of course, according to Rashi and the general understanding of this statement, we are not to bury the Gentile body alongside Jewish bodies (i.e., in the same cemetery) and if, therefore, it were possible to separate the bones, it would be preferable if that were done; but this is impossible, and therefore there is no choice.

To sum up: According to Jewish law, the fragments of a body must be buried. It is a *mitzvah*. If the fragments are unidentifiable, the mourning for the dead must depend upon official government announcement. The fragments of various bodies which cannot be identified may, by Jewish law, be buried all together. And finally, the fact that Christian bodies, or fragments of bodies, are buried there too, does not affect the situation materially.

43

RABBI PARTICIPATING IN A CHRISTIAN FUNERAL

A rabbi in San Francisco was asked by the husband of a Christian woman, who had attended his service and who had left a specific request for him by name in her will, to officiate at her funeral. He stated that any prayer the rabbi would say would meet with his approval; that his wife was very fond of this rabbi and asked that he officiate. (From Louis J. Freehof, San Francisco, California.)

THIS question is discussed in *Reform Jewish Practice,* Volume I, p. 144. But since it is referred to briefly, it must be useful to discuss the matter fully.

The Talmud (b. *Gittin* 61a) states that when the corners of the field are left unharvested for the benefit of the poor, then we must not prevent non-Jews from gleaning among the Jewish poor. The motivation for this humane brotherliness is stated in the passage: "*mipne darche shalom,*" "in order to follow the paths of peace." To follow the "paths of peace" is a widespread motivation in the law.

Sometimes the principle is stated negatively: "*mishum ayva,*" "in order to avoid hatred." But both phrases mean virtually the same thing: "to avoid hatred, to increase peace." A number of examples will be sufficient to illustrate the many-sided use of this humanitarian principle which is, of course, also practical and self-protective: A Jew moving from a house must remove the *mezuzah* if a non-Jew will now occupy the house. Yet, if removing the *mezuzah* will offend the new tenant, the *mezuzah* should not be removed (*Yore Deah* 291:2). Also, it was forbidden to have business or social dealings with non-Jews within three days of their festivals. But "for the sake of avoiding hatred and promoting peace," the law now is that we may have contact with them in their holiday period and may even give them gifts (*Yore Deah* 128:12).

This prevalent motivation used in the Talmud (*Gittin* 61a) for permitting non-Jews to share in the agricultural charities (the corner of the field, etc.) is used in the same Talmudic passage as follows: We sustain the poor of Gentiles with the poor of Israel; we visit the sick of Gentiles as with the sick of Israel; and we bury the dead of Gentiles with the dead of Israel, because of the paths of peace.

The only restriction placed upon this humane mandate is in the commentary of Rashi, who limits the meaning of the word "with." He says that "with" does not mean to bury Gentiles *in* Jewish cemeteries. The same explanation is given by the 12th century Italian rabbi, Isaiah of Trani (*Tosfos Rid*). But both are clear that we should conduct the funeral and console them. That this is not merely a passing statement in a Talmudic discussion is evident from the fact that it is taken as law by the later codifiers, Asher ben Yehiel in the *Tur,* and Joseph Caro in the *Shulchan Aruch* (*Yore Deah* 367:1). "We bury the dead of non-Jews and comfort their mourners."

Thus it is clear that Jews and the Jewish community should include in their charitable acts (whenever necessary) the burial of the dead of Gentiles. In fact, even when a Gentile funeral is conducted by Gentiles (as is, of course, usually the case) any Jew seated as the procession passes is in duty bound to rise out of respect and to accompany the funeral symbolically for four cubits (*Kol Bo Hilchos Avelus,* page 86c). This is cited also by Joseph Caro in his "Beth Joseph" to the passage cited from the *Tur.*

Thus if, for some reason, a Christian family asked that a Jewish funeral director should take charge of the funeral, he could not refuse to do so on religious grounds. Or if it were the body of a Christian when there is no one to take care of the funeral, it would be commendable, according to Jewish law, for the funeral director to do all that was needed. He would request some Christian cemetery to accept the body and provide a grave, but the Jewish funeral director should take, if necessary of course, the responsibility for the funeral arrangements.

While this is a general humanitarian requirement, nevertheless some may question (as in your inquiry) whether it is proper for a rabbi to conduct the funeral and give a eulogy. The law does not make distinctions in such matters between rabbi and people. But clearly whichever Jew officiates, rabbi or not, he is permitted to give a eulogy. The eulogy is especially mentioned in the form of the law as given in the *Tosefta* (*Gittin* Chapter 3). Of course, it goes without saying that the rabbi cannot with propriety read Christian trinitarian prayers. He may read from the Psalms, for example, and preach the usual eulogy.

All this is so clear in the law that it is strange that it should be questioned, or that a rabbi should have to explain himself for officiating at a Christian funeral. The same law in the Talmud which recommends such humanitarian action also includes "healing their sick." No one would ever question the propriety of a Jewish hospital serving non-Jews. But there is no difference in the law between feeding the hungry, healing the sick, and burying the dead.

Except for the restriction mentioned by Rashi against burying Gentiles in a Jewish cemetery, the law is definite that all funeral services, whenever necessary, should be provided for them. This is the recommendation of the Talmud and, judging by its continual restatement in the later codes, it can be deemed to have the force of law.

44

SOME KADDISH CUSTOMS

How old is the custom of reading the names of those whose Yahrzeit comes up during the week? Is there a traditional basis for hiring somebody to say Kaddish for the deceased? (From Rabbi Wolli Kaelter, Long Beach, California.)

As to the first question, our Reform congregations, at least up to the last thirty years, had the custom of reading the

names of the deceased and the Yahrzeits as part of the
Kaddish. Later some large congregations abandoned the
practice simply because there were too many names to be
read each week. Others, in order to keep the sense of
Yahrzeit from fading from our people, are experimenting
with informing the members of the Yahrzeit and reading
the names of the deceased whose relatives have signified
their intention to be present at the service. Other congregations, usually smaller ones, continue the older Reform custom of reading the names as part of the Kaddish. The question that is asked is: Does this reading of the names have
any basis in the Jewish tradition?

Clearly this custom of ours is related to *Yizkor* or *haskoras neshomos*. The *haskoras neshomos,* as all scholars
agree, began in the Rhineland after the Crusades. It was
conducted on Yom Kippur and obviously the names of the
martyrs were read, because we still have lists extant of the
martyrs. The Rhineland congregations kept a *Memor Buch,*
obviously for this purpose.

Then the custom of *haskoras neshomos* was extended in
eastern Europe from Yom Kippur, also to the last day of
each of the three festivals (cf. Isserles to *Orah Hayyim*
284:7). The question now is whether on these *Yizkor* services during the year a list of names was ever read (as we
do at Memorial Services and as some of our congregations
do at Sabbath services). First, we know that in eastern Europe there is a custom that lists of names of the deceased are
read. There is a discussion of the whole question in Greenwald, *Kol Bo Al Avelus,* p. 339 and then later on p. 400 ff.
Maharash Engel was asked the following question in his
Responsa V, 24: There is a custom in many congregations that if a person leaves money to the *Chevra Kadisha*
for this purpose, his name is read on the holidays and a light

is lit on his Yahrzeit. The question asked of Engel was, since oil is now expensive (it was during the First World War) may they light *one* light and read a whole list of names of those whose Yahrzeit it is that week? He gives this permission, but adds that we must be sure that the names of *all* the donors should be read whose Yahrzeit it is. Solomon Schick, in his Responsa Rashban (Orah Hayyim 213) speaks of reading all the names in a memorial list and says it is not necessary (as some claim) to list the men and the women separately.

Now all this concerns either the *Yizkor* at holidays or the Yahrzeit day of the deceased. Could such memorial services take place on the Sabbath? Yes, for those who died during the week (Maharil quoted by Beer Heteb, *Orah Hayyim* 284). There is no question that they may (see *Kol Bo* 339, 13, which gives various references to this effect; cf. also *Azulai Birche Joseph* to *Orah Hayyim* 284:15). However, this is not quite our custom. The names of the dead mentioned were always in the regular *Yizkor* place, after the Torah reading in connection with the general memorial prayer, *av horachamim,* never in connection with the Kaddish, as is our custom.

Therefore it seems clear that our custom of reading memorial names on the Sabbath in the Kaddish is original with Reform, but it has these many roots, as is mentioned above.

Now, as to the second question, how far back the custom can be traced of hiring somebody to say Kaddish (this will occur especially with families in which there are no sons surviving). The earliest statement I have found on this goes back to the fourteenth century. Jochanan ben Mattathias who was virtually the last rabbi in Paris before the expulsion (i.e., fourteenth century) is quoted by Joseph Caro in his *Bes Josef* to *Yore Deah* 403, and he speaks of people hiring a *melamed* to say Kaddish. Later references are fairly numerous (Magen Avraham, *Orah Hayyim* 132:2, near end). For example, it is discussed by Ezekiel Landau of Prague in his Responsa *Nodah b'Yehuda,* II, 8. Finally there is a full discussion of the whole question in Israel, in the magazine *Ha-Posek,* published by the late Rabbi of Tel Aviv, Hillel Posek. The question arose because the *shammas* of a Shul in Tel Aviv was hired to say Kaddish for as many as ten people at a time. Therefore he asked David Assaf, who is rabbi of Haifa and has written a book on funeral customs, whether this situation should not be changed. In the magazine *Ha-Posek,* beginning with paragraph 780, he has a long responsum which covers all the literature. He does mention, however, that while the custom is well founded among us Ashkenazim, the Sephardic Rabbi Ben Zion Uziel (in his *Mishpotey Uziel, Orah Hayyim* 2) objects to it on the ground that no one should take pay for what is a *mitzvah.* At all events, it is a well established custom.

What is the basis for the folk custom of sitting *shiva* for a child who has converted to Christianity? (Asked by Rabbi Morris M. Task, Bayonne, New Jersey)

The basic source of the custom is in a statement in Isaac of Vienna's *Or Zorua* (twelfth century). In the laws of mourning (at the end of the volume, 428) he transmits a report that Rabbenu Gershom (the *Light of the Exile*) sat *shiva* for his son who was a convert to Christianity. This statement is quoted by a number of the early authorities and I give you the references for completeness' sake: The Mordecai to *Moed Katan* 886, Meir of Rothenberg in his Responsa (edited Budapest, 544) and a later authority, Joseph Caro in his *Bes Josef* to *Tur, Yore Deah* 354. In all these references the authorities cited are careful to say that

the law is not according to Rabbenu Gershom. Now, therefore, if the original reference to Rabbenu Gershom in *Or
Zorua* meant actually that Rabbenu Gershom sat *shiva*
when his son was converted (i.e., because of the conversion) even so, the chief authorities say that this is not the
law.

However, a careful reading of the texts reveals that there
is a misunderstanding. Rabbenu Gershom did not sit *shiva*
when and because his son became an apostate. What he did
was to sit *shiva* for his son when the son died, in spite of the
fact that the son had become an apostate years before. That
this is the meaning of the passage in *Or Zorua* is clear from
the following: All the discussions in *Or Zorua* itself and in
the later sources which quote the incident, quote it in the
following setting: The tractate *Semachos,* Chapter II, says
that we must have no mourning of any kind for sinners and
those who abandon the community. Therefore the law is
that there must be no mourning, i.e., no *shiva,* etc., for
apostates. Nevertheless, Rabbenu Gershom sat *shiva* for his
apostate son when the son died, and the authorities all say
that we do not follow his precedent. In other words, we do
not sit *shiva* when an apostate dies.

How did the misunderstanding of the passage in *Or
Zorua* arise? Why was it wrongly taken to mean that Rab-
benu Gershom sat *shiva* when the son was still alive but had
converted? This was due to a peculiarity of the text in *Or
Zorua.* It says that Rabbenu Gershom sat *shiva* for his son,
K'sh'nish-tamede. Obviously, as Chones indicates in *Toldos
Haposkim,* page 208, the text should read "*sh'nish-ta-
mede.*" All the relevant contexts prove this (see Mordecai
to *Moed Katan* 886). The incident, therefore, is that when
Rabbenu Gershom's son, an apostate, died, he sat *shiva* for

him, which he should not have done. The wording of the text led people to the erroneous belief that he sat *shiva* for his son while the son was still alive and had just converted.

45

MARRIAGE WITH ETHICAL CULTURISTS

A member of the congregation is contemplating marriage with a girl of Jewish birth who was raised in the Ethical Culture Society. Does she need conversion before the marriage? (From Rabbi Michael A. Robinson, Croton-on-Hudson, New York.)

THE problem involved in the question is one which has been discussed in the Jewish literature for many centuries. The reason for the frequency of the question is the result of the phenomenon of the Spanish and Portuguese Marranos who for centuries kept escaping from those countries to Jewish communities, and coming to countries of Jewish residence, desired to be reaffiliated with the Jewish community. Some of these families of Marranos had not been practicing Judaism for generations (except perhaps in some rudimentary, surreptitious fashion).

Since these Marranos had been practicing Catholics for many generations, the question which arose was: Did they need conversion before being accepted into the Jewish community? The classic answer to this question by Solomon ben Simon Duran of Algiers (see *The Responsa Literature,* 218) was that as far as marriage was concerned, they are still Jews and that it would be wrong to convert them (because converting them would imply that until that conversion they were not obliged to obey the commandments, which is not so). In fact Duran says that as long as it was proved that the mother was Jewish, they are Jewish "up to the end of all generations." Of course there were later, stricter opinions based on the accusation that they could have escaped sooner than they did, but in general the opinion of the law with regard to marriage is that they are Jews (see also *Reform Jewish Practice,* page 78).

Now, of course, the liberality of this judgment on the part of the law towards these Marranos is due (besides their birth) to the fact that their non-observance of Judaism was due to compulsion and not to free choice. Our question therefore narrows itself to this: If a Jew in America, where there is no religious compulsion, joins the Unitarian Church or the Ethical Culture Society, is he or she still to be considered a Jew and therefore not needing conversion? I have discussed this question rather fully in *Recent Reform Responsa* (see p. 56). Here as you will see, the question pivots on the fact of whether such people who joined these two groups meant by their joining to abandon the Jewish community. If they did, they come under the heading of "those who depart from the ways of the congregation." This is described (on p. 58) as follows:

> "Maimonides (*Hilchos Avel,* 1:10) defines clearly what is meant by "those who depart from the ways of the congregation." He says those who depart from the ways of the congregation, namely, those who break off the yoke of the commandments, are not included in *Kelal Isroel,* in the doing of mitzvos, in honoring the festivals, in attendance at synagogues, and so forth. This statement is embodied as law in the *Shulchan Aruch, Yore Deah* 345:5. Clearly,

this describes those who join a Unitarian Church. They no longer attend the synagogue, they no longer observe the Jewish festivals. The fact that the form of church that they have joined is not trinitarian is no more relevant than if they had joined a Moslem mosque."

This gives us a means of judgment of the Jewish status of such people. If, for example, a man joins the Unitarian Church and gives up his membership in the Temple and breaks off his relationship with the Jewish community, he is no longer a Jew. If his joining is merely an additional membership to the synagogue affiliation, he may be considered a Jew.

In this light, we can judge the members of the Ethical Culture Society liberally. When Felix Adler carefully called his organization a "Society," he indicated that he did not mean that those who joined his Society should break with Jewish life. Two generations of experience with them indicates that they still consider themselves Jews, that most frequently they marry with Jews and associate with Jews.

Therefore on the basis of the spirit of the law, it is a reasonable answer to say that the young lady in question need not be converted to Judaism. She is a Jewess, but as happened frequently (especially in the cases of reconversion of apostates) the custom arose to have the people involved promise loyalty to Judaism (*chaverus*). If the bride will promise that she will continue to support her husband's membership in the Temple and will raise the children as Jewish, giving them a Jewish religious education, then there is no impediment to this marriage.

46

MARRIAGE WITH KARAITES

A Karaite young girl, whose family comes from Egypt
and who says she has always considered herself Jewish,
asks a rabbi to officiate at her marriage with a Jewish
young man. Shall he, as a Reform rabbi, officiate at the
marriage? (From H. M. Y., Cherry Hill, New Jersey.)

THE status of the Karaites in Jewish law has shifted a number of times. Sometimes they are received and sometimes
they are excluded; as for example, Isserles says plainly, we
must not marry with them (*Even Hoezer,* 4:37). No one
questions that they are of Jewish descent, but the question
involved from time to time is the question of their legiti-
macy. If their marriages were deemed invalid, then the children of course cannot be illegitimate in Jewish law, since a
child born out of wedlock is not deemed illegitimate in Jewish law. Only a child born out of a union that cannot be
legitimatized is illegitimate, such as a union between a man
and a too close relative, or between a man and a woman
married to someone else. So what is really held against the
Karaites is that their marriages are deemed valid as a general rule, but their divorces are deemed invalid. Therefore,
if a woman is divorced by Karaite law and remarried by
Karaite law, her offspring of the second union will be illegitimate. This is the basis for their rejection.

But there is no doubt that emotions were involved. In
periods when the groups were hostile to each other, the laws
were strictly interpreted. Therefore nothing is to be gained
for the present by following the ups and downs of the law. I
can tell you simply that one of the greatest authorities,

David ben Zimri of Egypt, who had more connection with Karaites perhaps than any other rabbi, is very liberal about them. (cf. *A Treasury of Responsa,* p. 122 ff.) In David ben Zimri's responsum on marriage with a Falasha, he speaks by analogy about the Karaites, and he takes the general point of view that their marriages are deemed valid but their divorces are deemed invalid, and because of this, if any Karaite is a descendant from a woman remarried after a Karaite divorce, such a person may be deemed a *mamzer* and cannot marry a Jew.

This is precisely the burden under which the *B'nai Israel* labors in the state of Israel today. The Orthodox rabbis, on the analogy with the Karaites, consider their marriages valid and their divorces invalid. Therefore the group is under the suspicion of *mamzerus*.

However, David ben Zimri continues that nevertheless, many of the Karaites have intermarried with Jews, and he says that by the law of average, the likelihood of illegitimacy, i.e., the percentage of divorce and "remarriage" and of children from this "remarriage" is so small a percentage that they could be easily considered legitimate and should be accepted into the community. David ben Zimri concludes that he agrees with Maimonides' son, the Nagid Abraham, that they should be received into the community. Similarly, Jacob Castro (died in Egypt 1610) contemporary of Joseph Caro, in his notes to *Shulchan Aruch* (*Hilchos Gerim*) said that Karaites simply must promise before a *Beth Din* that they will observe the oral law.

Beyond all this, there is a special consideration involved in the fact that we are Reform Jews. We accept the validity of civil divorce, at least in the United States. In some countries the Reform congregations give a form of divorce which really does not change the situation in the eyes of Orthodoxy, since these Reform divorces are considered by the Orthodox authorities as invalid (just like the Karaite divorces). Therefore we frequently marry people who are children of women who had been only civilly divorced and have remarried. The children of such a union are certainly illegitimate in Orthodox law. Yet we marry them without hesitation.

The reason for refusing a Karaite certainly does not have validity for Reformers. If we accepted the old ground for refusal, we could not marry a considerable percentage of people we do marry. Since the authorities agree that Karaite marriages are valid and Karaites are of Jewish descent, and since the only objection is the validity of their divorce and the consequences drawn from it, we should have no hesitation in officiating at the marriage of a Karaite and a Jew.

(Originally published in *Central Conference of American Rabbis Yearbook,* Vol. LXXV, 1965.)

47

THE BRIDE'S VEIL

Nowadays, it is customary for a bride who is married for the first time to wear a veil. Widows and divorcees who are remarried do not wear a veil. Does this custom, which is common to Jews and Christians, have any basis in Jewish traditional law? (From J. S.)

THERE is mention in the Bible of a bride being veiled (Genesis 24:65). We are told that Rebecca was traveling from

Padan Aram to Canaan to be married to Isaac. When they approached the residence of Abraham in Canaan, they saw a young man and Rebecca asked who he was. When she was told that this was Isaac, whom she was going to marry, Scripture simply says: "She took the veil and covered herself." Thus it well may be that the custom of a bride veiling herself is very ancient in Jewish tradition.

In the Talmud (b. *Kesubo*s 17a) where it speaks of rejoicing, dancing, etc., in the presence of a bride, Rabbi Samuel ben Nachman says that it is permitted to gaze on the face of the bride. But the Talmud adds curtly that the law is to the contrary. In other words, it is forbidden to gaze in the face of the bride. While this discussion may refer to the celebrations after the ceremony, the later authorities dealing with the matter applied that rule, also, for before the ceremony. Asher ben Yehiel in his compendium says of this passage that one may not look upon the face of the bride, but only upon her ornaments. Thus is the law transmitted in the codes. The *Shulchan Aruch,* in *Even Hoezer,* 65:2, simply states the law: "One may not look on the face of the bride." Isserles adds the note (following Asher ben Yehiel): "We may, however, look upon her ornaments."

Joel Sirkes, in the *Bach* to the *Tur* (*Even Hoezer* 61) reports a widespread custom in Russia of a solemn marriage ceremonial, with the veil put on the bride on the morning of the ceremony by the groom and the rabbi. From all this it is clear that the brides must have been veiled since earliest times. It stands to reason that if a ceremony, such as this one of veiling the bride, lasts as long as this seems to have lasted, it must have rooted itself in more than folk custom, and must have become embodied as part of formal law. Yet, while it is a fact that there are no definite prescriptions in the law requiring that the bride be veiled, and while it is mentioned generally only as a custom, nevertheless, a closer consideration of the legal tradition will indicate that the veil had a definite relationship, not only to the social, but also to the strictly legal side of the marriage contract and ceremony. The law is clear that when a bride enters the *chuppah,* she is then definitely the wife of the groom. It makes no difference, then, whether sexual relationship takes place immediately or for some reason is delayed. In the legal phrase, the *chuppah* "acquires" and she is now a wife (*Tosfos* to *Yoma* 13b).

The difficulty, however, is that it is not clear what is meant by the word *"chuppah."* The present form of the *chuppah,* a sheet of cloth held up by four posts, is not ancient. Isserles, who mentions this canopy in *Even Hoezer* 55:1, gives four explanations of the word *"chuppah,"* and these four cover the whole variety of its meanings in the legal literature. His note is worth citing as a summary of the various meanings. He says: "Some say that '*chuppah*' means when the groom brings the bride to his house for the purpose of marriage. Some say that the *chuppah* is the spreading of a cloth over the head of both bride and groom when the blessings are recited. Some say that the *chuppah* of a virgin is when she goes forth (from her father's house) with the *henuma* (which was a veiled litter or sedan chair or else a face veil)." And then he adds: "But the custom has spread nowadays to use the word '*chuppah*' for the cloth which we spread on four staves, under which the bride and groom are brought and the blessings recited."

It is evident that since Isserles speaks of "a custom widespread nowadays," he is describing a fairly new custom, and it is also clear that there were older meanings of *"chuppah"* which transfers the authority of the bride from her father to her husband. The *Tosfos* to *Yoma* 13b referred to above says that the *chuppah* refers to when the bride goes forth with the *henuma*. The *henuma* mentioned in *M. Kesubos* II, 1, is generally translated to mean a veiled litter or sedan chair, in which the bride was carried from her father's house to the wedding (see b. *Kesubos* 17b). Some translate it simply as a face veil, not as a sedan chair. Rashi to the passage in 17b simply translates the word as a veil and so do, in later times, *Tosfos Yom Tov* (Heller) and *Tiferes Yisroel* (Liphshutz). Therefore the veil has important legal significance. When the bride went forth veiled from her father's house (either in the veiled sedan chair or with her face veiled) this was considered "*chuppah*," and she was by that very process "acquired" by her husband.

However, in later times, it was not deemed a full legal marriage unless she was actually in her husband's house (or in a marriage house or tent built for the purpose). Therefore "*chuppah*" was interpreted to mean the husband's premises. Later, when it still was not deemed sufficiently legal unless all the blessings were recited, the custom arose to have the special canopy which we now call a *chuppah*, under which the blessings were recited. Thus it was always debatable in the law, just which of these various stages should be described as "*chuppah*" which transfers the bride to her husband's jurisdiction. Because there was this doubt, since the earlier definitions of *chuppah* did not pass out of memory, a composite custom arose with regard to the veil, to cover the doubt caused by the various definitions. So the *Bach* (Joel Sirkes) to *Even Hoezer* 61 says: "Because of these various doubts (of the meaning of the word "*chuppah*") the custom has arisen that in the morning, after the morning service (i.e., hours before the ceremony which will take place in the evening) the bride's head is covered with a veil or a cloth; and in Russia they are particularly careful to have the groom present at the veiling of the bride (because of the earlier opinion that by this veiling he acquired her as wife), and then later in the day, the couple go to the *chuppah* (i.e., the canopy) and is formally married with the blessings."

Ezekiel Landau in his commentary *Dagul Mirvava* to *Yore Deah* 342:1, cites this statement of the *Bach*. But he qualifies it as follows: "Only in Russia (Volhynia) where the groom is formally present at the veiling is this to be deemed *chuppah* (acquisition of the bride) but in our country (i.e., Bohemia) where the bride's family alone veil her at home, this veiling is not to be deemed the formal *chuppah*." Note, too, that the *Taz* (David of Ostrow) to the law in *Shulchan Aruch, Yore Deah* 342, also denies that the veiling is really the Chuppah.

It is clear from the above that at an earlier time the veiling had actual, solemn, legal significance. Therefore, even though later scholars, as the customs changed, denied that the veiling was to be deemed *chuppah* (any longer) it is clear that the veil is of great significance in the tradition. It may no longer be deemed a legal requirement (as Ezekiel Landau and the *Taz* imply) but it is certainly an ancient tradition which at one time was even of legal importance. Hirshovitz, in *Ozar Minhagey Jeshurun,* page 129, says that the veil must be transparent (i.e., lace) so that although the face of the bride is covered, the formal witnesses at the marriage should be able to recognize and identify her. This opinion of Hirshovitz is derived from an earlier source; see Raphael Meldola, *Chuppas Chassanim,* page 57, who quotes the prayerbook containing the customs of Leghorn (*Tefilla Zakka*) to the effect that we put a veil on the bride before the blessings because of modesty, but we raise the veil slightly before the groom formally declares, "Behold, thou art married," etc., so that witnesses can see her. He also quotes Matte Moshe giving the custom in Toledo to the same effect.

It may be added that the present day distinction that only a bride who has never been previously married wears a veil is also ancient. The Mishnah in *Kesubos* 2:1 (and also 2:10) declares that the testimony that the bride when she was married went forth with the *henuma* (the veiled sedan or the face veil) was proof that she was being married for the first time.

48

CUSTODY OF DAUGHTER IN CASE OF DIVORCE

Husband and wife are divorced. They have a daughter and the mother has custody of the daughter. The father had been given the right to have the child visit him on Sunday. On Sunday, when the child visits the father, he sends her to the religious school of the Reform congregation to which he belongs. The mother is appealing to the court to upset this arrangement because she wants the child to go to a Conservative Sunday school, which is the form of Judaism adhered to by the second husband. What are the rights of the natural father in that regard? (From Dr. M. Z., Panorama, California.)

THE basic question of custody of children in case of divorce was already discussed in *Reform Responsa,* p. 209ff. There it was made clear that the traditional law makes a

distinction between custody of a boy child and custody of a
girl child. The distinction is based upon the fact that according to the old traditional law, the duty of studying the
Torah was incumbent upon a boy and not upon a girl and
that, furthermore, the obligation to teach the boy Torah (or
to provide for the instruction) is an obligation incumbent
upon the father and not upon the mother.

Because of these two facts, the tráditional law of custody
works out as follows: Infant children are in the custody of
their mother. A girl child is permanently in the custody of
the mother. A boy child can be claimed by the father after
he reaches the age of six because at that age he must begin
the study of the Torah. This basic law is given in the *Shulchan Aruch, Even Hoezer* 82:7.

While the law generally is clear, there are a number of
modifying opinions. Isserles, for example, to the *Shulchan
Aruch*, says that if the court decides that the mother is not a
fit parent, then even the girl child may be taken away from
her by the father. Abraham ben David, in his note to Maimonides, *Yad Ishus* 21:17, says that the father can claim
the boy child *before* the age of six because religious education ought to begin earlier. Furthermore, there is some discussion and disagreement as to how long the father can be
compelled to support the children while they are in the custody of the mother.

If, then, the question asked were settled merely according to the classic statement of the law, the decision would
be that since the duty of teaching the Torah does not apply
to the girl child, the father cannot have any claim upon her.

However, it is evident that this matter cannot be decided
purely on the basis of the classical statement of the law,
because here the whole question revolves around the religious education of a daughter, a situation which could not

have arisen in the older law, where a daughter was not required to study the Torah. Since now it has grown to be our custom among Reform, Conservative, and to a considerable extent among Orthodox Jewry, that girls as well as boys are given religious education, then the father can claim custody of a daughter as well as custody of a son.

Of course, it may be argued that if we take into consideration modern conditions, then we might also say that nowadays husband and wife each has the responsibility of providing religious education. However, to this it may be said that while the equality of men and women religiously was proclaimed first by Reform and accepted, to some extent, by Conservative, it certainly has no validity in Orthodox Jewish law. There the right of the father as the provider of religious education is still paramount. Since, then, there is no Jewish consensus on the equal duty of the mother to provide education, but there is virtually an all-Jewish consensus on providing Jewish education for girls as well as for boys, then it would be logical to conclude as we have concluded, namely, that the father can claim, according to the general spirit of the law under modern circumstances, that he has a religious duty to provide religious education for his daughter.

What is more directly to the point, however, is this: The court has already allowed the father to have the company of his daughter on Sunday. On Sunday he takes his daughter to the religious school of the Reform Temple of which he is a member. The mother is now petitioning the court to take away this privilege from the father. Therefore, according to all legal systems, the burden of proof is upon her.

On what basis does she want to upset the present decision of the court? It can only be upon the basis that she wants the child to go to a Conservative religious school conducted by the congregation of which her second husband (not the father of the child) is a member. Is the court expected to decide that the Conservative religious school education is more Jewish or more worthwhile than the Reform in which the child is now being trained? Surely the court is incompetent to make such a decision, and we would protest against such a decision, if made.

Our conclusion, therefore, is as follows: Since under modern circumstances all agree that girls as well as boys must receive religious education, then the traditional duty of the father applies to the daughter too. Since he takes her to the religious school of the Reform Temple to which he belongs, he is fulfilling that duty. The mother, seeking to reverse the decision of the court, which gave Sunday custody of the girl to the father, can only do so on a claim that the religious education which she would want to provide for the child is superior to the religious education which the child now gets. This is certainly not an admissible ground for changing the past decision of the court.

49

ADOPTION OF CHILDREN OF MIXED RACE

There are a number of children born out of wedlock of Jewish mothers and Negro fathers. Are these children Jewish? They can be given for adoption to Negro families. Should they be given to those Negro families which call themselves Jewish, belonging as they do to "Jewish Negro" congregations in New York? (From Rabbi Isaac N. Trainin, Commission on Synagogue Relations, Federation of Jewish Philanthropies of New York.)

ONE might imagine that marriage between the races, producing half-breeds and people of skin colors which have not existed before, would indeed be a violation of the commandments implied in Leviticus 19:19 and Deuteronomy 22:9, where one is forbidden to sow with mixed seeds or to breed animals of different species. None of the earlier commentators offer any explanation as to why it should be wrong to mix breeds of plants or animals. The first to offer any explanation was Nachmanides (thirteenth century). Nachmanides, in his commentary on Leviticus 19:19, suggests a reason why such mixing of separate species is a sin. It is due to the fact, he says, that the man who creates such new breeds implies that God, Who created the present species and gave them the power to perpetuate themselves, had not done a perfect work at Creation, and that there is now need of new species of plants and animals, etc. In other words, the species as they exist are God's work and presumably are perfect. To make new species is, therefore, a sin. This is a general consideration, but let us consider specifically the question of mixing the human races.

In Numbers 12:1, we are told that Miriam and Aaron rebuked Moses for "the Ethiopian woman" (Cushite) whom he had taken. The *Targum* (evidently in defense of Moses) translates "Cushite" as "the beautiful woman" and the Talmud (*Moed Katan* 16b) also explains away the word "Cushite" by saying that this is really his wife Zipporah and that she was called "Cushite" because, being a Midianite, her skin was deeply tanned by the desert sun. The Talmud in the same passage explains away the Ethiopian benefactor of Jeremiah, Ebed Melech, and implies that he was a Hebrew named Zedekiah.

Nevertheless, all this explaining away of the word "Ethiopian" by *Targum* and Talmud does not necessarily indicate that racial prejudices were involved. Also, the Talmud (b. *Berachoth* 59b) states that he who sees an Ethiopian must make a special blessing: "Praised be Thou, Who hast made a variety of creatures," but this, too, is not anti-Negro prejudice because the same blessing must be recited, according to the Talmud, when one sees an unusually short man or an unusually tall man. So the law is recorded in the *Shulchan Aruch, Orah Hayyim* 224:9.

Nowhere does the Bible prohibit the admixture of races. Ezekiel, speaking to the Children of Israel in Chapter 16, verse 3, says: "The Amorite was thy father and thy mother was a Hittite." So, too, with regard to the vast mixed multitude which came out of Egypt. While this mixed multitude is sometimes deprecated as the source of sinfulness, there is no statement which I remember to the effect that the descendants of the Twelve Tribes kept from intermarrying with the mixed multitudes. (See above Chapter 30.)

Since the status of a child of a mixed marriage depends upon the status of the mother, a child born of a Jewish mother is a Jewish child and must be so considered, no matter what the color of its skin may be. However, the question asked goes further: Should we consider the members of Negro congregations who call themselves Jewish as being truly Jewish? The question must be settled before the Jewish Federation can give a Negro Jewish child to such a family for adoption. Whether any family is Jewish depends upon whether it is descendant from a Jewish mother. The rest, as we have mentioned, makes no difference. But if it is a family not descendant from a Jewish mother, as is the case with most, if not all the people in these "Negro Jewish" congregations, then they are not Jewish unless they are correctly converted to Judaism. Those who have been correctly converted to Judaism are Jews in every sense of the word. Those that are not so converted are only Jews if they are descendants of a Jewish mother.

May the child be given to such a family, if the family is not considered Jewish? This is, likewise, a religious problem. May we give a Jewish child to a Gentile family to be raised and, indeed, adopted? Clearly, most Orthodox authorities would say "no," but in this case, liberal opinion would say "yes." The liberal opinion would be based upon the realities of social life in America. If we Jews fight for the right to have Christian children adopted in Jewish families, we should not object under special circumstances if Jewish children are adopted in Christian families. In this special case, this dark skinned Jewish child will have no home at all unless given to this Negro family for adoption.

50

RABBINICAL FEES AND SALARIES

A congregation had decided that whatever fees a rabbi receives from weddings and funerals should be turned over to the congregation. It was assumed that the salary would be raised to make up for loss of fees, and that it is more dignified for the rabbi to receive only a salary and no fees from individual members. The question is asked by a colleague as to whether this deprecation of fees is in accordance with the ethics of the Jewish legal tradition and whether it would be wrong on his part to ask to have the decision reconsidered.

THE question of fees and salaries and the relation between

them has been an ongoing discussion in Jewish law almost from the beginning. The question grew complex and needed constant re-analysis and re-definition. To give a general picture of how widespread was the discussion, we need only mention a number of references in the law in which a detailed analysis of the question was deemed necessary.

There are full discussions of this question to be found, for example, in the following: A series of responsa by Simon ben Zemach Duran, from 142-148, and his long commentary to the *Ethics of the Fathers,* IV:5; Joseph Caro in his *Kesev Mishnah* to the *Yad (Hilchoth Talmud Torah,* Chap. III; Moses Isserles in the *Shulchan Aruch, Yore Deah* 246:21; also to *Even Hoezer* 154:21; also, *Tosfos Yom Tov* (Yom Tov Lipmann Heller) to Mishnah *Bechoros,* IV:6. Then there are the responsa by Joel Sirkes *(Bach)* 52; Meir Eisenstadt *(Panim Meiros,* I:79); Moses Sofer in his responsa *(Choshen Mishpot,* 164).

Such a continued and elaborate discussion reveals the fact that the question of fees and salaries is one which has undergone considerable evolution as the rabbinate gradually evolved, becoming first a special skill and then a full-time profession.

Originally no fees and no salary were deemed to be justified or permissible for any of the functions which we now look upon as the essential function of the rabbinate, namely, for teaching the Torah, for making decisions on the basis of Jewish law, for officiating at weddings or at divorces, etc. There was, first of all, the general ethical objection to getting any material benefit from the study of the Torah as is stated in the *Ethics of the Fathers,* "not to make worldly use of the Crown of the Torah" (I, 13) and "not to make it a spade to dig with" (IV, 5). The study of the

Torah was a religious duty incumbent upon every Jew (see Maimonides in *Hilchos Talmud Torah*); therefore, how could a person take pay for pursuing that divine mandate? Besides the duty to study, there was also a duty to teach the Torah. It was especially incumbent upon a father to teach his own child the Torah. In general, teaching of the Torah to anybody was a religious duty for which no pay should be accepted. The Talmud, in *Nedarim* 37a (basing its comment upon the verse, Deuteronomy 4:14, where Moses says, "And God commanded me to teach you,") elaborates Moses' statement as follows: "God said to me, 'Just as I, the Lord, taught thee without pay (*bechinom*) so thou teach without pay.'"

As for the making of legal decisions, that too was deemed to be a religious duty ("And they shall judge the people," Deuteronomy 16:18). Therefore the Mishnah in *Bechoros,* IV:6 says: "If a man takes pay for making a legal decision, all his legal decisions thereby become void." On the basis of these various opinions for complete "amateur standing," one can understand the stern statement of Obadiah Bertinoro in his commentary to this Mishnah, in which he says he was shocked at the rabbis in Germany who took fees for officiating at a divorce proceeding, and also at the witnesses who took fees for signing the divorce document (the Mishnah also prohibits witnesses from taking fees).

Nevertheless, even in the Talmud, as the need for special training grew, this general prohibition was mitigated step by step. A teacher could be engaged for pay to teach children. Yet could he be permitted to receive pay when the duty of teaching was religiously incumbent upon him? The Talmud says that teachers of children were paid, not actually for the teaching of the Torah which was their religious duty, but for teaching the *pisuk ha-ta'amim*, the punctuation and the accents, etc., which they were not *required* to teach (*Nedarim* 37a). Rav says that the teacher is paid for taking care of the children, i.e., not directly for teaching the Torah (cf. Rashi, ad loc.). The *Tosfos* to *Bechoros* 29a says that as for our present-day custom of receiving pay for the teaching of the Torah, it applies only to one who has no other means of support, or even if he does have other means of support, he is paid for the time that he is taking away from his other business. The comment of *Tosfos* has in mind the fact that so many of the rabbis in Talmudic times were working men and made their living from their labor and not from teaching the Torah (and in the time of the *Tosfos,* they were business men).

As for taking pay for making legal decisions, the law as such is embodied in the *Shulchan Aruch* (*Choshen Mishpot,* 9:5) namely, that if one takes pay for judging, all his decisions are void; but Caro himself adds that the judge may take pay for the time that he has taken away from his other business. This brief statement of his is more elaborately dealt with in his *Kesef Mishnah* to the *Yad,* (*Hilchoth Talmud Torah,* III:11) in which he says a man may take support from the community for all these functions, teaching, judging, etc., if he has no other means of support; and then he adds, since the time of the Rambam the custom is for rabbis to take salaries, and he justifies this situation by the statement of the *Tosfos* mentioned above.

Caro's statement as to the changes which have occurred since the time of the Rambam are to be understood in the light of the series of responsa 142-148 of Simon ben Zemach Duran and his commentary to *Ethics of the Fathers,*

IV:5. Duran, who formerly made his living as a physician, had to flee from the Belearic Islands, which was a part of Spain, during the persecutions of 1396. He could no longer practice his profession in Algiers where he was a refugee, and was forced to take a salary from the congregation. He reviews all the relevant literature to justify his taking the salary.

As for those who took pay for deciding legal questions, a distinction was made between those who were occasional judges and those who were appointed to devote all their time to judging, i.e., professionals (*Tosfos Yom Tov* to *Bechoros* IV, 6). With regard to divorces, Isserles says (*Even Hoezer* 154:2 in *Seder Ha-get*) that the arrangement of divorces is not to be classified as legal decisions and therefore no fees are justified.

The fact of the matter is that it simply became necessary to professionalize the rabbinate, and so Isserles (with reference to the responsa of Simon ben Zemach Duran) simply says, "Therefore it has become the custom in all places that the rabbi of the city has income and support from the community in order that he need not engage in other work."

However, the memory of the older level of the law before the rabbinate became a profession still remained, and the statement is often made by the scholars that if a person could afford to serve as a rabbi without pay, that would be the ideal situation. It is rather touching to read the responsum of Moses Sofer, *Choshen Mishpot* 160. A pupil of his had asked whether to accept a rabbinical position and the salary, and his teacher answers, "Alas, I am suspect in this matter; i.e., I take a salary." And then he refers to all the above opinions now permitting it.

As between fees or salary, there is really no choice as to

which would be deemed worthier or more ethical. The older law objected to both. Yet as can be seen from the arguments of Duran, the paying of the regular salary developed later than the receiving of separate fees for specific services. He bases his justification for accepting a salary (hitherto unprecedented) upon the fact that rabbis, etc., have "always" received "fees." But this was to be expected as a natural evolution; first separate fees were justified and then, finally, the custom of a salary was established. So there is really no historical preference for one form of income over the other. In fact, in later centuries, the rabbinical fees are considered to be the legal prerogative of the rabbi. Moses Sofer (in his responsa *Yore Deah* 230) refers to a responsum by Isserlein (three centuries earlier) in which Isserlein deprecates the acceptance of wedding fees. Moses Sofer says that since the days of Isserlein the situation of the rabbinate has changed; he is now engaged by the community (professionally) and the fees are an integral part of his income. (cf. fuller discussion *C.C.A.R. Yearbook,* Vol. LXV, p. 86-87.)

Of course a congregation and a rabbi have the right to agree as to the sort of emolument the rabbi should receive. There can be no legal objection to a contract confining the rabbi to one class of income or the other. If the congregation and the rabbi have agreed at the beginning of the rabbi's term that he should not keep the fees, they have the right to make such an agreement. But if the rabbi would like to have the matter reopened and the agreement changed so that he be permitted to accept fees, there can be no ethical objection in Jewish law to such efforts. Both salaries and fees have equal standing in the law except, perhaps, that fees arose earlier than regular salary. Both were equally frowned upon at the beginning, and both became acceptable as rabbinical duties became specialized and professional.

(Originally published in *Central Conference of American Rabbis Yearbook,* Vol. LXXVI, 1966.)

51

SECRETS OF THE "CONFESSIONAL"

A woman in the congregation was murdered by strangulation. A member came to the rabbi and said she had clues as to the identity of the murderer. She made the rabbi promise that he would not inform the police. What is the rabbi's obligation in this matter? (From E. A. G.)

FIRST, as to the "secrets of the confessional," Jews do not confess to a human being with the expectation of receiving "absolution" from him. Therefore, such confidential conversation between a congregant and the rabbi is in no sense "sacramental" and, therefore, does not have the status of something which the rabbi must guard against divulging. If he feels he must not divulge it, that feeling is based entirely upon a secular moral obligation, not upon a sacramental, religious one. The rabbi is thus not bound "theologically" against telling the police what has been told to him by this witness.

Let us now dispose of the question of the difference between giving information to a Jewish court and to a "Gentile court." The objection to a Jew testifying or having to resort to a Gentile court is an old one in Jewish law. It is based upon the fact that Gentile law might convict a Jew upon grounds on which he would not be convicted in a Jewish court. Jewish law requires two witnesses. A Gentile court would accept a single witness. Since a Jew is bound to the Torah, it is a sin to bear such testimony in such a court as would convict a Jew, contrary to the Torah. Of course, if a man is summoned to give testimony, that is another matter; or if the Christian courts in this case will use the basis of decision which is the same as in Jewish courts, there is less objection.

But with us, we accept the decisions of the non-Jewish courts in all matters (even though the principle of "the law of the land is the law" applies *strictly* only to financial matters). Therefore, we in modern life would decide that if this is a matter which you would have been bound to divulge to a Jewish court, you are also bound to divulge it to a Gentile court.

But are you bound to divulge it to any court? Are you in any real sense a witness? A Gentile court would not accept your testimony. It is "hearsay evidence." The same principle is basic in the Jewish laws of testimony. In *M. Sanhedrin* IV, 5, the witnesses are warned against testifying on the basis of hearsay evidence. In fact, Maimonides goes further and says that to testify on mere hearsay evidence is a grave sin (*Yad Hilchos Edus* XVII, 1). No matter how reliable the source is, if he himself is not an eye witness, he may not testify. Yet to inform the police does not constitute a formal testimony. It is only helping the police in their investigation. In these investigations, even a rumor may be helpful. Are you in duty bound to transmit to the police the hearsay matters which this woman has told you? This depends in part upon your judgment of the woman's own duty.

The law is clear (Leviticus 5:1 and *Shulchan Aruch, Choshen Mishpot* 28:1) that it is a sin to refrain from testifying if you have real knowledge of the matter. If this woman is merely retailing something that is hearsay to her, then your obligation to give the police "hearsay of hearsay" is hardly a strong obligation. But if what she told you seems based upon strong enough evidence that she would be accepted as a witness in a court in this matter, then (in the eyes of Jewish law) she has committed a sin in not testifying and, therefore, you were correct in urging her to give the information to the police. But you failed to convince her; and so it is correct to say that if you keep the information from the police (assuming it is sound information) you are committing the sin of aiding sinners (*masayeh yedey ovrey avera*) or what might be called in modern law, "compounding a felony."

The only question that seems to remain is this: Why is she refusing to give this information to the police? Is it because she is afraid that the murderers will harm her? In that case, it would seem to me she has a right to your protection. Therefore, if you should give the information to the police, it should be with the proviso that they permit you to keep from divulging her name.

To sum up, you are not a witness. You cannot testify, but you can aid the police with information. If what the woman knows is substantial, then she is committing a sin by not giving the information. But if she would be endangered by giving the information, then you must decide to what extent you can protect her, or whether the testimony is substantial enough to justify endangering her. You are not bound by any religious "confessional secrets."

The following statement of the situation in American law was provided by a legal expert:

With reference to your problem concerning knowledge of a felony (in this case, murder), there are two distinct problems:

a) The position of the parishioner.

b) The clerical position.

In both cases, it must be assumed that we are speaking in terms of Pennsylvania law. It is most likely that the law would be the same in all states, but nevertheless, the possibility exists of some variance.

The Parishioner:

Under the common law, as inherited by our present laws, all offenses, not specifically provided for by statute, continue to be punishable as heretofore. Under the common law, an offense designated as "misprision of felony" was defined as a "criminal neglect either to prevent a felony from being committed or to bring the offender to justice after its commission." While our modern Penal Code only provides for "misprision of treason," it would seem that the common law crime of "misprision of felony" is still an indictable offense. A search of the cases indicates that its modern application is in conjunction with an attempt to convict as an accessory after the fact. Mere knowledge of a crime, however, has been held not enough to convict as an accessory after the fact. Therefore, misprision of felony, while indictable as a common law offense, has not been generally used as a separate offense. The conclusion must be, however, that the parishioner has committed the common law crime of "misprision of felony."

The Cleric:

As you well know, communications made to members of the clergy in the course of repentance and request for absolution of sins are confidential communications and, therefore, privileged under the law. Where, however, a clergyman received information not in the framework of repentance or absolution, the law grants no immunity.

Since the fact situation at hand constitutes a crime in itself, it must be concluded that the advice sought from the pastor should be held in strictest confidence. Any other result would undermine the very *raison d'être* for the continued existence of confidential communications between parishioners and clergymen.

52

ANSWERS TO SOCIAL SECURITY OFFICE

Following are the answers given by the Chairman of the Committee on Responsa to questions by Charles S. Ferber, District Manager of the Social Security Administration. These questions were asked of Dr. Sidney L. Regner, Executive Vice President of the Central Conference of American Rabbis. They are for the purpose of determining whether cantors in Jewish congregations may be considered ordained, commissioned, or licensed ministers in the sense of the terms used in the Social Security Act. The answers below are to the specific questions asked by the District Manager.

(1) Question: What are the requirements to become a rabbi?

Answer: In Orthodox Judaism, a man had to study Talmud and Jewish law, and was then examined by some well-known rabbi, who gave him *semicha,* or ordination. In modern Orthodoxy, and in Conservatism and Reform, the candidate must graduate from a recognized rabbinical school, pass its examinations, and be ordained at the graduation ceremony of ordination.

(2) Question: What is the significance of ordination in the Jewish religion?

Answer: Originally it had a mystic significance. The spirit descended through "the laying on of hands," all the way from Moses. No one was truly ordained unless he was ordained by one who had previously been ordained by "the laying on of hands." This mystic, unbroken ordination ceased, owing to the persecutions in the fourth century. Since then, we still use the word, *"semicha,"* which means "laying on of hands," but it is essentially *"hatoras hora'a,"* which means the permission to the young scholar to teach independently of his master. Of course, the modern *semicha* has achieved authoritative standing and gained respect, but it is in essence a teacher's certificate (*Yore Deah* 242:14).

(3) Question: Is an ordination ceremony or ritual required before an individual becomes an ordained rabbi?

Answer: None is required. The Orthodox rabbi would simply give the paper of *semicha* to the student. Modern seminaries will have something of a ceremony of ordination, but that is only for the sake of dignity. It has no status as a religious ceremony or as a sort of "sacrament," and is not required.

(4) Question: Is a rabbi the only authoritative preacher and teacher of Judaism?

Answer: No; Judaism is essentially a lay religion. Any scholar can teach. There are certain functions which it has become customary for the "ordained" rabbi alone to perform, such as being in charge of the writing of a divorce, but any capable person may officiate at a marriage. All that the law requires with regard to marriage is that the man should know the law or, if he does not, he should have no dealings with the marriage ceremony (b. *Kiddushin* 6a). See the responsum in *CCAR Yearbook,* Vol. LXV, 1955, pp. 85-88, in which it is made clear that basically any competent person can officiate at marriages, but that in northern Europe the custom gradually moved toward restricting the right of performing the marriage ceremony to the rabbis of the community.

(5) Question: Are there any provisions in Judaism for licensing or commissioning of authoritative teachers and preachers of the faith other than through ordination? May a congregation license an individual to perform such services? If a congregation may do so, what is his title, and what are his duties? Is there a source in Jewish theology for permitting the congregation to confer such licenses or commissions? Does this authority extend beyond the particular congregation which licensed or commissioned the individual?

Answer: Congregations are required by Jewish law to appoint cantors to conduct the service, and these cantors have to have certain qualifications chiefly of character and maturity (*Orah Hayyim* 53:4). This does not permanently confer an enduring status, as does ordination, on the person. He is selected for a certain term, and when the term is over, he ceases to be cantor. Sometimes he is selected as cantor only for the High Holy Days. As far as I know, there are no documents of appointment as there are for a rabbi.

But the question asks further whether a congregation may ordain a rabbi or select a man to be its rabbi. All rabbis are selected by the congregation. In earlier days, special, formal "letters of rabbinate" were issued by the congregation to the man they selected. Since they usually selected a learned man, he, almost invariably had *semicha*. But if he did *not* have *semicha*, would the congregation's selection of him make him a rabbi? I do not know of any precedent for such an event, though there is nothing in Jewish tradition to prevent it. Contrariwise, many men in the traditional communities had *semicha* and yet did not serve as rabbis. If it would happen (though this would be comparatively rare, if it happened at all) that a man was selected who was not ordained, then he would be the rabbi only of that congregation. Perhaps the best answer would be that no congregation can confer *semicha*. Only other scholars can do so.

(6) Question: Does the Jewish religious community make any distinction between ordination, commissioning, or licensing of teachers and preachers of the faith? If distinctions are made, what are the differences?

Answer: This question is answered chiefly in the answers to the previous question. It could be added, of course, that a man who is ordained (*semicha*) is always known and recognized whether the ordained man becomes a rabbi or not. There was also, in past centuries, what might be considered honorific degrees conferred upon scholarly laymen (the degree "*morenu*"), which in many communities was used as a title when the man was publicly called up to the Torah on Saturday and holidays, but there is no official licensing other than the ordination or the temporary appointment of a cantor.

(7) Question: What authoritative body is established in Jewish theology for conferring ordination, licenses, or commissions, and what is the source of its authority?

Answer: There is no central authority in Jewish life for conferring any of the status mentioned above. Only another scholar (or a faculty of scholars in a theological college or yeshiva) confers ordination, and only a congregation selects its rabbis and its cantor. However, nowadays, cantoral schools have been established. The diploma given by these schools attests to the ability of the man to serve as a cantor. This might be looked upon in the future as a special status, but for the present it is no more status than that of any diploma of any school. The man becomes a cantor when a congregation selects him as such.

(8) Question: What are the requirements to be a cantor? Does the cantorial "Behold Me, Destitute of Good Works" recited at the beginning of the Additional High Holy Days Services fairly describe the duties and qualifications of a cantor? Are there any qualifications for being a cantor other than that he be a "grave, venerable, and righteous person, whose voice is sweet and acceptable to mankind"? Is a cantor anything other than "a humble conveyor of prayer" for himself, his family, and the congregation that deputed him?

Answer: The qualifications of a cantor are clearly described in the authoritative code, the *Shulchan Aruch,* 53:4: "The cantor must be worthy, which means free of sins, a man about whom there has been no evil report even in his childhood; he must be modest and acceptable to the people; he must have a pleasant voice, and must be experienced in reading Scripture." This is a guide to the congregation, telling it what sort of man to select.

(9) Question: Is there any ceremony or ritual required before an individual becomes a cantor? If there is, who performs such ritual or ceremony, and what is his authority to do so?

Answer: No.

(10) Question: What is a precentor and wherein does a cantor differ from a precentor?

Answer: There is no requirement for a "precentor" in Jewish law.

(11) Question: Does a cantor as such preach and teach the tenets of Judaism? Are the duties of a cantor akin to those of a rabbi as a preacher and teacher of Judaism?

Answer: The cantor is not a teacher, as a rabbi is.

(12) Question: Is it essential in Judaism that religious services or any portion thereof be conducted by a cantor, or may any individual competent to read the prayers, equally do so?

Answer: The services must be read aloud, usually with the traditional chant. The basic purpose of the audible reading is to fulfill the duty of worship for those who are unable to read the service themselves, but this reader need not be a cantor. Any member of the congregation can read the service aloud for the congregation. In fact, during most of the year, a member of the congregation (anyone, usually, who is commemorating the anniversary of a close relative) conducts the service. Some Reform congregations, therefore, do not have any cantor at all. The rabbi reads the service.

53

ANSWERS TO C.C.A.R. JOURNAL

THE questions asked by Rabbi Joseph Klein, Editor of the Journal, have a special interest beyond the fact that they are living questions, arising from our present religious and social experience. Hardly any of these questions can be answered definitely by reference to some clear decision in one of the codes. All of them require some evaluation of the legal tradition below the surface, down to its unspoken implications. In addition, they all somehow involve the unsolved problem of the relation of Reform to the legal tradition. This relationship will be analyzed by all of us for a whole generation. We no longer need to fear that the Talmud and the Codes will restrict our freedom to reform. Our movement is too strong to necessitate a struggle against the legal tradition. For where a decision is contrary to our conscience (as to the marriage of a *Cohen* with the daughter of a convert) we simply feel free to follow our conscience. Yet we respect the law and are confident that basically it embodies the spirit and idealism of our religious tradition. Therefore we look for guidance from it, rather than for governance.

This guiding line is, of course, somewhat hazy, and so our decisions cannot always be too definite. They will always include personal judgments. To the extent that such vagueness and subjectivism are undesirable, I ask the pardon of my colleagues.

The following are the questions sent to me, and my answers.

(1) Question: A man who believes Judaism best fulfills his religious needs comes to a rabbi and asks that he be converted to Judaism. The man's wife has no intention of accepting Judaism—she is a faithful attendant of her church—and their three children are enrolled in the Sunday school of the wife's church. Should such a person be accepted as a convert?

Answer: On the face of it, this candidate is the

noblest and most desirable type of candidate for conversion. Jewish law has always been discontented over the fact that most candidates for conversion want to be converted in order to marry a Jew. The *Shulchan Aruch* says definitely (*Yore Deah* 268:12) that we do not receive any proselyte who comes to be converted because he desires a Jewish woman. Nevertheless, many Orthodox rabbis reluctantly convert such candidates. They base it upon the conversion made by Hillel, in *Shabbas* 31, and by Rabbi Chiya, in *Menachos* 44, and the conclusion of Joseph Caro in the *Bes Joseph* that the court can judge whether even such a candidate is really sincere. We frankly convert such candidates who convert for the purpose of marriage; but because of the dubiety in the older Jewish law, the Conference made a clear-cut decision in its "*Report on Marriage and Intermarriage,*" 1947, namely, that we do not consider the desire to marry a Jew to be any drawback to the acceptability of the candidate for conversion.

However, it is clear that in the mind of the inquirer there is an additional problem. This is indicated by the statement in the question that the candidate's wife means to remain a faithful attendant of her Christian church and, so, their three children also. The problem, then, becomes clearer. If we convert this man to Judaism, we divide that household's religion. We ourselves object to all mixed marriages also on this ground, namely, that a religiously divided household is under great spiritual stress and is likely to be unhappy. We should not say, therefore, that this is the personal concern of the candidate; for surely we are not indifferent to the happiness of his home.

But there is a more definite approach to this problem. The moment he becomes a Jew, he is a Jew married to a professing Christian, with his children being raised as Christians. (We leave out of the discussion the complication in the law as to what extent he, being converted, is now "a newborn child" and has no relatives any more.) Certainly, becoming a Jew, he is the head of a mixed-marriage family. It is our act of conversion which makes him in this regard a sinner. We are, therefore, violating the definite law of "putting a stumbling block before the blind" (see discussion in b. *Avodeh Zara,* 6). It is clear, then, that because of the divisive effect on his household and because our very act of converting him makes him a sinner in Jewish law, we should not convert him. We have no right to change a righteous Gentile into a sinful Jew.

(2) Question: A young woman, whose grandparents on both sides were Jewish, converts to Christianity. Her parents were reared as Christians and in turn, raised their children in the Christian faith. She is engaged to marry a Jew and asks a rabbi to solemnize the marriage. Before meeting the young man she had never had any connection with Judaism nor had she associated in any way with Jews. May a rabbi officiate at such a marriage without a prior conversion or without some promise on the part of this young woman that she will formally identify herself as a Jewess?

Answer: This question is one which is fairly clear in the law. There was plenty of opportunity in the history of the law to clarify it. The Marranos kept on coming from Spain and Portugal for centuries. Some of the later waves of refugees were already Christians for six or seven generations. What was their status in Jewish law? Did they need to be converted if they wanted to live as Jews again? The general basis of the decisions is that all who are children of a Jewish mother are Jews. Especially are their marriage rights unimpaired. The classic responsum is that of Solomon ben Simon Duran of Algiers (*Rashbash,* 89). He said that as long as their maternal line is Jewish, they remain Jewish "to the end of all generations." He is definite that it would be illegal to attempt to convert them, for such an attempt would imply that without such conversion they are not Jews and not obligated to perform *mitzvos*. But they are Jews and should not be converted. This is clearly the law.

However, it was generally customary to let them go through some ritual, or at least to promise *"chaverus"*; that is to say, to be loyal to Judaism. Thus, see Mogen Avraham to *Orah Hayyim* 326, end of Note 8, who reminds us that whatever requirements we make, they are not strictly required (see full discussion in *Reform Responsa*, p. 192 ff.).

Therefore in the case of this young lady, we must tell her that she is not required to be formally converted, but since she has lived as a Christian, we would ask her to study and declare in some way her desire to be loyal to the Jewish faith.

(3) Question: A man divorced his wife in a civil suit but turned down her request for a *get*, thereby interfering with her chances to marry again, inasmuch as the Orthodox man to whom she was engaged would not marry her until she received the *get*. The divorced husband now wishes to marry another woman and has asked a Reform rabbi to officiate at his second marriage. The rabbi is well aware of the circumstances surrounding the dissolving of the man's first marriage and had, indeed, urged that he give his divorced wife a *get*. Under these circumstances, should the rabbi officiate at the man's second marriage?

Answer: Since Reform (in America, at least) accepts the full validity of the civil divorce, there is no impediment to this man's remarriage. I do not see how a

Reform rabbi in America can refuse to marry him. He is, however, a mean fellow who refuses to allow his former wife, since he refuses to give her a *get*, to be married to the man of her choice. It is certainly our moral duty to persuade him to be considerate and to urge him to go through the ceremony of a *get*, even though to him as a Reform Jew it will have little meaning. We may even go so far as to speak to him and his new intended bride and say that unless he gives the *get*, the Orthodox rabbinate would consider this intended marriage invalid, though of course we do not. If after all pleading he refuses to be of help to his former wife, I do not see how we can refuse to officiate at his marriage.

(4) Question: A woman, married to a Jew for forty years, dies. Her husband produces a marriage certificate proving they had been married by a prominent rabbi who is no longer living. The husband claims his wife was also converted to Judaism by this rabbi but lacks a certificate of conversion as proof. The deceased woman had never been a member of a synagogue nor had she ever identified herself with Jewish life. All the children of this couple have married outside the Jewish faith and none have identified themselves as Jews. The cemetery officials question the right of the husband to have his wife buried in a Jewish cemetery despite his possession of the Jewish marriage certificate. What should be the position of the rabbi when the cemetery officials ask him to rule on whether or not this woman may be buried in the Jewish cemetery?

Answer: The question does not state what sort of a congregation conducts the cemetery in question. If it is a Reform congregation, then there is no problem at all. Reform Judaism in America had decided seventy-five years ago to permit the burial of an unconverted spouse in the

Jewish cemetery (see *Reform Jewish Practice,* Vol. I, p. 137 ff.). Of course, the presumption, then, is that the Christian funeral service is held in the chapel or in the home, but that in the Jewish cemetery there be no Christological services or symbols on the grave.

But what if this is not a Reform cemetery and there is no documentary proof that she was converted? The question of a person claiming to be converted without giving documentary proof has received considerable and complicated attention in the law, going back to the Talmud, in *Yevamos,* 47a, and has been discussed in the *Tur* and the *Shulchan Aruch, Yore Deah* 268:10, 11. Of course, if this family had lived as Jews, their claim would be accepted with almost no question, but they have not lived as Jews, and that would make the Jewish authorities more dubious.

Yet, in general, the tendency of the law is to accept such claims of having been converted. See Joel Sirkes (*Bach* to *Yore Deah* 268) who says, "At all events, it is our custom to believe a man's claims and to marry him to a Jewess." If the mood of the law is to accept such claims even for marriage, then surely they would be accepted for burial. Besides, the fact that they have a marriage certificate from a prominent rabbi creates a presumption, if not an absolute proof, that the Gentile woman had been converted.

(5) Question: A Jewish father and a non-Jewish mother, who has not been converted to Judaism, adopt a child. The child has been enrolled in a Jewish religious school. Is this a Jewish child?

Answer: Orthodox responsa are increasingly concerned with the question of adoption, a question which almost never was discussed before in Jewish law. Certainly the Orthodox law would require (based upon the Talmud in b. *Kesubot* 11a) that the infant should go through the formal process of conversion. The Central Conference of American Rabbis made a definite decision in its *Report on Marriage and Intermarriage,* 1947, that we should not subject an infant to the ceremonies of conversion. An infant boy, of course, is to be circumcised, but we would not dip an infant girl into the *mikvah.* Instead, the Conference formally decided that the children be enrolled in the Cradle Book of the Congregation and then enter the religious school so that the ceremony of Confirmation be deemed the substitute for formal conversion.

I do not think it would have been the mood of the Conference at the time or even now, to insist that the child is *not* to be considered a Jew until the whole process is completed. Certainly most of us will agree that the intention of the parents would be sufficient for us to deem the child attending our school or enrolled in our school as already Jewish.

(6) Question: An elderly man wishes to marry his childless, equally elderly sister-in-law, the widow of his deceased brother. An Orthodox rabbi has refused to officiate at the marriage and insists that the man must undergo *chalitza.* They then go to a Reform rabbi and argue that their marriage is valid on the grounds of *yibbum.* What should the Reform rabbi do?

Answer: Scripture prohibits a man from marrying his deceased brother's wife (Leviticus 18:11). The only exception is when the husband dies childless; in that case the brother is *required* to marry the widow in levirate marriage (Deuteronomy 25:5-9). This elderly couple to which the question refers asks to be married on the basis of the Biblical law of levirate marriage (*yibbum*). The Orthodox rabbi refuses to officiate but insists that the man give his brother's widow *chalitza*. Should we officiate?

It is possible that a Reform rabbi might officiate at this marriage, but not on the ground mentioned by the couple, namely, to officiate at a *"yibbum,"* although, in a sense, *yibbum* is a factor. Already in Talmudic times levirate marriage was deprecated. See the opinions of Bar Kappara and Abba Saul (b. *Yevamos* 109a). The later authorities are divided on the question of the desirability of levirate marriage. The Sephardic scholars would recommend it but the Ashkenazic scholars (northern France, Germany, etc.) who lived in the lands where monogamy prevailed, all opposed levirate marriage. See the opinion of Joseph Caro in *Shulchan Aruch, Even Hoezer* 165:1, and the contrary opinions of the Ashkenazim cited by Isserles in his note (*ibid*). Levirate marriage, therefore, may not be performed in the Ashenazic (monogamic) lands.

If a Reform rabbi would consent to officiate, it would be basically on other grounds. The justification would be that not every prohibition in the Scriptural law is of equal validity to us. Some biblical laws with regard to marriage actually run counter to our conscience. The biblical law reveals the inferiority of the status of women. It is a principle in Reform that men and women should be of equal status before the law. That is why the Orthodox *get* is not acceptable to us, since it gives to the husband alone the privilege of giving divorce. Therefore Reform congregations in the United States accept the validity of civil divorce, or in some countries will grant the woman the divorce on her initiative.

There is the same inequality in the status of women in the laws of forbidden degrees of kinship. A man may marry his niece but a woman may not marry her nephew. More specifically, in the case which we are discussing, a man may marry his deceased wife's sister, but a woman may not marry her deceased husband's brother. Furthermore, the particular prohibition involved in this case (that a woman may not marry her deceased husband's brother) is after all not a prohibition based upon consanguinity of the proposed partners but only on affinity. Finally, there would be stronger grounds for refusing to marry this couple if they were young and there would be a likelihood of children being born of this union.

All these arguments in favor of officiating at the marriage might possibly apply even if the widow and her deceased husband had had children; but since she and her deceased husband were childless, it becomes even more possible to officiate. While there is the division of opinion mentioned above (stemming from the Talmud), dividing the Ashkenazic from the Sephardic scholars as to whether *yibbum* or *chalitza* is preferable, nevertheless the levirate marriage cannot be entirely deprived of its firm biblical status. So all scholars agree that a levirate marriage can easily be legitimate. If, for example, a man and his childless brother's widow did have sexual relationship without formal marriage, the bulk of legal opinion is that she thereby becomes his wife and this becomes a valid marriage. See *Mishna Yevamos* VI:1 and the discussion in *Shulchan Aruch, Even Hoezer* 166:7, especially the discussion in *Pis-che Teshuva.*

For all these reasons it is possible that a Reform rabbi might officiate at this marriage of the elderly couple. Nevertheless, one should hesitate before officiating at a marriage to which most of the Ashkenazic authorities would be opposed.

(7) Question: A Reform congregation has printed a Hebrew verse from the Bible on its letterheads in which the Tetragrammaton appears. A member of the congregation argues that this is in violation of the law against taking the name of God in vain, as letters are often thrown away and even burnt. A similar argument was used when a biblical verse containing the four-letter Name of God was engraved over the synagogue Ark. What position should the rabbi take on this question?

Answer: While Reform congregations do not follow strictly the laws about writing the name of God in secular papers, etc., and would not deem it necessary to do as Orthodox people do and spell the name of God, "G-d," nevertheless, when it comes to the Tetragrammaton in Hebrew, we have a strong sense of reverence.

In general, the law is that unless the Name is written with conscious intent, as a scribe does when writing it in the Torah, the Name is not actually holy. However, it is chiefly out of reverence that Orthodox leaders would object to printing the Name of God on papers that could be taken to unclean places (although the printed Name is not really holy.) There are Orthodox authorities, for example, who while objecting to printing the Name of God in newspapers, would defend the embroidering of the Tetragrammaton on the Torah cover, where it would be protected. (See Shalom Mordecai Schwadron in *Yerushalaim D'Dahava* by Ben Zion Katz.) But to print it on paper which can be taken to all sorts of places is generally objected to. I believe we would share that sentiment. But it is only a matter of sentiment, rather than strict law, that we object to the use of the Tetragrammaton regularly in the Temple letterhead.

(8) Question: What should be our position with respect

to sitting *shiva* on Chol Ha-moed Succos and Pesach? Despite the tradition which declares that one should not sit *shivah* on these days, is it proper for mourners to receive visitors who come to offer their sympathies?

Answer: Again, this is a question of our feeling in the matter, with due consideration of the law. The law is definitely that there should be no regular *avelus* on Chol Hamoed (see *Orah Hayyim* 548:4). Nevertheless, the law itself has certain mitigations. In that same section it says that while there may not be public manifestations of mourning, yet certain matters that are not public (*b'zina*) are permitted. And also in Number 6 it says that we may make efforts to console the mourners during the festival. Since we do not follow the rules of *shiva* strictly, it would seem without objection that we should allow people to do what the *Shulchan Aruch* says in *Orah Hayyim* 548:6, permitting them to come and give their consolation. What is forbidden is, after all, a strict ritual of *avelus,* not merely meeting people for the human consolation derived from it.

(9) Question: Catering for a Bar Mitzvah reception following a Sabbath service has become a commonplace fea-ture of present-day Jewish life. Kosher caterers who come into the synagogue will deliver and prepare the food before the Sabbath begins. What position should we take with respect to non-kosher caterers who deliver the food on the Sabbath and prepare it in the synagogue kitchen?

Answer: This question, also, touches an unsolved larger problem in the relationship between Reform and the legal tradition. How strict should we be in Sabbath observance? We have to go by our feelings in the matter. We certainly would not ask a Jewish caterer to work for us on the Sabbath, nor would we make an arrangement with a

Gentile caterer, asking him specifically to come on the Sabbath and work. We simply ask him to cater the Bar Mitzvah. The day which he picks for his preparatory work is his choice. We are not paying him for the day's work. We are paying him for the job. All this would be strictly in the line of Jewish law with regard to Gentile employment.

But this, also, happening in the synagogue, makes a difference. According to the law, even the general contract permitting a Christian to work on his own time, would not be permitted if the work is done on a Jewish street, because it would look as if the Jew commanded the work to be done on the Sabbath, and we are concerned with the look of things (*maris ayin,* i.e., with the impression it makes on the public). We must therefore decide this matter of whether we can have a Christian caterer work on the Sabbath preparing food, according to the impression it would make on the congregation. I think there are some congregations that might not mind it. I think that most would be unfavorably impressed, for the sake of *maris ayin.* If the congregation would not object to it, I do not think the rabbi should raise an objection. But as a contrast, the Gift Corner, which is run by Jews and involves buying and selling on the congregation premises, should not be permitted to be open on the Sabbath.

(10) Question: What position should a Reform synagogue take with respect to biblical dietary laws when food is served within synagogue premises? Granted that the Talmudic extensions of biblical dietary laws are not upheld by the Reform movement, and that the Pittsburgh Platform of 1885 declared obsolete "all such laws as regulate diet," is it not incumbent upon a Reform synagogue to prohibit serving within the synagogue at least those foods which are forbidden in the Bible?

Answer: An honored colleague was asked by a family at the marriage at which he was to officiate, to wear a hat during the ceremony. He conceded to their traditional sentiments. After the ceremony, they went into the dinner and *trefe* seafoods were served; and he rebuked them, quite justly, on the ground of their hypocrisy. There is considerable inconsistency (to say the least) among our people in the matter of foods. But we are concerned, not with consistency, but with the sense of propriety.

There can, of course, be no discussion from the legal point of view on the question of forbidden food. Yet a large proportion of our people follow certain restrictions, and these restrictions have become a tradition with them. Laws which are rabbinical extension of the Bible (even though the rabbis themselves may consider them as directly derived from the Bible and therefore *m'd'oraiso*) no longer have meaning to our people, such as questions of meat and milk and the salting and soaking of meat. But the forbidden animals are still deemed forbidden in the sentiments of our people. This certainly, if not religious, is reverential, and the synagogue should not discourage it by bad example.

54

THE WOMAN'S WIG

Mr. Alfred Rubens of London asks the following question which came up in the course of his research for a book on "Costumes." Grunwald, in the article, "Costumes" in the Universal Jewish Encyclopedia, says that when the women's wig (*sheitel*) was introduced in the late Middle Ages, the rabbis violently opposed its use. What is the evidence of this opposition and what was its basis?

THERE can be no doubt that Jewish women (some of them) wore wigs long before the Middle Ages. The Mishnah and the Talmud make mention of women wearing *peah nochris* ("the lock or hair of a stranger"). The Mishnah (*Shabbas VI, 5*) speaks of what a woman is permitted to carry out into the courtyard on the Sabbath and it mentions: "Her hair, the hair of others, and a wig (*peah nochris*)." In the Talmud (b. *Nazir* 28b) there is a discussion of a woman making a vow to be a Nazarite. When the term of a Nazarite vow is over, the Nazarite must shave the head. Now, may her husband annul her vow on the ground that he objects to a wife with a shaved head? In the discussion of the question, one of the discussants says: "But she may wear a *peah nochris* (a wig)."

If, then, women wore wigs in Mishnaic and Talmudic times, how could rabbis in latter Middle Ages object to it? There are a number of objections which they could and did adduce from the older literature itself.

The first reason may be described as puritanical. They considered the sight of a woman's hair to be sexually provocative (*ervah*). The Talmud (b. *Berachos* 24a) says that the sound of a woman's voice, the sight of her skin and the sight of her hair are all provocative. This puritanical attitude became a fixed motif in the law. The *Shulchan Aruch* (*Orach Chayyim* 75:2) says that it is forbidden to pray within sight of a woman's hair.

Therefore it became an established custom for women to cover their hair entirely with a cloth. That custom of women covering their hair was already well established in Mishnaic times. In Mishnah *Nedarim* III, 8, the law is given that if a man vows not to have any benefit from the "black-haired," his vow does not include women. The Talmud

(*Nedarim* 30b) explains this by saying that women's hair is always covered by a cloth (so their black hair is not seen).

It will be of interest to the writer of a book on "Costumes" to know that (at least in France in the twelfth century) women always used a *white* cloth to cover their heads. This is clear from Rashi's comment to the Talmudic passage.

Joshua Boas (sixteenth century, Italy) in his commentary, *Shiltey Ha-Gibborim* to Alfasi on the passage on the Sabbath law cited above (that a woman may go out on Sabbath wearing a wig) does not disapprove of the custom. He gives the wigs an Italian name, *"Coronale."* In fact he says that the sexual provocation objected to in the Talmud applies only to a woman's own hair, not to a wig.

But Joshua Boas seems to be the only one who permits the wigs. All traceable later opinions oppose it. Issachar Eilenberg of Posen (sixteenth-seventeenth century) in his *Beer Sheva* (Responsa 18) attacks Boas's permissive decision and cites (from a manuscript) the contrary opinion of another and contemporary Italian, Rabbi Samuel Judah Katzenellenbogen. Katzenellenbogen says that when the Rabbis of the Talmud permitted the wig, they permitted it only if worn under the usual head covering.

So it is clear that by the sixteenth-seventeenth century when the custom grew widespread of wearing wigs (evidently it started in Italy) the women began to wear them instead of (not under) the white kerchief. This is evident from the responsum of Jacob Emden of Altona (1697-1778). In his responsum I, 9, he says: "The wig is prohibited if placed on the top of the head in place of the hair (i.e., covering the hair); but it is not prohibited if it is put under the kerchief and on the side of the temples." Therefore, the hair was again visible to any passer-by who, of course, would not necessarily know whether it was the woman's own hair or not. So the old puritanical objection was raised again against women showing their hair in public. Eilenberg, who quotes Katzenellenbogen, decides that the Mishnah permits a woman to go into a courtyard, but not into a public place. To appear in public, that is a violation of *"das Yehudis,"* i.e., the decencies required of a Jewess.

The next scholar to give a full discussion of the matter was Eleazar Fleckeles (1754-1826) Rabbi in Prague (cf., *Teshuvah Me-ahavah* I, 47-48). He raises a new objection, namely, that the hair comes from the dead and it is forbidden to have any benefit from a dead body.

Moses Sofer of Pressberg (1763-1839) the leading authority of Hungarian Jewry, in his will forbids the women of his family ever to wear a wig. This will was so greatly honored that it was published with a long commentary by Akiba Joseph Schlessinger and widely studied. In the book called *Lev Ha-Ivri,* at the passage in Sofer's will where he forbids the wig, Schlessinger lists many other authorities who forbid it. I cannot cite the exact page since my copy of *Lev Ha- Ivri* has no pagination. But the passage is easy to find by following the text of the will. Schlessinger's commentary is well worth reading, not so much for the arguments (for they are only a rehash of the earlier arguments mentioned) but for the strong indignation expressed, indicating that the objections are against what was deemed immoral, and also against a new fashion in the fear of all novelty.

55

SPORTS AND ATHLETICS

ATHLETICS and competitive games in Talmudic times had, to use an American sporting expression, two strikes against them. In Mishnaic and Talmudic times, public sporting spectacles, public games, etc., were associated with the Greek and Roman heathendom, against which Judaism fought its greatest battles. The Greeks with their public athletics in the stadiums, the Romans with their gladiatorial contests, man against man, man against beast, and beast against beast—all of these were hateful to the Jews for a number of reasons. One, these public spectacles were always dedicated to the gods and hence were part of heathendom; and then, also, a great deal of betting took place at these contests, and gambling was strictly forbidden by Jewish law. The Talmud (in *Avodah Zora* 18b) forbids attending circuses, stadiums, etc. In the discussion of gambling, too, besides the expected mention of dice play, there was reference to sporting contests. The Talmud (*Sanhedrin* 25a) develops the Mishnaic objection to those "who fly doves," speaks of racing pigeons, one against the other, and also (25b) of racing any other animals.

These two objections (heathendom and gambling) were carried over in all medieval discussions in the responsa literature and additional objections were developed. However, the very fact that the question came up century after century, indicates that the people themselves did follow the various sports and therefore the rabbis had to be asked to pass their judgment on the popular practice. Thus it was with mixed dancing, which never was suppressed, and so it was with gambling, concerning which there is a wealth of material in the responsa literature. As for direct references to what might be called games and sport, there is a fair amount in the responsa. Of course, one rarely finds any outright approval of a game or sport because of the shadow of the negative tradition mentioned above.

The subject which occupies most space in the responsa is hunting. Jews from ancient times fished and trapped animals. In medieval Europe, where game was plentiful and hunting was the dominant sport among the nobility, this occupation found its way into Jewish life and there are references to it in almost every century. Isaac of Vienna (early thirteenth century) in *Or Zoruah*, II, "Laws of Sabbath," 86:17, discusses the possibility (upon Talmudic grounds) of permitting hunting with dogs, but he says: "But I say whoever hunts animals with dogs, as the Gentiles do, will not have the joy of the Leviathan feast," (i.e., will not go to heaven). This is cited almost precisely in the next century by the famous authority, Meir of Rothenburg, in his Responsa 27 (edition Berlin).

But hunting continued among the Jews and there are responsa on the subject in almost every generation. In *Pachad Yitzchok*, by Isaac Lamperonti (seventeenth century) there is one responsum by Sabbatai ben Elisha, another by Isaac Lamperonti himself. It seems clear to the scholars that hunting with dogs is forbidden on the basis of *Or Zoruah*, quoted above. However, when the result of these various decisions is finally codified in the *Shulchan Aruch* (*Orah Hayyim* 316, 2, in the note of Isserles) it is still uncertain whether hunting with dogs is absolutely forbidden. Isserles simply says that on the Sabbath, urging a dog against a beast constitutes "forbidden" hunting, and then adds: "And *some say* that even on weekdays it is forbidden to hunt with dogs."

When gunpowder came into general use, and hunting of animals could be followed even without dogs, the questions took another form: Is it permitted to shoot animals? This involved a question frequently discussed in the responsa: Is it permitted consciously to make an animal unfit for food? (Since the animal must be properly slaughtered, if it is shot, it becomes unfit.) This question is, also, not quite settled in the law and is debated extensively. But Samson Morpurgo (1681-1740, Italy) in his responsa, *Shemesh Zedakah*, 18, uses another argument, that God gave us the animals for food, but not to torture. *Shechita* is painless, but shooting hot lead into the body of an animal must be terribly painful and, therefore, is forbidden on the ground of cruelty to animals.

The question is discussed as late as the eighteenth-nineteenth century. Ezekiel Landau of Prague (1713-1793) was asked about a Jewish estate owner who hunted. He adds one more argument to all the preceding ones in the various responsa: He says that it is against Jewish law for a man to bring himself into danger by entering the forests where animals lurk. It is doubtful whether Jews did much hunting in eastern Europe in the early nineteenth century because the only question relating to this matter, answered by Moses Sofer of Pressburg, (*Yore Deah* 52, 53) is whether birds and animals found with bullets in them are kosher or not.

While hunting, especially with dogs, was objected to but nevertheless practiced, horseback riding was found less objectionable. Israel Bruna of Ratisbon (fifteenth century) was asked whether Jews may be spectators at horse races and at tournaments. He permits the first on practical grounds and objects to the second without giving an explanation. Of course, he is dubious because the whole sport seems to him to be rather un-Jewish. His wording, perhaps, will be of interest to the modern reader (Responsum 71): "I was asked whether it is permitted to be a spectator at the pleasures of the Gentiles, when, in their games, they race their horses, and the man whose horse comes first, wins gold. Is this to be forbidden just as hunting of beasts and birds is forbidden in the Talmud in the first chapter of *Avodeh Zara*? I permitted it, because this is not primarily for pleasure, but to teach skill to buy horses, in order to escape from one's enemies, as I have seen people do." (In other words, it was of practical advantage, he thought, for Jews to become expert judges of horses.) Then he adds as follows: "But I doubt whether one (i.e., a Jew) may be a spectator when they run against each other with lances, etc." (i.e., at the tournaments).

The responsa literature is only interested in the legal questions involved, but incidentally (one might say without intending it) they reveal social history. Moses Minz, rabbi in Germany in the fifteenth century, in his Responsa 73, is discussing the oft-discussed question of whether one may annul a hastily made vow. The whole responsum deals with this question, but *incidentally* he mentions the reason that the man made the vow: "I was asked concerning this man who loved horseback riding and whose delight was constantly to ride in and outside of the city. His mother and father-in-law rebuked him. He, in anger, made the vow, 'If I ever stride my horse again, I will give a hundred gulden to charity.' " It is evident that horse lovers could hardly have been rare.

With regard to ball games, the law was generally liberal. The only restrictions are whether ball games may be played on the Sabbath or on holidays. The *Tosfos* (eleventh, twelfth century, to *Beza*, 12a, at the bottom of the page) simply says: "It is customary for the people to play ball on the holiday in the public domain. The ball is called *Pelota*." In *Sheboley ha-Leket*, 121, Rashi is quoted as describing the *Pelota* as a ball covered with hide. Moses Isserles (sixteenth century, in *Darche Moshe* to *Tur, Orah Hayyim* 308) cites the statement of the *Tosfos* that it is permitted to play ball on holidays, even in public. Evidently this game, or ball games of various kinds, were quite popular.

It is interesting to record at least one sport that had met with no disapproval at all and which, also, must have been widespread, since the famous rabbi who records the question involved, demonstrates that he understands the sport well. He must have seen a lot of it. The rabbi, Asher ben Jechiel (thirteenth century) emigrated from Germany to Spain. The matter concerned a wrestling match between two Jews. When one was "thrown," he was injured and lost the sight of one eye. The question asked was whether the opponent is liable to damages for the injury. Asher ben Jechiel's answer (*Responsa* 101:6) is as follows: "These two men wrestle with each other by their common consent, and if one injured the other, it is without any intent to do so; for their only intent when they both wrestle is to cause each other to fall. Now, when one exerts himself against the other, it is impossible for him so to control his strength that the other shall fall gently and not be hurt; for they wrestle with all their strength and each tries to make the other fall."

In general, sports and games came into medieval Jewish life with a bad heritage from pagan times. The people however, influenced by their environment, enjoyed various sports as is reflected by the frequent discussions in the responsa literature. Hunting, especially with dogs, was largely prohibited. Horseback riding and racing was more or less permitted (although Israel Bruna says nothing about betting, which would be frowned upon). Ball games were widely played. Wrestling seems to have been completely approved.

56

HOMOSEXUALITY

A group in the Temple is planning a discussion program on the question of homosexuality. What is there in Jewish law on this subject? (From I.B.C., Florida.)

CONSIDERING the prevalence of homosexuality in the East, one can say in general that it is remarkable how little place the whole question occupies in Jewish law. After the biblical prohibitions, there is almost nothing in the Mishnah, Talmud, and Codes on the question. The Talmud itself explains (perhaps unconscious of the fact that it is explaining it) why there is so little discussion of the question. In b. *Kiddushin* 82a it discusses the prohibition of seclusion (*yichud*) with any of the forbidden sexual degrees of relationship; i.e., a man must avoid being, or must not be permitted to be, alone with a woman with whom he is forbidden to have sexual relationship. Then the Talmud says that Jewish people are not under the suspicion of homosexuality (i.e., it is highly improbable among Jews) and therefore it is not forbidden for a Jewish man to be alone with another Jewish man.

There is an interesting development of this Talmudic statement in the way this dictum (that Jews are not suspected, etc.) is carried over to the *Shulchan Aruch*. The

Shulchan Aruch (in *Even Hoezer* 24) states the law as derived from the Talmud that since Jewish men are not suspected of homosexuality, they are not forbidden to be alone with each other. Then Joseph Caro adds: "However, in these generations when sinful men have increased, it is better to avoid isolation with another male." Moses Rifkes (Poland, seventeenth century) in his *Be'er Ha-Gola,* gives the Talmudic reference for the first part of the statement; but as for the latter part of the statement ("Nowadays when evil men have increased," etc.) he notes carefully: "These are his own words; there is no reference for this precaution in the Talmudic literature, and Joseph Caro makes the precaution on his own authority." Why should Joseph Caro have made such an extra precaution which the Talmud does not require, against males being secluded together? The *Bes Shemuel* (Samuel of Furth) explains, in the name of Joel Sirkes (Poland, sixteenth century), that in the land in which he (Joseph Caro) lived, homosexuality was rampant, but "not in our land," hence it is not required for males to avoid isolation (see *Bach to Tur,* same reference). Of course this is correct historically. The Arab lands were notorious for homosexuality and Joseph Caro knew that. But to the rest of Jewry it seemed farfetched to prohibit males to associate with each other for fear of homosexuality.

Now as to the Biblical sources: They are Leviticus 18:22 and 20:13, prohibiting male sexuality with males; also Deuteronomy 23:18, which prohibits male prostitutes who were maintained in connection with the idolatrous temples. So, more specifically, I Kings 14:24, speaking of the evils of Judah when it became corrupt, says that the people copied "the abominations of the nations around them and had male prostitution." The prohibition is carried over into the

Mishnah, *Sanhedrin* VII, 4, where it is briefly mentioned among the whole list of sexual relationships. Then the fullest discussion in the Talmud is in *Sanhedrin* 54b. There is a discussion whether illicit intercourse is punishable by death if it is involved with a person under the age of nine. The Rambam in *Hilchos Issure Biah* 1:14 summarizes this Talmudic discussion and says that both the active and passive partners are culpable (as the Talmud says) but the punishment of death should not be inflicted upon a boy under nine (evidently a young boy would hardly initiate such action). But Maimonides adds that although the punishment of death does not apply in this case, they should be punished by the courts. In other words, such intercourse with a boy under nine is *potur* from the death penalty, but *asur* (forbidden per se) and should be punished.

All in all, considering how much detail there is in the law on every kind of forbidden sexual relationship, the very paucity of biblical and post-biblical law on the matter speaks well for the normalcy and the purity of the Jewish people.

57

FREEZING OF BODIES (CRYOBIOLOGY)

According to a newly developed scientific technique, cryobiology, it seems possible to freeze a human body and after considerable time, perhaps months or years, thaw out the body and revive the person. The question asked is: Is it permissible by Jewish law and Jewish legal tradition to take the body of a person dying of a disease at present incurable and freeze it for a long time, even years, and then to revive him when a cure for his sickness will have been discovered? The suggestion involves many difficulties in the law, as the questioner correctly points out, namely, has a person the right to consent to such a procedure with regard to himself? What is the status of his wife and children? Are they in mourning as if the person were dead? When shall he be revived? Who will decide, etc.? (From Rabbi Joshua D. Haberman, Trenton, New Jersey.)

I believe that we may assume that these wider questions involving cryobiology are for the present largely theoretical. Most of the questions raised involve freezing the body for years and then reviving it when some cure will have been found for the sick person's disease. It is hard to believe that it would be possible to freeze a body for five or ten years and then revive it without the body having deteriorated at all. In other words, in the case of all strange remedies discussed in the law, the question is always asked how provable a remedy it is, and whether there are not dangers involved in it.

But the basic question here is another one entirely. The proposal is to freeze such bodies in cases only of people already dying or virtually dying of an incurable disease. So it amounts to the delaying of the death of a dying person. This is clearly prohibited by Jewish law. While one may not do anything at all to hasten the death of a dying person, one may also not do anything at all to prevent his dying. Such a person has the right to die. Please see *Reform Responsa*, pp. 119-122. Of all the material quoted there, I quote from page 120:

Roughly contemporary with this Spanish scholar is the famous German mystic-legal work "The Book of the Pious," from which many customs and laws are often cited. In this book (p. 100, 315-18) it says: "If a man is sick and in pain and dying and asks another man to kill him mercifully, this request must *not* be fulfilled, nor may the man take his own life. Still, you may not put salt on his tongue to keep him alive longer." Then it continues: "Ecclesiastes says, 'There is a time to live and a time to die.' " Why does the author need to add this obvious fact? The answer is that he has in mind the following situation: "If a man is dying, do not pray too hard that his soul return, that is, that he revive from the coma.   He can at best live only a few days and in those days he will endure great suffering. So, 'there is a time to die.' " (See also the long note, 4, in "Sefer Chasidim," ed. Margolies, p. 34; also note to 723.)

In other words, the answer would be that if there were a trustworthy remedy already available for the disease but the remedy involved freezing, it would all be permitted. But if there is only speculation that some day a remedy might be discovered and on the basis of that speculation the process of dying is prevented, that is contrary to the spirit of Jewish law.

58

PORNOGRAPHIC LITERATURE

What material on the question of pornographic literature is found in our Jewish traditional writings? (From Rabbi Joshua O. Haberman, Trenton, New Jersey.)

THE question of pornography in speech and writing would concern the ethical rather than the legal literature, but the following is what there is in the ancient literature and the tradition based upon it.

The chief source is Deuteronomy 23:15. In discussing the duty to keep the camp of the Hebrew army sanitary, the verse in Deuteronomy expresses itself as follows: "For God walketh in the midst of thy camp. Therefore shall thy camp be holy, that He see no unseemly thing in thee." The phrase translated "unseemly thing" in Hebrew is *"ervas dovor,"* and so "unseemly thing" can be translated as "unseemly word." In fact the *Targum* uses the word *"pisgom"* which means "word," and Ibn Ezra explains the phrase to mean "nothing unseemly in deed or word."

More specifically, in Leviticus *Rabba* 24:7, Rabbi Samuel ben Nachmann says that the phrase in Deuteronomy refers to pornographic speech (*nibbul peh.*). In fact the Talmud in *Ketuboth* 5b, speaks of the fingers and the ears and refers to the stick which is mentioned in the Deuteronomy passage for digging up the earth and covering the dirt, and also refers to the fact that the word used in the Deuteronomy passage for "weapons" is *"ozen,"* which also means "ears." Upon this the Talmud says that the passage implies that if a man hears unfit speech, in other words, pornographic speech, he should use his fingers to stop up his ears so as not to listen.

There are a number of more direct statements about pornographic speech. The Talmud in *Shabbas* 33a says that misfortunes come to us and young men die prematurely because of unseemly speech. This is based upon the verse in Isaiah 9:16, which refers to "the mouth that speaketh unseemly words." The Talmud in *Ketuboth* 8b says quite straightforwardly, "Everyone knows why the bride enters the *chuppah* (here the word *"chuppah"* means the connubial room) but the man who will make sexy jokes about it will be punished by God's decree."

Therefore (and here we come closer to legal decision) the *Shulchan Aruch* in *Even Hoezer* 25:1-2, speaks of the duty of a man to avoid such speech even when he is alone with his wife. This is also based on the statement of the Talmud in *Chagiga* 5b. Actually the whole matter of the avoidance of pornography, although it is more ethical than strictly legal, is organized as a series of legal regulations for self-control in speech (*Even Hoezer* 25:1, etc., and *Orah Hayyim* 200:9).

This about covers the strictly legal material.

59

USING THE BLOOD OF THE DEAD

The USSR for thirty-five years has been using the blood of the recently deceased for the benefit of patients who need transfusions. This blood is useable for transfusions up to three months; then the plasma can be extracted and frozen and be good for five years. What is the attitude of Jewish legal tradition to this procedure? (From Dr. Harold Bernstein, Rockville Center, New York.)

FROM the point of view of Jewish legal tradition, which in many ways expresses Jewish ethical feelings, there are many objections to this procedure insofar as it applies to the bodies of deceased Jews and insofar as the blood is to be used for the benefit of Jewish patients. The objections are as follows:

1. The blood is deemed an integral part of the body and it is a duty to bury the entire body of the deceased, including the blood. Thus if a body of a murdered man or a slain soldier is found with his blood soaked into the earth around him or into his clothes, the blood soaked objects must be buried with the body.

2. It is forbidden for the living to derive any benefit from the bodies of the dead. This objection is often applied to the planned use of cornea and of bone from a bone bank, etc.

3. It is especially forbidden by Jewish law to eat blood. This is a biblical prohibition and is the reason for the thorough soaking and salting of meat before it may be eaten.

The first legal principle concerning the duty of burying the entire body, limbs, eyes, blood, etc., applies as a general rule. However, if it is demonstrable that certain parts of the body are a remedy for a sick person who is in grave danger, then the necessities for healing would constitute an exception, as it also constitutes an exception to point two, namely, not to have any benefit from a dead body. It is, therefore, necessary to go into the question of the legal status of healing, as to what may be used for healing the sick.

The laws are based upon the verse (Leviticus 18:5): "Observe My commandments which a man shall do and live by them." From this verse the conclusion was drawn that whenever life is endangered, the rule is that the ritual and Sabbath laws are suspended (in fact, all laws are suspended except those involving idolatry, murder and immorality). In this spirit the long chain of legal tradition is finally codi-

fied in the *Shulchan Aruch, Yore Deah* 155. There the law
can be generally stated as follows: If a patient is not dangerously sick, he may use anything which is forbidden by
rabbinic law (i.e., by secondary laws, except idolatrous
spells, etc.). If a patient, however, is *dangerously* sick, then
he may use even things prohibited by biblical law (which is
primary). Thus the principle is that anything at any time
may be used for the benefit of a patient who is gravely sick.
The Sabbath must be violated in his behalf, food must be
given to him on Yom Kippur, and all forbidden foods are
permitted to him. But if he is not *gravely* sick, these permissions are, as has been mentioned, somewhat restricted.

How this works out can be seen in a responsum of Judah
Lev Zirelsohn, the famous rabbi of Kishenev (*Lev Yehu-
dah*, 45). He was asked the question, what to do when the
doctor recommended that a patient with anemia eat liver
which is full of blood, the liver to be cooked in butter (here,
then, are two prohibitions, the blood itself and the meat
with butter). He said, "If the patient has an ordinary tendency to anemia, the doctor should be asked whether there
are not other more acceptable remedies, but if it is *perni-
cious* anemia, then the patient not only may take the remedy, i.e., the blood and the meat with butter, but it is his
duty to take it, since the saving of life is primary."

More specifically with regard to the use of blood is the
responsum of Jacob Reischer, Rabbi of Metz (seventeenth-
eighteenth century). He said that the people of his community use as a remedy for various sicknesses (not necessarily grave ones) dried goat's blood, and he says that this is
permissible because the blood has been so dried up that it
has become like another substance.

A similar responsum, and more modern, is by David
Hoffman, the great German legal authority of the past gen-

eration (*Melamed L'Hoyil, Yore Deah* 34). He was asked whether a man may take medicine made from blood which has been chemically broken up and in a new form. He says the blood may be used since it has now been so changed that it can be considered as another substance. See also Grodzinski (*Achiezer* III, 31:3).

There are a number of secondary elements involved in the question. One consideration involves the method by which the material is taken into the body of the patient. The law makes a distinction between "the way thing are enjoyed" (*k'derech hanaoson*) and "the way things are not enjoyed" (cf., *Yore Deah* 155:3). If, for example, forbidden food is given to a patient in such a way that he enjoys it as food, it would be frowned upon. But if it is taken in a way so that there is no enjoyment, it is permissible. A transfusion of blood involves no direct eating or enjoyment from eating and therefore is permissible so far as that is concerned.

Of course the special difficulties in this question are due to the involvement in the USSR procedure with the bodies of the dead. If it were not for that fact it would be a rather simple problem. A well known Orthodox authority, the late Hillel Posek of Tel Aviv, editor of the rabbinic magazine "*Ha-Posek*" (in No. 96-97, 9th year, Responsum 1082) gives a general and unrestricted permission for the use of blood transfusions. He says that in the first place the prohibition against the consumption of blood is essentially a prohibition against eating the blood of cattle or birds. It does not apply to the blood of fish or any other animals, including man. Of course because it may look like forbidden blood, then if a person's teeth or gums are injured and some blood appears on the bread he is eating, he may not eat that bread, but that is only because of the appearance of the blood. However, the unseen blood that may be sucked from the gums and swallowed is not forbidden. This law is clearly stated in the *Shulchan Aruch, Yore Deah* 66:10. Maggid Mishnah (Don Vidal of Tolosa) in his commentary to Mai-—monides' laws of forbidden foods (2, 3) says such blood is absolutely permitted.

Then Hillel Posek comments further that whatever prohibition there is, is only a prohibition because of appearance (that the blood looks like forbidden animal blood, hence it may not be eaten or swallowed, as the legal phrase is, "in the way of enjoyment"). But inserted in the veins, etc., which is not by way of enjoyment, there is no prohibition at all against the procedure, even with regard to sick people who are not in danger. But all this general permission applies to blood taken from living people. Hillel Posek did not know, as the present writer did not know, of the practice in the USSR of taking the blood from the dead. Hence the limitations which I mentioned above.

To sum up, the general attitude of Jewish law would be as follows: There would be some hesitation about using the blood from Jewish bodies because of the special requirements with regard to their burial and the prohibition against benefiting from them. But this is only a general hesitation because it is overridden by the outright permission to use any valuable remedy for a patient who is in danger. For such a patient the blood itself can be used. If the patient is not in danger, then the blood plasma, which changes the appearance of the blood and its original form, may be used.

60

PSYCHODELIC DRUGS

Is the use of the so-called psychodelic drugs as a spur to religious insight known or justified in Judaism? Aside from the claimed inspirational effect of the drugs, would Jewish tradition condone the use of such drugs? (Mrs. Maurice Samuel, Editor of *Keeping Posted,* UAHC, New York.)

THE question of the use of psychodelic drugs is a difficult one to discuss on the basis of Jewish legal (and other) literature. Yet the very reason for this difficulty is to the credit of the Jewish experience and tradition. Though the Jews have lived for centuries in contact with the Orient and in the Arab lands (where the use of various drugs, opium, hashish, etc., was prevalent) there is no statement of which I am aware in the entire legal literature as to any sort of drug addiction. They knew, of course, of the existence and the use of anesthetic drugs, as in the discussion in the Talmud (*Kiddushin* 21b) which deals with the painless piercing of the ear of a Hebrew slave. But the whole Jewish literary experience seems to know nothing of drug addiction, nor for that matter does it know anything of addiction to alcohol (i.e., the actual disease of alcoholism as opposed to occasional drunkenness). The question therefore must be discussed by analogy with related matters, as is frequently necessary in the discussion of certain modern topics and their connection with our traditional literature.

First, then, as to the use of a drug as a spur to religious inspiration or revelation or illumination: The ancients, of course, had a great belief in the significance of dreams and considered that knowledge could be imparted by God to man through a dream. That is why Deuteronomy 13:2 couples "that prophet" with "that dreamer of dreams," but it is noticeable that the "dreamer of dreams" is used in a deprecatory fashion of the false prophet, since dreams are so complex and therefore easy to misinterpret and to be used as a means of misleading. Jeremiah discusses the prophets and the dreamers and (even though he believes there can be true dreams) he speaks of the false prophets in relation to dreams. See Jeremiah 23:25: "I have heard what the prohets have said, that prophesy lies in my name, saying: 'I have dreamed, I have dreamed.' "

The Jewish philosophers of the Middle Ages who were deeply concerned with the question of revelation and the vehicles of revelation generally agree with the opinion of Maimonides, namely, that while revelation *may* come through dreams, such revelation is usually symbolic and mystic and needs to be interpreted. The true revelation comes through the clear intellect. Therefore the more the intellect is developed and refined and kept free from confusing passions, the more likelihood there is of Divine communication and revelation. All this is discussed clearly by Maimonides in his *Hilchos Yesodey Torah,* VII, 6. He bases this opinion upon the statement of Rabbi Jochanan in the Talmud (*Nedarim* 38a). In other words, the essence of the Jewish position seems to be that the proper road in the search for God is through the calm intellect and not through the superheated emotions.

Now as to whether it is proper to take drugs at all: Again this question can only be discussed by analogy. The one available analogy is that of drunkenness. Judaism has never been ascetic, forbidding the drinking of wine. On the contrary, it has made wine a part of many a religious service. Nevertheless it is sternly against drunkenness. The Bible, especially in Proverbs, denounces drunkenness. The priests are prohibited in Scripture from conducting the sacred service if they even taste liquor. See Leviticus 10:8: "And the Lord spoke unto Aaron saying: 'Drink no wine nor strong drink, thou, nor thy sons with thee, when ye go into the tent of meeting, that ye die not; it shall be a statute forever throughout your generations.' " After the Temple was destroyed, the prayer services were considered to be the substitute for the Temple sacrifices. Therefore the same prohibition against drunkenness at the Temple sacrifices was applied to prayer. The Talmud says (*Erubin* 64a): "A man who is drunk shall not pray. If he does pray, his prayer is an abomination." Also in *Berachos* 31b the Talmud says that if a man who is drunk prays, it is as if he has worshiped an idol. It is clear, therefore, that any sort of befuddling of the clear mind was considered a *hindrance* to a true and sincere religious life.

But there is a further consideration involved: Medical opinion (in a report to the American College Health Association) indicates that many addicts of LSD have gravely endangered their health and tend to increase the danger of general addiction, feeling a compulsion to recruit others to the use of the drug. With regard to the danger to health, Jewish law is clear: It is forbidden to a person ever to endanger himself (except, of course, under the special conditions of martyrdom for the sake of religious conviction, when one must accept death rather than give up the faith). But in general the law is clear that a person must never endanger his health or his safety. These various laws are summed up in the *Shulchan Aruch, Yore Deah* 116. See especially the statement of Moses Isserles to 116:5 in which he says: "A man must be careful with regard to all matters that bring him into danger, for danger is even more serious than (other) prohibitions." (b. *Hullin* 10a).

To sum up: According to the spirit of Judaism, the path to religious knowledge is the clear mind, not the confused emotions. Any sort of drunkenness or bemusing of the senses is an impediment to true worship, and any willful endangering of the health is strongly prohibited by the Jewish legal tradition.

BIBLIOGRAPHY

TALMUD, CODES AND COMPENDIA

Aaron of Barcelona, *Sefer Ha-Chinuch,* 13th Century.

Aaron of Lunel, *Orchos Chayyim,* 14th Century, Jerusalem Reprint, 1957.

Abudarham, David, 14th Century, Jerusalem, 1959.

Alfasi, Isaac b. Jacob, and *Commentaries.*

Asher ben Jehiel, to the Talmud.

Babad, Joseph, *Minchas Chinuch,* Lemberg, 1889.

Babylonian Talmud.

Benveniste, Chaim b. Israel, *Kenesses Hagedola (V'Sheorey K.H.)* Turkey, 1603-1673.

Berachia, Aaron of Modena, *Maavor Yabbok,* 17th Century.

Bes Talmud, ed. Friedmann and Weiss, Vienna, 1881.

Cohen, Israel Meir, *Mishna Berura,* Chofetz Chaim, New York, 1943.

Eliezer b. Joel Halevi, *Ravia,* Germany, 12th Century, ed. Aptowitzer, Berlin, 1918 ff.

Eliezer b. Nathan of Mainz, *Raben,* Germany, 12th Century, ed. Ehrenreich, Samleul, 1926.

Epstein, Jehiel, *Aruch ha-Schulchan,* Vilna, 1923.

Felder, G., *Yesode Yeshurun,* Toronto, 1954

Felder, Gedaliah, *Nachlas Zvi,* New York, 1959.

Greenwald, Jekuthiel, *Kol Bo Al Avelus,* New York, 1941.

Hirshowitz, Yeshurun, *Ozar Kol Minhagey,* Lemberg, 1930.

Ibn Gayyat, Isaac b. Yehuda, *Shaarey Simcha,* Furth, 1862.

Isaac of Vienna, *Or Zorua,* 13th Century, Zhitomir, 1866.

Israel of Krems, *Hagahos Asheri,* 14th-15th Century.

Jacob ben Asher and Commentaries, *Arba Turim.*

Jaffe, Mordecai R., *Levushim.*

Jeroham ben Meshullam, (Rabbenu Yeruchem), *Toldos Adam V'Chava,* Provence, 14th Century, Israel Reprint of Venice Edition.

Jerusalem Talmud.

Katz, Jacob Zvi, *Leket Hakemach He Chodosh,* London, 1964.

Kol Bo, 13th Century, New York Reprint.

Lev ha-Ivri, *Ethical Will of Moses Sofer,* Lemberg, 1864.

Maimonides, *Yad ha-Chasaka.*

Margolis, Ephraim, *Shaare Ephraim,* New York, 1952.

Meir ha-Cohen, *Hagahos Maimoniyos,* 13th Century.

Midrash Rabba.

Mishnah.

Moelln, Jacob b. Moses, *Maharil,* Mainz, 14th-15th Century.

Moses de Leon, *Zohar,* Spain, 13th Century.

Moses of Coucy, *Semag,* 13th Century.

Moses of Przmyzl, *Matte Moshe,* London, 1958.

Rabbenu Yeruchem, see Jeroham ben Meshullam.

Sefer Chasidim, ed. Wistinetski-Freimann, Frankfurt am Main, 1924.

Shulchan Aruch and Commentaries, Large Vilna Edition, New York Reprint, 1962.

Sifre, ed. Friedmann, Vienna, 1864.

Tekuchinsky, Jehiel Michael, *Gesher ha-Chayyim,* Jerusalem, 1960.

Tosefta, ed. Zuckermandel, Pozewalk, 1881.

RESPONSA AND SIMILAR WORKS

Arik, Meir, *Imre Yosher,* Muncacz, 1913.

Asher ben Jehiel, *Responsa,* Venice, 1607.

Ashkenazi, Isaac, *Vaya'an Yitzchok,* London, 1961.

Ashkenazi, Joel, *Mahari Ashkenazi,* Muncacz, 1893.

Ashkenazi, Zvi, *Chacham Zvi,* Lemberg, 1900.

Azariah, Menachem of Fano, *Sziget,* 1892.

Bachrach, Yair Chaim, *Chavos Yair,* Lemberg, 1894.

Benamozegh, Elijah, *Ya'aney Vo-esh,* Leghorn, 1906.

ben Mattithyah, Benjamin, *Responsa Benjamin Zeev,* New ed. Jerusalem, 1964, etc.

Bruna, Israel, *Responsa,* Stettin, 1860.

David ben Zimri, *Responsa Radbaz,* Venice, 1745.

Deutsch, Eliezer, *Peri Hasodeh,* Faks, 1906; *Duda'ay Hasodeh,* Seini, 1929.

Deutsch, Simon, *Or Ha-emes,* Frankfort am Main, 1967.

Duran, Simon ben Zemach, *Tashbetz,* Lemberg, 1891.

Ehrentreu, Enoch, *Checker Halacha,* Munich, 1904.

Eisenstadt, Meir b. Isaac, *Ponim Meiros,* Amsterdam, 1705.

Enzil, Yekuthiel, of Przmyzl, *Responsa,* Lemberg, 1882.

Ephrati, Simon, *M'gay ha-Haregah,* Jerusalem, 1961.

Feinstein, Moses, *Igros Moshe,* New York City, 1959 ff.

Fleckeles, Eleazar b. David, *Teshuva Meahava,* Prague, 1815.

Geonim, *Responsa,* Various Volumes.

Glick, Abraham Isaac, *Yad Yitzchok,* Mihalifalva, 1903.

Haas, Solomon, *Kerem Shelomo,* Pressberg, 1840.

Hagiz, Moses, *Shtay Ha-lechem,* Wandsbeck, 1773.

Hoffman, David, *Melamed L'Ho'il,* Frankfort am Main, 1927.

Isaac bar Sheshet, *Rivash,* Lemberg, 1805.

Isaac of Fass, *Berech Yitzchok,* Salonica, 1803.

Isserlein, Israel, *Terumas Ha-deshen,* Venice, 1519.

Katz, Ben Zion, *Jerushalayim D'dahava,* Drohobicz, 1910.

Katzenellenbogen, Ezekiel, *Kenesses Yecheskel,* Altona, 1732.

Klein, Abraham, *Beeros Abraham,* Tyrnau, 1928.

Landau, Ezekiel, *Nodah B'Yehuda,* Stettin, 1861.

Landau, Nathan, *Kenaf Renana,* Przmyzl, 1886.

Landau, Samuel, *Shivas Zion,* Prague, 1827.

Landsofer, Jonah, *Meil Zedaka,* Sedilkow, 1835.

Leiter, Wolf, *Bes David,* Vienna, 1932.

Leon of Modena, *Zikne Yehuda,* Jerusalem, 1957.

Lerner, Meir, *Chaye Olam,* Berlin, 1905.

Lev, Aryeh, of Cracow, *Shaagas Aryeh,* Neuweid, 1736.

Meir of Padua, *Responsa,* 16th Century, Furth, 1756.

Meir of Rothenberg, *Responsa,* Cremona, 1557.

Messas, Joseph, *Mayim Chayim,* Fez, 1911.

Minz, Judah, *Responsa,* Furth, 1766.

Minz, Moses b. Isaac ha-Levi, *Responsa,* Cracow, 1617.

Mizrahi, Israel, *Peri Ha-Aretz,* Salonica, 1755.

Morpurgo, Samson, *Shemesh Zedaka,* Venice, 1790.

Oppenheimer, David, at end of *Chavos Yair,* 1664-1736; Lemberg, 1890.

Oshry, Ephraim, *M'maamakim,* New York City, 1959.

Reischer, Jacob, *Shevus Yaacov,* Lemberg, 1860.

Roller, Mordecai, *Beer Chayyim Mordecai,* Neamtu, 1923, Cluj, 1923, 6.

Rudnick, Isaac, *S'dey Yitzchok,* London, 1961.

Samuel ben David, *Nachlas Shiva,* Furth, 1792.

Schick, Moses, *Responsa,* Satmar, 1904.

Schick, Solomon, *Rashbam,* Muncacz, 1900.

Schwartz, Joseph, *Ginze Yosef,* Oradea, 1930.

Schwadron, Sholom Mordecai, *Maharsham,* Warsaw, 1900 ff.

Shafran, Bezalel, *Rabaz,* Jerusalem, 1962.

Shapiro, Eliezer, *Minchas Eliezer,* Muncacz, 1902.

Slonik, Benjamin, *Massas Binyamin,* Metz, 1776.

Sofer, Isaac Zvi, *Mispar ha-Sofer,* Jerusalem, 1961.

Sofer, Moses, *Chasam Sofer,* Lemberg, 1894.

Taubes, Moses, *Chasam Sofer,* Lemberg, 1841.

Ungvar, Eleazar Lev b. *Pekudas Eleazar,* Satu Mari, 1931.

Uziel, Ben Zion, *Mishpetai Uziel,* Tel Aviv, 1935; Jerusalem, 1964, etc.

Walkin, Aaron, *Z'kan Aharon,* New York City, 1955.

Weil, Jacob, *Responsa,* 14th Century, Hanau, 1610.

Weinberg, Jehiel, *S'rida Esh,* Jerusalem, 1961.

Yeruchem, Chaim, *Birchas Chaim,* New York City, 1956.

Zirelsohn, Judah Lev, *Ma'arche Lev,* Kishenev, 1932; *Lev Yehuda,* Kishenev, 1935.

Zuckerman, Kalman, *Minchas ha-Kometz,* Jablonow, 1937.

Combined Index for "Reform",
"Recent"and Current Reform"Responsa"

Abortion and German measles, II,
    188
Adoption: I, 200
    baptism of child before, II, 97
Aguna, I, 86
Apostate:
    burial of, II, 127
    daughter, I, 192
    priest (Cohen) I, 196
    reverting, I, 195; II, 120
    Shiva for, III, 181
Ark:
    closed when Torah removed, I,
        43
    curtain (parochet) I, 62
    embroidered Name of God, III,
        22
    in south, I, 66
    not centered, I, 65
    people stand when open, I, 44
Artificial insemination, I, 212, 217
Ashkenazim:
    Age at Bar Mitzvah, III, 70
    Chanukah Lights, I, 25
Athletics and Sports, III, 231

Bar Mitzvah:
    at age of 12, III, 70
    Gentile stepfather, III, 91
    of retarded child, II, 23
    Sabbath afternoon, I, 37; II, 19
    stepfather called up, I, 32
    Sunday, I, 35
    Yom Kippur, I, 38
Bas Mitzvah, II, 19
Bastardy, I, 201, 203
    Karaites, III, 186
Birth Control, I, 206
Blood from the Dead, III, 242

Breaking glass at weddings, II, 182
    Jacob Z. Lauterbach, II, 183
    Hillel Posek, II, 186
    see also, Wedding
Breast feeding, II, 226
Burial:
    arrangement uniform, I, 156
    Christian cemetery, I, 140
    delayed, I, 150
    enemies side by side, I, 136; II,
        61
    infant in grave of parent, II, 139
    mass burials, III, 169
    mother's ashes in son's grave, III,
        145
    non-Jews in Jewish cemetery, III,
        155
    rabbi at Christian funeral, III, 175
    sinner, burial of, II, 131
    tombstone in absence of body,
        III, 141
    see also, "Cemetery"

Caesarean operation:
    on a dead woman, I, 213
    on a dying woman, I, 212
    Maimonides discusses, I, 216
Cemetery:
    alignment of graves, III, 132
    Arlington, I, 141
    first grave, III, 138
    municipal and Jewish sections, I,
        161
    outright possession preferable, II,
        148
    section in general, II, 144
    Sefer Torah carried into, II, 43;
        see also, "Burial," "Tombstone"
Chanukah, I, 29
    lights, I, 25

255